IN THE HEART OF
BANTULAND

A LUBALAND HEADMAN.
A type of Hunter-Chief in Lubuland, Katanga

IN THE HEART OF BANTULAND

A RECORD OF TWENTY-NINE YEARS' PIONEERING
IN CENTRAL AFRICA AMONG THE BANTU PEOPLES,
WITH A DESCRIPTION OF THEIR HABITS, CUSTOMS,
SECRET SOCIETIES & LANGUAGES

BY

DUGALD CAMPBELL

FELLOW OF THE ROYAL ANTHROPOLOGICAL INSTITUTE

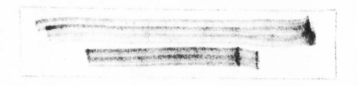

WITH MANY ILLUSTRATIONS & A MAP

NEGRO UNIVERSITIES PRESS
NEW YORK

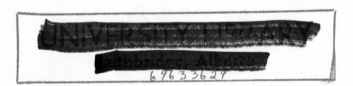

Originally published in 1922
by Seeley, Service & Co. Ltd., London

Reprinted 1969 by
Negro Universities Press
A DIVISION OF GREENWOOD PUBLISHING CORP.
NEW YORK

SBN 8371-1456-X

PRINTED IN UNITED STATES OF AMERICA

CONTENTS

11

12 Contents

Contents

CHAPTER XXV

LIST OF ILLUSTRATIONS

In the Heart of Bantuland

CHAPTER I

Dead Man's Land

THE expression used almost continuously during the late war of a man "going West" is a pure Africanism, for every Bantu negro when he dies "goes West." One of the peculiarities of Bantu languages is that the only geographical directions recognised and fixed are west and east, sunset and sunrise. There are no words for north and south. The west has always been associated among the Bantu tribes with darkness and death, misery and misfortune. The West was the home of the slavers whose coming with firearms and rum brought devastation and sorrow to countless peoples, and " to go West " to tens of thousands of Africans meant literally to go to sure and certain death ; *the red road* from the interior to the West Coast it was, alas ! only too truly. In these parts of Africa where I have lived for the past twenty-nine years of my life, the West Coast is known as *Mbonshi* or " dead man's land." The root word signifies " Hell," and is so translated in many missionary publications. Just as *Kabanga* means the East, and suggests to the native the origin and beginning of things, the source of life, light, and fertility, and a man when he is buried must be laid " facing the east, sir ! " so the West connotes darkness and

death, and, to the negro mind, the savage state out of
which he is trying to emerge, and he finds there one of
several solutions to the colour question. " Did not God
create you white people in the daytime and us blacks
during the night ? " " In the white man's country it was
dawn long ago, whereas it was s⁺ill night in the black man's
land." A crude truth !

Catumbella, three miles from Lobito Bay, one of the
great, new seaports of Africa, used to be called by the
Portuguese *o bocca d'inferno*, " Hell's mouth," or " doorway," so that, from the European as well as the African
point of view, the Bantu name of " dead man's land " for
the West Coast was no misnomer.

Benguella, fifteen miles north of Catumbella, was joined
to Catumbella by means of a small, single line of railway,
and an iron bridge, and in early days if the trip was accom-
plished in three hours we were well satisfied. Like most
West Coast towns Benguella was built on a sand-belt close
to the sea, and was therefore unhealthy, malarious, and
fever-stricken. Most of the houses, government buildings,
and traders' stores were built of *adobe*, or sun-dried bricks,
and covered by corrugated iron, or thatched roofs. The
walls of these were usually from two to three feet thick,
which, despite the intense heat outside, kept the interior
cool. Some of these buildings have stood for over a
hundred years, and in the early days when natives from the
interior made raids on the coast town to plunder the
traders, those thick walls, which were loopholed, served as
fortresses, and many an epic story could be told of a handful of traders putting up a stiff fight against overwhelming
hordes of savages.

Angola has been known to Europeans from the fifteenth
century, and the Portuguese have been living and trading

there for three hundred years, though—with the exception of two or three explorers—they have rarely ventured far inland.

There is only one Portuguese known to us who has travelled far, and traded widely in the interior of Africa ; his name is Silva Porto. The story of his romantic life as I have heard it told round the camp fires again and again by notorious old slave-traders who travelled with him, and others at the coast who knew him, would fill a portly volume, and his unique abilities were well worthy of a better cause. As a boy, about seventy years ago, he stowed himself away on board an old sailing ship from Lisbon, and during the slow voyage was made to work, helping the cook in the galley. On reaching Benguella he went ashore, and from there made his way inland with a native caravan to Bihé, 150 miles from the coast. There he established himself, and founded a trading station and colony at Belmonte, which eventually became the Government headquarters. He set himself to collect caravans with which he travelled all over the interior, trading. Then, trade goods, firearms, and rum were cheap, and much sought after by the natives. Slaves, ivory, beeswax, and gum copal were abundant, and to be had for next to nothing. As a consequence, in a short time he became incredibly wealthy, and was highly respected by both the King and the people of Bihé, with whom he lived on the best of terms. By and by the Portuguese authorities having decided on the effectual occupation of the country, brought up a large force, which was attacked by the King with an army. The King was subsequently defeated, made a prisoner and deported to the Cape Verde Islands where he died in exile. I saw him there when returning to Africa twenty years ago. He wore an old silk hat and frock coat, and standing among some of his exiled elders as he spoke to me, he looked every inch a king. Old Silva Porto was so worried over the failure of the Government to pacify the country, and his own political part in it, that he gathered together and piled up all his gunpowder in the centre of his house, and, wrapping himself in the Portuguese flag, he blew himself and his house to pieces.

From the two coast towns of Benguella and Catumbella two great caravan routes bifurcated into the interior. One ran S.E. via Kakonda towards the Barotse hinterland, and S.S.E. to the great horse-breeding and cattle-raising country of the Tunyama. The other stretched east over the hills from Catumbella to Bihé and the far interior.

This latter is the route I followed in my three journeys from one side of Africa to the other. Here at the coast one met during occasional visits many of the " black-ivory " hunters, as the Portuguese then styled themselves.

One of the most typical, and by far the most interesting old-time slave and ivory traders of Catumbella was a jolly fat Dutchman named " old Pete," manager of the " Dutch house." He not only lived, but thrived in the steamy, sweltering coast towns, despite dinners which lasted two to three hours daily, plus unlimited *vinho tinto* and rum, and a frequent forty to eighty grain dose of quinine. I have seen his book-keeper come rolling out of his room, and, staggering from side to side of the passage like a drunken man, he would say : " Ah, Mr. Campbell, dat man vill kill us all." " What is it, Mr. Kortekaas ? " I would ask. " Ah, he be shust gif me eighty grains of quinine one dose." Old Pete was, like most of the early travellers and traders, something of a doctor, dentist, and Jack-of-all-trades rolled into one, and there was nothing that he would hesitate to attempt. I remember seeing him one day in the backyard with a rough pair of old dental forceps pulling a suffering Portuguese about by the mouth, the latter howling with pain and hanging on to him with both hands, but unable to get free of the forceps until the tooth came out. He used to take great pleasure in scaring new-comers by pointing out enormous, long, fat cockroaches that trooped out of the wall-cracks during dinner in the evening, and saying : " Ah, that is a mosquito. That is a jigger ! " " But," asked a young lady missionary, " how could such a great creature get into one's toe ? " " Ah vell, shust vait, Miss, shust vait and you shall see." He was hospitality personified, though he was never scrupulous about recouping himself at the first opportunity, and adding it to our accounts. Like most Hollanders I have met on the coast, he spoke fluently nearly every European and African language required. I have seen German, Portuguese, French, Dutch, English, and native travellers and traders at dinner, when Pete would entertain them all in their various languages with his inexhaustible fund of stories acquired during over thirty years on the West Coast.

The Benguella of to-day is of infinitesimal importance, having been superseded by Lobito Bay, which is probably the finest seaport round the coast of Africa, with a magnificent bay. I remember twenty-nine years ago rolling about on the sea in front of the glaring walls of the old customs house at Benguella in an old rat-eaten steamer, when almost within sight of our ship—a few miles away—this same natural seaport stretched out its inviting arms. Later, on my return there in 1899, I drove out to the bay in a mule cart with my fat friend Pete K——. Nothing was visible round the beach save a few squalid fishing hamlets, close to which, bobbing in the bay, were to be seen a number of dugouts manned by ragged natives, who, after supplying their own needs, sold the remainder of their fish in the open market of Catumbella.

Here at the coast one met members of a hundred different tribes speaking as many different dialects. The local tribes speak mostly the three principal coast dialects : Kimbundu, Umbundu, and Portuguese.

All other natives east of the Kwanza River on the Bihé border are called by their more civilised coast neighbours Gangellas, a term of reproach meaning " heathen," and are considered as fit only to be slaves.

Crimes and murders were of common occurrence around here, and low-type traders frequently plundered native caravans of their rubber, ivory, etc. If the native took his case to the Fort there was seldom any redress, for, alas ! too often the local authority was in league with his friend the trader. "*Nos somos aqui para encher as algibeiras,*" " we are here to fill our pockets," I have been told by officials on many an occasion. I once compelled one of these sharks to disgorge and restore a load of rubber he had stolen from one of my carriers ; there were, however, some decent Europeans to whom the native trader took his goods year after year and by whom he was treated fairly.

As I have said, crime and bullying were generally encouraged by the Portuguese. I have watched a group of traders standing at their store doors with arms akimbo, or holding their fat sides in hilarious laughter, at two Ndombe natives, to whom they had given rum, and long sticks, and who were belabouring each other viciously while the blood flowed freely from their heads and bodies. They were goaded to this for the sake of the rum and money they were given by these civilised lovers of the noble art. Strolling out at night, as I used to do, one frequently heard howls and cries proceeding from traders' backyards where slaves were being flogged, and I have been shown spots in the yards where there had been buried slaves who had been murdered for " bad conduct " or for

" disobedience." Close to the town on the west side I passed the *dambo Maria* where poor half-caste Mary had been murdered by her paramour, and a walk of an hour or so on foot over the hills would take one to heaps of bleaching bones and skulls of slaves who had been left to die, or been done in because they were of no value at the coast and not worth taking back inland, and the owner would allow no one else to derive profit from his slaves.

If you had travelled up with me from Catumbella to Bihé you would have got sufficient evidence to convince you that the negro who coined the name of " dead man's land " for the West Coast made no mistake. The first day's travel over the hills was a revelation to a new-comer ; bodies lying about here and there in the open in various stages of decomposition, and others lying about in the huts built by travellers which, however inclement the weather, one shunned with horror, preferring the company of a live hyena or a lion to those foul-smelling slave corpses ; full-length skeletons also, days, months, weeks, and years old, skulls and vertebræ, leg and arm bones, etc., lying loose on each side of the road, or in little heaps. At the first camp we reached, a slave hunt was in progress, but, as the slave ran into our camp and sought our protection, the hunters with their dogs and guns had to return to Catumbella without their quarry.

On we go inland from day to day, with similar experiences ; slave camps and caravans meet us on every hand, convincing us, if proof be needed, that slavery is a real, live, going concern under the white man's flag in " dead man's land." I am writing of my experiences twenty-eight and even twenty years ago.

On our way up to Bailundu and Bihé we pass through the Humbe country, a splendid pastoral district where are large herds of cattle, though the natives are loth to sell their stock. This is also called by travellers " the goitre country," as a large number of the people are afflicted with Derby- shire neck, and for this they wear thick, heavy brass wire collars. On the ninth or tenth day we reach Bailundu, beyond which a tramp of a few days more brings us to the highlands of Bihé, 5000 to 6000 feet above sea-level. Here domestic animals thrive, even horses, and European fruits and vegetables do well, and it is not uncommon during the cold season to find ice $\frac{1}{4}$-inch thick on the water. This is the natural boundary of the west coastlands. This country is inhabited by a hardy race called Ovimbundu, who are enterprising traders, and used often to go far into the interior of Africa for two or three years at a time trading. They are the Arabs of West Central Africa.

Here in Bihé I spent my first two years and acquired a thorough knowledge of the language. The method I adopted was to live in a native village and listen to the natives speaking among themselves. Also, on every avail- able occasion, I attended the native law courts where the best Bantu was always in evidence. Sometimes a lawsuit would take weeks to thrash out, and as a general rule good native advocates and orators only would be permitted to speak. There one found unique opportunities for getting at the back of the black man's mind. Thousands of proverbs, clear and obscure, besides idioms and legal instances both recent and several generations old, would be quoted. Songs ancient and modern, customs and laws in vogue and obso- lete, would all be called into requisition at such times ; this, added to the bamboozling paraphernalia of native law-courts, and intricacies of native law, were beyond the heroic attempts of ear, pencil, and notebook, to record. However, I have never had cause to regret that I took such an amount of pains and trouble to acquire my first native language. That one particular language has proved

a key to the opening up of the archives of every other
language I have since mastered.

The native doctors and diviners that one met at every
turn in Bihé, and of whom, and whose language in those
young days I understood so little, provided me with one
of the most fascinating and all-engrossing studies of native
life and thought. The field of their operations, and all
their un-European *modus operandi*, has to do with the real
" dead man's land " of Africa—the world of spirits. The
unity of the negro race, living and dead, past and present,
is the great doctrine taught and enunciated, by those
masters of the Black and the White art—*The devil doctors
of Bantuland.*

CHAPTER II

The Slave Trade

SLAVERY is one of the world's oldest institutions and was recognised by Jews, Mohammedans and the early Christian Church. When missionaries argued with Tipu Tib and his hordes on Tanganyika, or with the black Bihéans of Angola, Abraham was quoted and Europeans pointed to as the original cause and promoters of export slavery. Slavery was recognised by law and precedent until less than one hundred years ago, and it is only within the last few decades that the world's conscience has been roused and slavery become branded as execrable and incompatible with our modern standards of civilisation. From time immemorial Arabs and Bihéans have gone into the interior from the East and West Coasts to supply the markets of Islam and Christendom. Barter goods were carried with which to trade, such as rum, guns, gunpowder, etc. They also carried wherever they went a veneer of civilisation, and they, not missionaries, were the first bearers of the Koran and the Crucifix to the untutored natives of inland Africa. Though I have been in touch with and lived amongst the scenes of slavery as carried on by Arabs and Rugaruga from the Congo to Lake Nyasa, my chief and most intimate experiences, gained at first hand, have been acquired while travelling between Catumbella and Katanga in company with West Coast slave caravans and traders. For months on end I have been a daily witness of the horrors of this vile traffic, while powerless to do anything towards putting an end to it or mitigating it in any way.

It must be borne in mind that slaves were classified in different categories, and that all slaves did not necessarily represent poor innocent, downtrodden humanity. Some of the slaves disposed of were sold on account of crimes committed, and these represented, as a rule, the incorrigible class of recidivists who in Europe would have been sentenced to sweat out the remainder of their lives in the galleys, or on the treadmill. I have on occasions redeemed several of this type, and in every instance have regretted it. This type of slave is bad and, generally speaking, not worth the twenty or thirty yards of calico paid for his (or her) redemption. Shakespeare's Blackamoor in *Titus Andronicus* is a real live picture of some of these I have known. One I knew actually did mutilate a woman, and another dug up a newly filled-in grave and stripped the dead woman's body of ivory bracelets, cutting off the hands and feet to do so. Another I knew in the Katanga. . . . Well, the Congo law had evidently no means of punishing such cases! Of course, African chiefs do not understand our incarceration methods of punishment, and so adopt that of graded mutilations or enslavement. What Van Diemen's Land was to Britain, and parts of Angola were to Portugal, so the West and East Coasts, too, came to be looked upon by African chiefs—a land of exile for their criminals and undesirables, and slave caravans the ships to carry them there. Of course, those taken in war, or raids, represented a mixed class, but the larger percentage were of the slave element. The coming of each fresh caravan with guns and gunpowder meant war and raids, killing, burned villages, and devastated countries. Many of the once populous countries round the Katanga : e.g. Luba, Lamba, Lala, etc., as well as thickly peopled corners of N.E. and N.W. Rhodesia are thinly peopled to-day because of raids to procure slaves to supply the Angola markets.

The first slave caravan with which I travelled from Bihé to Msidi's country, in the Katanga, was composed of some three hundred slave traders. The men who carried my loads were all of the budding slave trader type, or slave traders down on their luck, who, with the wages I gave them for the trip, would trade and return rich in slaves and ivory. I have seen a slave caravan of about three thousand men which broke up into several camps for convenience, but which held together for protection from extortionate or quarrelsome natives by the way. I have seen slaves bought in the interior for next to nothing. A young boy or girl could be bought for four yards of calico, or a handful of gunpowder and a few percussion caps. Full-grown men and women were sold for eight to twelve yards of calico. Babies were considered of no value but rather a drug on the market, as they prevented the mother from carrying a load of rubber or ivory. Sometimes they would spear the child or give it a knock on the head with an axe or club. Rubber and ivory had first consideration.

On buying a slave the usual mode of procedure was as follows : the slave after purchase was thrown on the ground, generally knocked about a bit to emphasise the new master, then roped and shackled. If a young man, he had his neck put in a heavy forked stick ; sometimes a stick with a fork at each end would be used to hold two. Women were merely roped waist to waist or neck to neck during the daytime, but at night wooden shackles were put on their hands and feet, and they slept with these on till the morning, when the peg in the shackles between the two hands and feet was knocked out, and they were free for work and travel.

Bihé, Benguella, and Catumbella were the principal slave markets of that part of Angola where I lived. Slaves brought from the interior were usually, though not always, kept a year in Bihé and fattened up before being taken down to the coast to be sold. Many slaves were disposed of in Bihé to traders, or kept by the Bihéans for domestic purposes. Often the slave, if ruffianly disposed, developed into a full-fledged trader, and many such I knew who could beat their masters at the game. When put into any position of trust in the caravan, as a rule, the ex-slave was more cruel and merciless than his quondam master, and the *shikote*, " hippo whip," was his inseparable companion. At Catumbella high prices were given for healthy young slaves, some bringing from £15 to £30. I have seen the slave market in full swing at the West Coast and traders up against each other for the best slaves. *Marfim negra*, " black ivory," was the trade name as distinguished from *marfim branca*, or " elephant tusk "!; when sold and shipped to S. Thomé, or Principe, they became *Serviçaes*, or " contracted servants." On account of the enormous demand for slaves for the Cocoa Islands, the human article was at a premium for many years, and could only be bought inland for guns and gunpowder. Many of these were bought from cannibals and from revolted Congo State soldiers, who were thus through Portuguese channels supplied with arms and ammunition, by means of which they devastated the south-western corner of the Congo State, and waged war for many years against the authorities. Some of the world's best cocoa was grown on the Portuguese islands of São Thomé and Principe on the West Atlantic. The same slave-grown cocoa has made some of our great cocoa and chocolate manufacturers famous, and produced ameliorated conditions of life and garden cities for the cocoa workpeople. What about the cocoa slaves who sweated out their lives in bondage under the most cursed conditions on the two islands referred to? On the two occasions when I was at home, twenty-one and thirteen years ago,

I lectured wherever I went on the horror of the slave trade, and pointed out that every cup of cocoa drunk and every cake of chocolate eaten was soaked in the blood of men and women. Many were stirred. The Anti-Slavery and Aborigines Protection Society took action. Nevinson was sent out to investigate, and the result was an exposure of many cocoa and chocolate manufacturers who were unconsciously and indirectly fostering the slave trade. Then C. A. Swan, a missionary and my old colleague, was sent as a Commissioner in the interest of cocoa manufacturers to give a true account, and the results of his trip and investigations are found embodied in his book, *The Slavery of To-day*. I wrote two booklets on slavery describing the enslavement of a Luban boy called Goi and a Luban woman named Bwanikwa, who had been sold ten times by different masters. These were scattered in thousands throughout Britain. Much interest was thus created on behalf of slaves, and " Cocoa slavery," as it was called, brought down upon it the condemnation of every right-thinking man and woman who read the story. Some offered me money to redeem slaves, others declared a boycott of cocoa and chocolate, but more radical measures were required, and at last the British Government brought pressure to bear on the Portuguese Government, who promised great things and eventually did *a little*. My frequent letters from Africa to the Anti-Slavery and Aborigines Protection Society had much to do with the spasmodic activities of our own Government and the eventual black-listing of slavery once for all by the Portuguese authorities.

I have gone ashore on these islands, visited the plantations in the interior, and spoken to slaves there in their own tongues, as well as to the planters. Most of these slaves hailed from the Congo State and Rhodesia. Sometimes life on the plantations became so unbearable that the slaves attempted to escape into the forests, when man-hunts would be organised with guns and dogs, and many were shot to strike terror into the hearts of the others. A Portuguese steamer from Africa *en route* to Europe with a friend of mine aboard, when within twelve hours' steaming from São Thomé, sighted a capsized boat. The weather was rough, and heavy seas running, but they lowered a boat which reached the derelict. Two Africans were found clinging to it. They were taken on board and after care and nourishment told their story. They were slaves belonging to a cocoa plantation, and three days before had attempted to escape in an open boat. Having no knowledge of bearings, they rowed towards the east. They were caught by a storm and the boat was capsized. They had passed three days clinging to the boat's bottom without food before being rescued. I remember seeing a big slave caravan on the march at Lake Dilolo with about three thousand slaves and slavers all told. It hailed from Lubaland, away up in the Congo. Smallpox had broken out and was claiming its victims at each camp. The Lunda, Luena, and Chokwe tribes, through whose countries they were passing, carried off stragglers and laggards, one of whom I saw dragged away before my eyes. These man-thieves followed caravans like vampires and preyed on the sick and slow who were left behind. Great gangs of slaves were chained or roped neck to neck, some were in fork sticks and shackles, but all had loads of rubber or ivory tied to their heads and shoulders. Many were skin and bone, others with babies pick-a-back or on the tops of loads; some were in advanced stages of pregnancy, and one had given birth to a child by the roadside. These things did not delay the great westward-bound stream of slaves. Even little children barely able to walk were dragged or driven alongside the caravan, with protruding eyes and distended stomachs. When they saw me they shrank in horror, believing that they had at last reached the country of " big devils." White men are called *Ovindele*, or " big devils," and their home *Mbonshi*, " hell," or " dead man's land." In 1886, Livingstone referred to slavery as " this trade of Hell "—strong words, but nevertheless true.

Often when burning with a sense of injustice and impotence at the cruelty and wicked inhumanity of the slave trade I have struck little blows of my own. The first of these was when returning from Benguella to Bihé after accompanying a sick European to the coast. I was riding an ox, and had turned a bend of the path when I came face to face with a Mulatto slaver with whip in hand, pipe in mouth, and gun on shoulder driving a man-slave in front of him in a fork stick. I ordered him to halt, and calling for my rifle told him to " knock off that shackle." He was slow to do it, so I pushed a cartridge into the breach, and in a minute he called out for an axe, hewed the shackle to pieces, and the man stood free. " Now," I said to the slave, " if you want to go with that man you can do so ; you are free. If you want to follow us, I will protect you." I need hardly say which course he chose, while I kept my rifle on the slaver until he was well out of sight. While on a visit to his relatives he had been sold to this man for a keg of rum. It is not often natives sell their relatives, but rum is responsible for a lot of misery. On another occasion in the Congo State I freed two gangs of slaves, numbering in all fourteen. This nearly cost me my life, for guns were pointed at me from all over the slavers' camp. One item in this was touching. I had rescued among the first gang a quaint old Lunda man. In the second gang rescued was an elderly Lunda woman, and when in the evening the two gangs met in my camp,

THE LAST SLAVE CARAVAN.

This photograph is particularly interesting as it shows the last caravan of slaves laden with ivory to reach Biké Angola, from the Congo.

to our surprise the old Lunda man ran into the arms of the Lunda woman, who turned out to be his wife. After the sale they had been separated, having been bought by different masters. Both lived with me for many years on the Luapula River. The old man was an expert wood-carver, and the old woman a potter, and as they had no children I gave them a little girl-slave I rescued, who grew up in their house and is now married and has a child of her own. I sent them back to their own country some years ago, and the old man became the Chief of a village of freed slaves near to Kalene Hill at the apex of North-West Rhodesia.

The " red road " to the West Coast, as Livingstone called it, was littered from end to end with bleaching bones and skulls. The " Hungry Country," near Bihé, being the end of the long slave road to the interior, was *literally white* with these by the roadside, and as long as these remained there was visible proof of Portuguese complicity and guilt. As a number of Europeans travelling west from Rhodesia saw these, and photographed them, it was necessary that there should be a big official sweep-up of the roads. Orders were given to this effect, and there was a big " spring cleaning " of the Portuguese house from Catumbella to Moxiko.

The " Hungry Cokwe country " was a veritable ossuary, literally a chamber of horrors. I have seen bones and dead bodies to right and left of the road, and even astride it. Invariably we looked to see if the dead slave had been hamstrung, or knocked on the head with an axe, one or other of which was usually done to prevent their falling into other hands. If a slaver showed the least sign of humanity he became the laughing-stock of his fellow-traders, the butt of their jibes for many a day. Nine years ago the Portuguese Government woke up, and one day *it issued an edict freeing all slaves in the Colonies.* This resulted in a few claiming freedom, and obtaining it, and later others followed their example. I have in my possession, given me by such a freed slave, a *Carta de Liberdade*, signed by Portuguese officials and witnessed with the slave-owner's mark—a most interesting and epoch-making document which I wish I could produce here. Many of these ex-slaves when freed headed for Lunda and Lubaland. I found a number of villages of freed slaves when up there two years ago and conversed with them in their own tongue. They received permission from the Congo authorities to settle and build, but most are more concerned about finding their lost relatives than settling down permanently anywhere at present. The first effects of freedom are manifest in the desire of the slaves to be near those they can look up to as masters, hence they are settling round European Government posts, and mission stations. The slave spirit engendered by a life of bondage will take long years to eradicate, and the evil effects of association with the slave traffic which has left its cloven mark not only on the slave, but on many of the Portuguese and men of other nationalities who have engaged in it, will take decades to disappear. From the last letter received via Angola it appears that there is much room for improvement in the official attitude to slavery, and there is evidence obtainable that slavery in Angola is not yet as extinct as the Dodo, in fact, that it still exists under another name.

[NOTE.—This, of course, must be read strictly from the historical point of view. I am well aware that, since the days referred to, the cocoa and chocolate manufacturers in question have done everything in their power to right what was wrong, and can truthfully say to-day " Nous avons changé tout cela."]

CHAPTER III

Government & Socialism

OF the Bantu negroes, who to the casual observer seem to have no form of stable government, it could be truly said that they are the most excessively governed race among the world's peoples, as they are, *chez eux*, the most respectful and law-abiding.

The nominal form of government is by king and a council of elders, with district chiefs and village headmen. The Bantu idea of king, as among the Teutons of barbarous times, is, *the man who can.* For this reason, one has seen again and again an interloper, by a swift *State stroke* brushing all law aside and killing a weakling, seize the throne and establish himself, to the people's satisfaction and his own, as their king. Thereupon he is accepted with little demur, and, like Msidi and many others, quickly inaugurates his reign by putting to death all who oppose him or are likely to do so. At the same time he will call to his side powerful blood relations to whom he will give chieftainships, doing the same also to such other powerful men as, from interested or mercenary motives, will lay their guns at his feet. Another Bantu view of government is that the king is *the man who provides.* A king who fails to recognise the fundamental law of savage life, namely, that a native population, like Napoleon's army, marches on its stomach, is certain to meet an untimely end.

Every native king must attend to cultivation and provide bread and beer for his people, and show them, as well by example as precept, how it must be done. In the hoeing season from sunrise to sunset all chiefs may be seen in the fields with their people, and often, as in Rhodesia, they vacate their villages and live for months at a stretch out in their fields, digging and planting. At such times the king's wives brew quantities of beer, and make food, and the people come to dine and drink after work at the great bark beer-bins. I have seen three such great bark casks, 4 feet high by 2 feet wide, full of strong millet beer, and the people sitting around, chatting, drinking, and singing. Often with drum and song and the chief at their head, long lines of people would be seen in the fields during the early part of the cultivating season, hoeing and singing, keeping time with the music, their hoes rising and falling to the beat of the drum and the words of the song :

> " In our country there'll be hunger,
> In the Katanga there'll be hardship.
> Raise your hoe high, my boys,
> Dig down, dig deep, my boys."

Again and again elephant and big-game hunters arrogate to themselves headships of villages and districts by obtaining a following as the result of success in the chase. These are good shots, usually brave, good soldiers, and being able also to protect the people from wild beasts and enemy raids, and provide them with wealth and cloth from ivory sold, they become popular leaders.

A king will not readily refuse a chieftainship to a hunter of repute whose ivory brings trade and wealth to the country and cloth to his people, besides guns and gunpowder. These men, however, often become arrogant and cause much trouble. In times of famine when ordinary people are starving, the population of a Nimrod district or village are found sleek and well fed. This causes ill-feeling, and I have known a trumped-up case of witch-craft brought against such a hunter, which case ended in his being tried, sentenced, and burned to death.

There are tribes like the Wemba and Matabele, who, in pre-European days, lived by gun and spear, but to-day, all these warrior clans have had to beat their spears and battle-axes into agricultural implements, and be content to hoe their peaceful furrow. The " spear-boundary " was the only original and recognised frontier of Bantuland, hence to-day the perpetual squabbles over local frontiers that have to be settled annually at Indabas in each adminis-trative district by the Administrator of Northern Rhodesia. The Arab boast that " only the gun is king in Africa " corresponds with Pringle's song in " The Emigrant's Cabin at the Cape " a hundred years ago.

> " The death-fraught firelock in my hand,
> The only law of the desert land."

Mushroom kingdoms like the Yeke kingdom of the Katanga existed all over Africa, half a century being the usual length of each settled form of government ; but within each the same laws of inheritance and succession always obtained, and dynasties here and there can go back over a long succession of kings and legal successors, e.g. the Wemba and Lunda of Northern Rhodesia.

In different countries and during different years the forms of taxation imposed were not always the same. But labour, viz. cultivation or help in building, was a form of tax that never varied. Once a year each sub-chief had to send or take to the capital his quota of men to help to till the king's gardens and later to fence them. When the site for a new capital was chosen and building about to commence, each headman had to send a stated number of men—the number being fixed by the chief, according to the population, to help in building the chief's kraal. The king claimed all ivory, plus a leg of each animal killed, with the titbits, viz. kidneys, liver, and heart. The king would sometimes send for a marriageable daughter of an under-chief or headman. Such a marriage would confer higher status and favours on the father-in-law. If the king saw a pretty girl when on a visit to his villages, or heard of one, he would send for her and make her his wife, to which there could be no refusal. Hoe-making districts would be taxed in a certain number of hoes. Fishing districts would pay a tax in fish, and oil-producing districts were taxed in oil. All taxes were in kind, which was the only currency. *Mafuta*, " oil," also signified " wages," from the verb *futa*, " to pay," just as " salary " originally meant " an allowance of salt." Lion and leopard skins were claimed as *Royal Property*.

The army was made up of units under local captains, *batwale*, sent from each district throughout the country. There was also the king's particular regiment made up of the pick of the young men, who usually married and lived round the chief's kraal (*musumba*) to be in readiness for emergency. In war, and for defence, a citizen army was formed of every able-bodied man. Women were expected to do all the provisioning, and many used to follow the men into the field as wives and carriers. To equip and arm his soldiers the king had to sell his ivory, lion and leopard skins, with slaves and all else of marketable value. Guns and gunpowder, with flints and percussion caps, were bought up in peace time, and in time of war these were handed out to the soldiers. A special head-dress was usually worn, and sometimes red shawls. The Angoni soldiers wore feather busbies, and officers had distinguishing marks. Msidi's people in war adopted red caps or turbans by which they knew each other in battle. Every one con-

tributed to the upkeep of the fighting-men, and in time of
war there was little respect shown for private property.
Even the king's kraal and wives were not immune at such
times. From time to time as caravans of trade goods
arrived, these were bought, and the lion's share handed
over to be divided among the king's army. When travelling
through their own country, or that of friendly tribes, the
army was quartered on the villages, which had to supply
them with food and drink. In wars of offence they supplied their own needs wherever they went by plunder and
pillage. In war-time all soldiers were not at liberty to go,
but a regiment was chosen, and officers appointed, by the
king, who attended to all important matters *in propria
persona*. Protection was granted with all the power at the
king's disposal to every one of his subjects, provided they
kept within the limits of the law. In cases of sorcery,
adultery, or murder, a man put himself outside the pale
of the law, and therefore forfeited the law's protection.
Sometimes a chief went to war to protect a single subject
who had been kidnapped or treated badly by one or more
of a neighbouring tribe. When the Belgians arrived to
take over Msidi's country they found it already broken up
owing to Msidi's stubborn refusal to hand over his court
orator and favourite, named Kasanda, who was held
responsible by the Sanga people for the murder of one of
their women. The man in question was only indirectly
responsible, in that he owned a slave who in a drunken
bout seized a gun and shot the woman. The relatives,
through their chief, demanded the slave's master to be
handed over for execution, which Msidi refused. He
protected Kasanda, and this brought about the guerilla
warfare that ended in his downfall. Each member of a
family, village, clan, and tribe, claims and obtains the
protection of his fellows, this being the law of the land.

" My country right or wrong " is certainly and fundamentally African law.   Negro respect for authority is
proverbial, but the said authority must have solid support
at the back of it, for the element of power is omnipotent
in the savage mind.   As Kipling makes little Kim say, " A
big stick is a good reason."   England lost the Katanga
because Mr. Alfred Sharpe, who was sent to make a treaty
with Msidi, turned up at Bunkeya Capital without a force
to support his claim to be England's representative.

The Bantu proverb runs, " When the lion's dead the game
can go where they like."   The lion, to the negro mind,
personifies *law and authority* as he moves about, the
animals have got to be careful and not get in his way, but
to keep to the beaten game path.   Thus the negro has
tremendous respect for the power that can make itself
felt.   In the good old days he was kept in his place by ear-
cropping, eye-gouging, nose-slitting, lip-removing, hand-
lopping, and many other forms of legal corporal punishment that had great power in the land as deterrents of
crime.   The thought of a spear-thrust through his feet
for spitting in a public place, or a spear-thrust through his
heart for insulting another man's wife, made him an out-
and-out respecter of law and order.   The loud-mouthed,
blustering, over-dressed, and noisy-mannered negro that
one meets in the streets of Johannesburg or Elisabethville
to-day is not the product of native law or village life, but,
wholly and solely, the outcome of contact with our modern
civilisation.   The negro fresh from the kraal sets himself
at once to understand the European and does not always
wholly fail, but how many Europeans take half an hour's
trouble to study and try to understand the negro ?   We
have him in our houses as servant, we use him as cook, thus
putting our life in his hands, we use him as nurse-boy for
our children and run the risk of the moral contamination

of our families. We use him as store and office boy, where
he often learns—by opportunity—how to steal and forge
cheques with impunity. We use him in a hundred different
ways, and yet we are indifferent as to his character, and do
not even trouble ourselves intelligently to know where he
goes at night, or what he does outside house, store, or
office hours. Is it therefore to be wondered at that he
becomes vicious and bad under our tutelage ? Let us once
and for all recognise and remember that the native is not
naturally lawless, but has an inborn respect for law and
authority. The native is also a born humorist and, however ridiculous it may seem, his whole idea and code of
censorship of morals, public and private, is wrapped up in
the sharp sayings and witty warnings of the court and
village jester, who from time to time dons the motley.

As it was in the days of Aristophanes and the early
Greek drama, so it is in Central Bantuland. Under the
cap-and-bells are exposed civic corruption and sharp
practices. The court jester is a Government official, and
he has power to rebuke even the king in public, and warn
him that if he doesn't behave and govern well, the people
who made can unmake him. The language he uses is,
unfortunately, somewhat indecorous and unparliamentary,
unfit for a European drawing-room, but it is well understood by the nude people for whose ears it is intended, and
the king has to take it all in good part. The village jester
performs a similar function for the humbler folk, and many
a reproof and warning is thrown about, wrapped up in the
sugar of wit, received amid roars of laughter, and never
fails to reach its mark. Sarcasm and jest are the two
sharpest *shamboks* with which to punish your pachy-
dermatous negro and will not land you in the law-courts.

All government is by the will of the people ; whether it
be the choice and coronation of a king ; the selection of a

man to fill a new chieftainship; the framing, proclamation, and promulgation of a new law; the removal of the
village from one site to another; the declaration of war
or the acceptance of terms of peace; everything must be
put to the poll and come out stamped with the imprimatur
of the people's will. No permanent form of negro government can exist save that based four square on the people's
will. Sometimes the people demand a change of king or
the repeal or change of a law. The king may get wind of
this and, by accepting the inevitable, retire on a plea of
old age, weakness, or inability to continue his public function, or from some other justifiable reason. He and his
elders, with the people, may appoint a successor, after
which he may make his public abdication, handing over
spear and bow and arrows, with the other paraphernalia
of chieftainship, and saluting his elders and people as a
common man, saying: "I'm no longer So-and-so, your
chief. Behold your chief!" He then retires from the
lion skin, the seat of authority, to an adjoining hut where
he takes up private life, leaving his successor seated there.
So also with change of laws. It must be discussed, agreed
to by all, then be proclaimed publicly, and promulgated
all over the country by public crier.

The Lunda is one of the greatest colonising tribes known
in Central Africa. They have to-day three self-governing
colonies outside their original tribal home at the Matiamvo
capital. From the centre their pioneers struck east and
settled in what is to-day Lovaleland and founded colony
No. 1. They then went further east and founded on the
Lualaba River colony No. 2. They continued still further
east to Rhodesia and founded colony No. 3 on the Luapula
River, where they have governed since the seventeenth
century. They say that the tribal name Lunda means
" colonist," and comes from the verb *ku-lunda*, " to add

to," or " to colonise." *Baku-Lundampanga* means the " annexors of country to country," or simply " the colonists." Often, like Msidi, kings have conquered and colonised, but to-day the results of their conquests are nil and their colonies have either been wiped out or become assimilated by the autochthonous peoples. Not so the Ba-Lunda ; their colonies stand to-day and have absorbed, and still continue to absorb, local elements. It is known, and it is their boast, that they have conquered and assimilated peoples by means of the hoe rather than the spear.

All Bantu government has not been based on tyranny and founded by tyrants, though there have been many tyrants, and people have suffered from their tyrannies. Mutilation as a legal form of punishment or summary execution is not tyranny, for the same existed in England up till comparatively recent times. " In 1837 the punishment of death was removed from about two hundred crimes, and it was still left applicable to the same offences as were capital at the end of the thirteenth century. Pocket-picking was punishable with death until the year 1808 ; horse-stealing, cattle-stealing, sheep-stealing, stealing from a dwelling-house, and forgery until 1832 ; letter-stealing and sacrilege until 1835 ; rape until 1841 ; robbery with violence, arson of dwelling-houses, or sodomy until 1861."

Msidi of the Katanga was an undoubted and typical tyrant, whose boast to the helpless was : " I'm the world ; and there's no escape nor doorway, even Above." Many a man and woman so far defied him as to take the one doorway of escape from his tyranny. Many a threat of a return to earth in vengeance was pronounced by a condemned subject of Msidi. Many a divination test, too, proved that the threat had been fulfilled, and that the avenger was at work devastating in some direction or another as lion, or leopard, or in snake form, and killing without mercy. The only cure was to dig up the bones of the dead witch or wizard, and burn them publicly, from the ashes of which fetish horns would be compounded as a protection and prevention against the demon's power.

Despite the seeming anomaly, all Bantus are pronounced socialists, and socialism, I was going to say kingly socialism, is their fundamental and fixed form of government. In view of the rise everywhere of questions relating to socialism and economy, much that is instructive may be gathered from a study of existing conditions in the lives of Central Africans. The social status of equality observed by the primitive peoples of mankind is now the aim and ambition of the most highly civilised communities ; and in Central Africa we have a complete object lesson before us of the result of life under conditions of equality.

In Bantuland the spirit of enterprise among the people is restrained, even crushed, with the constant fear of exciting the envy and cupidity of their fellows. For example, one who builds a better house than his neighbour will have his house pulled down. If a man exerts himself to cultivate, breed animals, or amass riches, he courts the enmity of his fellows, and becomes doomed to a premature death. One of my best headmen was a case in point, and he only saved himself by running to the European for protection. Ambition to excel, which is such a common attribute of human nature, receives no encouragement. Coinciding with this we often find the people living in anarchy and ignorance, without a constitution as we know it, without a history, and without even definitely established habitations. They lack even the ambition of conquest, and are content to pass their lives in a state of mental atrophy.

Socialism from the African point of view—like blood friendship—is a form of mutual exchange. The Luba verb *ku-pana*, " to give," is used in the reciprocal form, and means, to give reciprocally. From the native side there is no giving without receiving, and the man, black or white, who receives without the intention of returning at least an equivalent, is looked on as a thief. Hospitality is one of the most sacred and ancient customs of Bantuland, and is found everywhere until European individualism comes along, when " ancient hospitality," as the poet says, is

"With unceremonious thrift bowed out of doors."

A native will give his best house and his evening meal to a guest, without the slightest thought that he is doing anything extraordinary. African Socialism is not one-sided, for if the chief receives he has to give. If he is served it is because he is servant of all. If I benefit from the Bantu socialistic laws I must be prepared to forego my own rights, fields, house, and all else for the common good. Bantu socialism is not a poor man eating up the wealth of a rich man, but each one living, digging, building, hunting, fishing for the public weal—all for one, and one for all.

CHAPTER IV

Native Laws

NATIVE law is the sacred synonym of the revealed will of the spirits, by keeping and rigidly observing which a man ensures to himself success and peace in this world and a happy future across the border in " dead man's land." The chief's decision may be taken for final, but every man has right of appeal to the spirit courts, which have the last say. This may take the form of the poison cup or any other of the many tests which are presided over by the gods, who are considered the final arbiters in all matters of legal difficulty.

Law is the line drawn, a path to walk in, a doctrine to be received and obeyed without demur. Two words are used—*Mushilo* and *Lifunde*. The former means a specific " prohibition," " command," and is much used by doctors in prohibiting their patients from doing certain things that are considered to be injurious, or from eating certain foods ; the latter means a law taught and promulgated, a doctrine generally understood as to be obeyed, and pertaining to the chief and country where it is in force and where its sanction obtains.

To keep a law is equivalent to guarding the said law with all the armed forces at the command of the chief and people, for in Africa laws are made to be obeyed. It is not enough passively to submit to a law, but each is expected to uphold and champion the law and to teach and explain it to others. To see a law broken and not to take up cudgels to bring the guilty to book is often equivalent to condonation and guilt, and is punishable. The peculiar verb used for breaking a law considers the law as a wall built up across the path, and the law-breaker walks bodily through it, or literally bores or breaks through the law (*kupula mafunde*). The other word, *Mushilo*, considers the law as a line drawn, or a path to walk in, and to cross that line is to transgress or go out of the path. A stronger verb is used, *shilula*, which, while equivalent to "transgress," also means to rub out the line, or to nullify the law by tramping on it, an act of tribal disloyalty.

Land laws have been, and still are, one of the perpetual sources of tribal warfare. Boundaries are always well defined, recognised, and their laws understood among natives, and for any chief to encroach on the boundaries of another chief, or in any way attempt to remove the ancient landmarks, is to wake and unleash the dogs of war. (I was waked up in the middle of the night four years ago on Bangweulu owing to a fight between two chiefs over the attempt of one to encroach on the other's boundary). Boundaries may be, but are not always, rivers, mountains, or any particular geographical feature. Sometimes a tribe occupies both sides of a great river or mountain, and the boundary may be a big tree or rock, or gully.

The land in every instance belongs to and is vested in the chief and people, who are only, however, tribal trustees, and have no power whatever to sell the land or to alienate any of it to any one under any pretence whatever. The land is tribalised and belongs to the tribe in perpetuity. I have heard an old chief when dying say to his successor proudly as he handed over the chieftainship : "Look, I have not lost a single stretch of the land entrusted to me ; all the boundaries are intact ; see you do likewise and guard well our inheritance, the land of our ancestors." Of course, where the spear makes the law, all other laws become " scraps of paper." Old Msidi used to boast of his " spear boundary," and claimed all the countries raided by his armies, many of whom, for fear of a second visitation, gladly paid tribute, e.g. the Mashukulumbwe and Angola natives.

A man may cultivate as much land as he and his wives can hoe, to supply their personal needs, but the land does not belong to him and, as already remarked, he may not sell a yard of it. All individual land tenure is only temporary, and holds only so long as the land is used. All land is nationalised, and this tribalisation of land system obtains all over Bantuland as against the system of individual possession in vogue among European peoples. A form of primitive socialism rules among the Bantu peoples, and though the individual self-consciousness is not fully developed, the clan consciousness is all-powerful.

Fences are used to keep out pigs and wild animals, but not for the purpose of enclosing a private piece of land. The land is socialised.

Property laws exist, and only here does the right of the individual assert itself and give him claim to separate consideration. A man's field is inviolate, and a thief found stealing corn is roughly handled. A most amusing form of punishment in force not many years ago, was to take the thief with the corn he stole, and dress him up in a corn-jacket, and parade him through the village while the mob rough-handled him, calling out as they did so, in sarcasm, " O come all ye people and see this pretty man with new-fashioned corn-jacket." An ordinary case of violation of property laws was tried by the chief, but if a man entered another's house or field at night to steal, he could be (and often was) speared at sight.

Laws of inheritance and succession form an intricate code,

POTTERY INDUSTRY.

Women are the potters and make clay cooking-pots and water-jars of graceful design, and decorated with pretty patterns.

many of which seem to point back to an early Semitic origin, dating from Arab or Hebrew domination or influence. A brother can inherit a dead brother's wives and goods, and failing a brother a nephew is chosen to succeed the deceased. Among some tribes like Yeke the son can.inherit and may take over all the father's wives save his own mother. The inheritance ceremonies are elaborate, and the festivities often last for weeks, during which great quantities of food and beer are consumed. Drumming and dancing are kept up night and day, and there is great rejoicing and general jollification.

Laws of war exist in name only, for the chief object of both parties is to get in the hardest blow first. Very often he who draws first blood is considered the victor, as was the law among the clans of Scotland. If a chief is taken prisoner he is frequently kept as a hostage and, on professions of loyalty, willingness to pay tribute and help to fight the conqueror's battles, he gets a new name and insignia of chieftainship, and is reinstated among his people as a friend and ally. He and his people are henceforth treated well and receive a new status.

" Thou shalt not steal " was not brought to Africa as an article of the Decalogue and taught for the first time by missionaries. There are five different verbs in every-day use to describe forms of stealing, and all with different shades of meaning :

Ku-tola, to pick up (what is not your own).
Ku-bula, to take (other people's things).
Ku-pompola, to pilfer.
Ku-iba, to steal.
Ku-sompa, to plunder.

There was Jabiri, my old Arabic teacher, who " only borrowed," or, when caught, said so. His name was Kopakopa, " the man who only borrowed." He stole a fowl and ate it, but when found out said he was going off to buy another to replace it. When found wearing another man's shirt he said, as he went and brought it back, " Please, I only borrowed it." No mercy was ever shown to a thief when caught. A man will disown his own son or brother if caught, but will share the booty if not found out. I remember some Bihéan traders in camp in Lovaleland. One of their number woke up in the middle of the night to find that a Luena man had got through the doorway unperceived and had his arm round a load of guns. The trader quietly stretched out his hand and, seizing his axe, raised it and pinned the thief through the back. The camp was roused and, bringing firewood, axe and hoe handles they soon had the midnight robber on the burning pile. He was burned to death. In the same connection a queer thing happened just about the same time to a trader. As there had been many scares and night thefts in the camps along the road, each Bihéan kept his axe handy by his bedside. The man in question, who lived near me when I was in Bihé, had been sleeping with his one leg raised, propped against a post in the hut, with the result that the leg became " dead." In the dark hours he woke up suddenly to see what looked in the dark like a man in his hut. He speedily seized his axe and raising it behind his head brought it down with full force, cutting through his own knee, which he had mistaken for a robber. He was carried home to Bihé in a hammock, where he lived, in the village of Kwanjulula, hobbling around with a stick. This killing of a robber was the law of the road.

Prior to European government, a man had his hands and ears cut off for theft. In the Wemba country this severe form of punishment was only meted out to those who stole from the chief. In other countries any criminal stealing from anybody was mutilated by the cutting off of hands or ears. Sometimes a thief was enslaved and sold to Arabs or Bihéans. Sometimes heavy fines in kind were imposed and paid. *No stealing was winked at*, and if a man was suspected, and denied the theft, tortures were resorted to in order to make him confess.

Assault was always punishable, and these cases were dealt with by the chief or headman at the local courts. As a rule the man who " started " the quarrel was fined, and had to pay a basket of fowls, a goat, a sheep, or a number of hoes. On account of this law it was common to hear the defence pleaded : " Chief and gentlemen of the court, this man started me " (*wantendeka*). If the assault was repeated after warning the person was sent away to a distant village.

Adultery laws were one throughout Bantuland in this respect, that the husband would be justified if he killed the aggressor, which was the reason why *he was given an arrow at marriage* with the words pronounced by the bride's father : " This is to kill the seducer of your wife." Among the Wemba a man would be fearfully mutilated for adultery with a chief's wife. Sometimes all his relatives also would be mutilated, even his mother. Eyes picked out with the thumb and removed with fish-hooks, or bored out with antelope horns, or simply extracted by means of the strong finger of the executioner boring into the eye-sockets were common occurrences among the people of Bembaland. Sometimes the woman was killed or mutilated, the breasts being cut off. The chief Kafwimbe on the Luapula was notorious for this form of punishment to women. Of course, most of those so mutilated died afterwards in a very short time. Of one of those mutilated women who lived and recovered there is an old song still sung. She was the headwife of the chief Mwimuna, who went to make war on the aforesaid Kafwimbe ; the latter, however, fore-

stalled him by attacking his village, catching his queen
and cutting off her ears and breasts. The words of the
song roughly translated are :

> " O Mwimuna who went to war,
>   With your flintlocks against Kafwimbe,
>   Look behind you and see your queen,
>   They've cut her ears and breasts off."

Arson laws are strict. If a man burnt down another man's
corn bin he had to replace the corn destroyed and build a
new bin. If a man burned another man's house he had to
build a new house and replace the goods, or pay the value
of the goods destroyed. If a man burned another's fence
and field of corn he had to build a new fence and pay over
a larger field of food. If a man set fire to a house and the
whole village caught fire and was burned, the man was
enslaved with all his relatives. These were the laws of
accidental burning. If any of these were done with
malicious intent and forethought the matter was more
serious. The man was flogged and beaten, and had to
pay up heavy fines in goods and stock as well as court fees,
and had to replace the bin, house, or fence burned. If a
village was destroyed both he and his people were enslaved
and liable to be sold to the first slave caravan that arrived.

Laws of murder, like the other laws, were rigidly enforced,
and not even natural affection was allowed to interfere
with the cause of justice. I knew a witch doctor who
condemned his own mother and then was the first to drive
an axe into her body to prove that he had no sympathy
with, or complicity in, the act for which she was burned.
If a man with intent kills a man, he is executed. If a man
kills a woman he is killed and his sister enslaved to raise up
children to the dead woman. I knew a case of a man
who for adultery followed his wife to her field, killed her,

and cut her into pieces. The murderer fled to the forest and hid in a thicket, but he was followed by the dead woman's brother and killed. But for the presence of a Government official a blood feud would have ensued; the murderer's relatives would have been killed also, and his two sisters enslaved. If a man kills a man accidentally he has to pay a heavy fine. If a man says to another, " Let's go out fishing," but the man refuses, and the other in the presence of witnesses presses him to go, and while they are on the river or lake the canoe is capsized, and the man who suggested the journey escapes, he is held guilty of murder, and executed as a criminal.

If a man marries and his wife dies in childbirth, he is held guilty of murder, but being only a man he is not equal to a woman, and his sister is killed instead. (This is under the African law of potential motherhood).

Laws relating to witches and wizards, who are treated as murderers, are amongst the most vital of the whole Bantu code. These people are recognised as being anti-social; their practices cut at the root of tribal life and unity. " Thou shalt not suffer a witch to live," is a fixed law in force throughout all Bantuland. For witchcraft only one form of punishment was meted out, and that was the death penalty. Witchcraft, or black magic, is prohibited all over Africa. One of the main difficulties for Europeans lies in this : that witchcraft and poisoning are apt to be looked on as identical. Sometimes a whole family is burned with a mother witch, and the only loophole of escape is in publicly expressing horror at the mother's wickedness and being among the first to hack and cut at her, prior to burning.

Marriage laws are binding, and I have seen many a black Darby and Joan struggling on through their marital difficulties and incompatibility of temperament, with the oft-repeated snub : " It's just because I married you that I continue to live with you." Such a thing as a man taking a marriageable girl to his house without a regular betrothal and marriage ceremony would be considered a disgrace to the relatives and the community. Birth, marriage, and death are the three great events of life, amongst which marriage holds a central place.

Divorce laws are at the disposal of all those who can, poor or rich, produce legal reasons why they should not continue to live together. Repeated adultery on the part of the wife, and barrenness on the part of either party, are two of the most fruitful causes of divorce. If the girl is proved to be at fault the marriage present must be returned. If the man is to blame he has to pay up heavily to the girl's people. It happens in Africa, as elsewhere, that there are sometimes abuses of law and miscarriages of justice, but on the whole the law is allowed to take its course. Better severe primitive laws than no laws at all.

Compensation is sometimes paid if a man assaults or insults another, often also for adultery and arson. On two occasions I had to pay compensation, once when a cow I had gored a boy who had been teasing it ; again, when out hunting I lit the grass thoughtlessly and a native fence round a garden was burned down. I paid the man the price of a new fence, and damages to the gored boy's relatives. A boy, a girl, a man or woman, as well as a four-footed animal, have all a certain fixed money value which is decided by law and is used in regulating compensations. A woman, or any female animal, has a special potential value owing to the inherent power of motherhood, and this is taken into consideration in the judgments given and in the settling up of lawsuits.

Fines are paid into court for court fees, and fixed compensations have to be laid at the chief's feet to be examined, to see if the amounts are correct before being handed over to the person indemnified. "An eye for an eye, and a tooth for a tooth" is the Medo-Persic law all over Bantuland. If there is one thing a negro does not understand it is European philanthropy, which he does not believe in, and if there is one other thing he does believe in it is blindfolded justice. The story is told of a man (and many such could be told) who gave his boy three shillings more a month with the remark, "That is because you have done well recently." The boy looked at the money and then at his master. "What is the matter?" said the master, surprised. "Please, sir," said the boy, "you still owe me fifteen shillings for the past five months' work." "What do you mean?" "Well, sir," said the boy, "I'm not worth more to-day than I was then; you are trying to rob me."

Punishments are innumerable and every new chief or slave trader gloried in inventing a new form of punishment. If a man was a good hunter he sometimes had his eyes taken out by his chief to prevent his ever killing game for any other chief. If a man showed musical talent he was similarly treated so that he could never play far away from the chief's hearing. More will be said on this subject in the chapter on "Cruel Customs." There are thousands of Neros in Africa. However, as all punishments were intended to be preventive, and there were no prisons or police, it is marvellous how effective this crude system of maintaining law and order was in a country where of all countries might was right and "gun was king."

A case at law had first to be heard by the village headman, then taken to the local chief, who, if he failed, sent it on for trial at the court of the paramount chief. The chief's orator, the accuser and the accused, with witnesses and relatives, then went off to the king's kraal. On arrival

they were shown huts and received hospitality. No case
was tried the same day ; they had to sleep. Next day the
chief's messenger would call to tell them that the court
was open. They would go, and on arrival fall on their knees
to greet the chief. When the chief greets them in reply
they seat themselves and the case proceeds. The accused
speaks first and states his case. The accuser is called and
follows. Then the king's orator restates the case to the
king. After that the local chief's representatives speak,
then witnesses. The king's orator again restates to the
king what they have said, and after consultation with his
elders—if the case is serious—the king speaks again and
gives his decision. Court fees are paid in with the fines
imposed. The white chalk acquittal is given to the winner
of the case and he, greeting chief and elders, leaves amid
great noise, cheering, and rejoicing. The losers greet
the king and court respectfully and go quietly back to their
village.

CHAPTER V

Peace & War

A PEACEFUL country is an old country, or as it is called in local parlance, "the country of the old fowl," i.e. a country where the fowls are not swooped down upon and carried off by raiding parties. One of the most welcome sounds that greet the ear of the traveller on emerging from the forest and approaching human habitations is the voice of chanticleer, often long before one sights the smoke of the village, or hears the merry voices of children playing on the outskirts of the forest, or on the approaches leading to a group of beehive-shaped huts. In the days when fire and sword swept through the land from end to end, villages were burned to the ground, and there are few countries from east to west that one has not seen in the throes of war. Villages were being continually rebuilt, and newly built villages were the miserable symbol of countries recently devastated by war. Cultivation and abundance of food was another evidence of a peaceful country, and for five miles and often more, from the centre of a group of hamlets, one would come on smiling stretches of cultivation: fields of golden-tasselled maize, or wavy millet, olive-green gardens of cassava, patches of potato vines, beans, and deeply dug beds of the much-coveted monkey-nut. I have bought fat chickens at ten for two yards of calico, worth tenpence; goats and fat-tailed sheep for the equivalent of half a crown. In times of war these would be wiped out, and a fresh start had to be made by securing new stock, and many a village

I have helped, and given a fresh start to in this respect.
The natives appreciate help of this kind, and by and by they
return the compliment in the form of a good present in kind.

The hoe *versus* the gun signifies peace *versus* war.
There were many tribes that lived entirely by the gun
and made subject tribes supply their food. This was the
real African regime of militarism such as was found among
the soldier tribes of Zulu, Hausa, and Masai origin, with
many others now defunct. In the cultivation of their
own country the work was done for them by slave labour
and by subject peoples on whom they preyed, and they
themselves merely superintended the operations. Much
of the grain grown was used for brewing beer, which the
warrior tribes consumed in enormous quantities. Often
drinking continued for months at a time, until all the grain
was used up with the exception of a little left for seed
purposes. One of the most common arts of war employed
to reduce their enemies to subjection was to burn all their
grain bins, and destroy the fields of food, and by this means
compel them to sue for peace at any price. Sometimes this
proved a shortsighted policy of killing the goose that laid
the egg, and produced famine that reacted and punished
even the conquerors.

Casus belli are innumerable ; often real, sometimes
imaginary, but more often the repetition of Æsop's old
tale of " The wolf and the lamb." (Of course, Æsop was
an African !) The *casus belli* of the Sanga war that ended
in the break-up of Msidi's kingdom, was the shooting of
Masenga, a Sanga woman. In the Lunda country I have
seen war declared on a district because a man infringed
the law of forest rights, and dug honey out of a tree growing
in the country of another chief. I remember war being
declared by old Mieri Mieri, a notorious brigand chief,
near Fort Rosebery (before Government days) because

Chinama, a local chief, picked up an elephant that had been shot in the former's territory. I met him on the warpath in paint and feathers, and succeeded in persuading him to settle the matter amicably.

Nkole law used to be one of the fertile causes of inter-tribal war. Somebody caught somebody, who was a far-off relative of somebody who knew somebody who robbed or shot a man, whose relatives put the matter before the chief, who constituted this interference a *casus belli*, and declared war. Any infringement, however trivial, of hunting or fishing rights was considered poaching, and poaching laws were severe, often ending in war and heavy fines in slices of territory and slaves. A hunter shooting an elephant or other head of big game which may die in a neighbouring country, has, in the case of an elephant, to give up a tusk and the choice pieces of meat, or if other big game, a hind leg with the breast, liver, heart, and kidneys. Failure to do so would involve his chief and people in immediate war. When all was said and done the only real and basic law in Bantuland prior to the advent of European government was the law of *Might*. The Arabs never tired of saying " The gun is king of Africa," and it proved in every instance the last argument of African chiefs. Even in personal quarrels this applied, e.g. if a man entered another's field he was speared or shot; if he entered another's house to steal his goods or his wife, he was summarily dealt with—" treat him as you would a hyena " was the law, i.e. shoot or spear him.

The laws of ultimatum differed in various countries, and depended largely on the arms used by the tribe in question. Though the symbol of war varied, the symbol of peace was, in every instance, the same, viz. *a hoe*. Among very primitive peoples the symbol of war was usually an arrow or a spear. Among tribes who had been in touch with the coast and traders the war symbol was a cartridge of gun-powder wrapped up in paper, with a bullet or two inserted at the end.   Sometimes a knife or any sharp steel instrument was sufficient to suggest war, and used as a war symbol in issuing an ultimatum.   *Chela* or *Chuma* are words used for metal, and used synonymously for weapons of war. It is also used as we use it in English, metaphorically, thus : " I shall show you my metal " ; " a man of metal," etc.

If, again, a chief was well supplied with guns and gun-powder, he might, out of pure swagger (*filumba*) send a loaded gun as an ultimatum.   In every instance the hoe had to accompany the weapon.   Whatever the choice of ultimatum symbols, hoe and bullet, hoe and gun, the choice of either decided the issue.   If, as rarely happened, a war of extermination was decided on, no choice of hoe accom-panied the message or messenger.   An enemy, or enemies, would be caught in the woods, the heads cut off and sprinkled with gunpowder, and these would be laid on the road, or cross-roads, leading to the enemy's country. This was done by the Wemba and Arabs in N.E. Rhodesia to defy the government of Nyasaland when they made their first attempt to take over the country thirty years ago.

When war was decided upon after appeal to the local deity, or fetish, a declaration of war usually took the visible form of small pieces of ant-heap into which were stuck a few red feathers of the war-bird (*Nduba*) and these were laid at the various approaches to the enemy's country. Wars of defence were often undertaken with vigour and every possible preparation hastened to give the oncoming enemy a warm reception.   I was once camped in a large village (*Chivas*) on the Luapula River, when messengers arrived from Kazembe with a declaration of war, and within five minutes the whole village was like a beehive. Blacksmiths got out their old dusty goatskin bellows, tongs, and hammers. They rushed here and there for charcoal, and in a very little time the smithy was full of horny-handed blacksmiths and their helpers. Men rushed up with their spears and arrows, and axes, and old flintlocks to be repaired, and soon the sparks were flying, and the stone anvil sounding with heavy blows of sledge and small hammers. Old guns were hastily repaired and cleaned up, spear-heads were sharpened, or forged, with arrows lying in little heaps, while every conceivable kind of metal weapon was put into shape, handled, and burnished for war. Others rushed to the forest with their axes and cut and carried in stout poles to strengthen and repair the stockade, while another lot dug a deep moat round the village and cleared away all long grass and bush. Women set to work to pound and grind meal and prepare food to withstand a possible siege, while boys and girls ran round everywhere, helping in any and every way they could Before many hours had passed the palisade was strengthened, a clearing made all round the village to avoid the unseen approach of a lurking enemy, and men had donned war-paint and feathers and were performing a wild war dance to show their readiness to give a good account of themselves.

Wars of offence and aggrandisement were conducted more slowly, and with greater care and deliberation. In the case of Msidi he used to send and consult the great Ju-Jus— Makumba and Ngosa—on the eastern side of the Luapula River. To obtain an audience of the oracle he had to send presents of cowrie shells and slaves before enquiries could be made as to whether he would be successful, or otherwise, if he made war in such and such a direction. In every instance the god's advice would be followed out in every detail. The Wemba tribe consulted their famous war fetish called *Lilamfia*. This was kept by members of a guild called the *Bachamanga welamfia,* and was compounded of, among other things of potent medicinal value, a small piece of the skull of a famous Lungu warrior chief called *Chikoko*. To make this, a slave's throat was cut and the blood used on the fetish, which was made to spin round and round, and where it pointed when it stopped spinning was an indication as to the direction in which they should go and make successful war. Most of the Wemba warfare was of an offensive nature, and only on a few occasions were they forced to take the defensive, and those were when attacked by the Angoni-Zulus. Their wars were as a rule of a very brutal nature, and associated with much cruelty and mutilations, many of which would hardly bear description. Like Msidi of the Katanga, their name was a terror in all the surrounding countries and among every tribe save the Angoni-Zulu.

Internal wars were more the rule than the exception throughout the Luba country in the Congo. I have been visited in my camp by messengers with tusks of ivory offered in payment for help to kill a brother, or a cousin, and replace him by an ambitious relative. The messengers were greatly surprised that I should refuse such a tempting offer. Said they : " Just let them see you've got men and guns and can shoot and we'll win our cause without a blow." These internal struggles are very sanguinary and protracted, and due in most cases to some covetous cousin who is determined to oust the other out of the chieftainship. He first secures a following by means of bribes and promises, and then sets to work to undermine the other's influence surreptitiously. By and by, when he feels sure of success, he strikes the open blow and declares war. I know of two brothers who quarrelled and after a fight agreed to separate and divide the country in two. These have since become two rival clans with different names, and live peaceably side by side in Rhodesia.

Just as the law of symbolism is seen in sending a hoe and a bullet to an enemy, so one chief will send his spear (which is equivalent to his sceptre) to another, to request his help in fighting an enemy. As remarked elsewhere, in travelling one's help has been sought again and again by chiefs at war, and ivory and slaves offered as payment. I have known traders who have enriched themselves by such mercenary methods, and on the occasion referred to in Angoniland (*vide* Chap. XXVI) the war was said to be due to a white man who supplied the guns and powder and helped the natives against each other. As these men usually act in countries outside European spheres of influence, it is very difficult to reach them with the law, however long its arm.

Guerilla warfare used to be much indulged in throughout the Katanga by the Aborigines. They would lie in wait along the road and kill and capture their enemies. Sometimes they would make surprise attacks during the night, and shoot fire arrows into the thatch of their enemies' huts in the dark, and when the occupants were clearing out they would shoot or spear them, catching at the same time many prisoners. Sometimes, like my erstwhile friend Mulowanyama, they would take to the hills or the caves of Sangaland, whence they would emerge for periodic raids and forays on their more powerful but less secure neighbours. For years the West Coast caravan road was endangered by bands of Mulowanyama's bandits. On one occasion they plotted the life of my colleague, but fortunately he was detained in Angola and the plot miscarried, though his messenger was caught and killed at the Lualaba River. Once I fell into one of their traps near the Lualaba River, close to where the messenger was killed. Leaving camp one morning with my carriers, I ran full tilt into a trap. A band of these strapping hillmen sent by the rebel chief blocked my road. I sauntered boldly up to them as they lined up along my path, barring my way with gun in hand, and pans primed for work. I took the bull by the horns and greeted them in the most friendly fashion, presuming on their chief's once expressed friendship. I talked, and talked, and argued, and presumed they were out after elephants, and held out my hand to wish them well. They looked at their guns and at each other, then at me and my men. Meanwhile, I was talking away thirteen to the dozen, and eventually wishing them " Good day " I ordered my men forward. I sidled off, with my hand waving " Good-bye " or " Go you well," but with my left eye turned well back and my rifle and cartridge belt handy, my chief desire being to avoid any shot from behind. Their sulky, hang-dog expression, and their shuffling manner, considering that they were armed to the teeth, convinced me, with what I afterwards found to have been good reason, that they had orders to bring my head to the cave.

Later on the same chief with his gang was driven by a powerful Congo State force into his cave where, with all his people save three, he miserably perished. This action, however, cost the State the life of Lieutenant Froment, a brave Belgian official, who was killed by a shot from an elephant gun at the first charge.

Bantu negroes on the battlefield are not the formidable and bloodthirsty foes one would expect to find. I have been the eyewitness of a lot of native skirmishing in the bush and in the open, and it is certainly not the bloody affair one had been led to anticipate. Very often the side that draws first blood is considered the victor and the other side retires. Lots of their shooting is mere noise and wild display. I have watched a fight on two consecutive days when guns banged on every hand and men were shot at all around me, but the net result in casualties was nil.

Greeting a Village Headman in Kazembe's District.

Head-dress of Women and Children, Chokwe Tribe, Angola.

Of course this does not apply to trained fighting tribes like the Yeke, Wemba, or Zulu. The Arabs, too, and their bands of Rugaruga mercenaries, are a bloody lot who slay and spare not, whose object was, as a rule, ivory, slaves, and loot. The Swahili are, many of them, good shots, and I know one who in war shot an old friend of mine from a bastion at three hundred yards. He is to-day chief of a big village in North-Western Rhodesia.

Hostages are often respected and treated well, at any rate so long as the object for which they are held is also respected, and people usually maintain good behaviour so long as they know that their hostages are treated well. When the object is attained the hostages are returned to their people laden with presents and messages of good-will. Prisoners of war receive scant mercy, and are as a rule treated cruelly. Frequently, on return from war, some of these are sacrificed at the graves of the dead chiefs. Others may be sacrificed at the triumph of the victorious general and army. Those who remain are kept as slaves, given to the soldiers, and may be sold at any moment to a passing caravan. I have seen great gangs of prisoners of war, men, women, and children, all of whom were treated brutally, and were emaciated owing to the length of their journey from the scene of war, and the heavy loads they were compelled to carry. Among cannibal tribes many of these were killed and eaten by the way. A real war dance is, once seen, not readily effaced from the tablet of memory, and is a sight the details of which haunt one the remainder of a lifetime. I remember one at which quite three thousand people were present. The chief had gone with an army to punish an old enemy who was hand in glove with a rebel chief. The village was surrounded and attacked and the males killed, the women and children were captured together with twenty-two good-sized tusks of ivory. On his return the chief waited a few days outside his capital while preparations were duly made for the day of triumphal entry. The people, gaudily dressed and painted up for the occasion, gave the warriors a roaring welcome, and then gathered in an open space in the middle of the town which had been prepared for the big war-dance (*tomboka*). I went along and watched, as I thought it might possibly prevent any undue cruelties. Five great war-drums, ranging in size, boomed out victory and defiance, besides *marimba*, telephone drums, and drums and musical instruments of other kinds, all in charge of the big bandmaster. The band struck up, and amid the thunder of the war drums and the acclamations of the people the chief took his seat on the lion skin. Each warrior danced into the middle, the head or heads of those he killed dangling from his mouth. He pranced about, firing his matchlock, and, tired and sweating, placed his heads at the feet of his chief, who promptly put his foot on each. As each warrior danced he deposited his heads till the pile grew into a great grim heap. When all the warriors had finished these gruesome proceedings, Queen Mahanga sent every one wild with her renowned dancing—which recalled the Salome scene. Women ran in front of her dropping green leaves in her path as she danced. Then, when she had finished, the chief wobbled forward in State dress like a great sausage, sword in hand, and despite his cumbersome robes brought the dance to an end dancing himself, amid thunders of applause and songs and orations of praise to the chief and his warriors. I came away sick at heart from the devilish sight, glad to be back at my house three miles south from the capital. The consequences of defeat are seen in the grovelling servility on the part of the conquered and a readiness to suffer any insult or ignominy. They pay up with alacrity all war taxes imposed, whether in slaves or service of any kind. " We do it to save our necks " is the reply given.

CHAPTER VI

Cruel Customs

NATIVE slave traders are past-masters in the art of torturing slaves. The torture may take the form of the slow excision of an external organ, or the cutting out of pieces of live flesh, refined sarcasm (to which I have often heard a native express his preference for the hippo whip), flogging with the *shambok* often till death, twisting back the thumbs or fingers until they touch the forearm, pulling out hair and eyelashes, burning with hot irons, and other excruciating tortures. I have seen them cut V-shaped notches—like saw-teeth—in the edges of two pieces of split bamboo, then place these up the side of the head and tighten them by means of a rope under the chin and over the head, screwing the rope until the V-edge of the bamboo cut into the temples and almost drove the man mad. I have rushed in to save a young slave while the master, after flogging him with a scourge of thorns, held the axe over his head threatening his life.

Prisoners taken in war were also tortured in all manner of ways, many being done to death on the return journey. One official is called *Teta matwi*, which means "the ear slitter"; another is called *Teta miongo*, "the vertebræ cutter," who uses an axe for this purpose; another is called *Yamagazi*, the "bloody man," who uses spear and axe to cut and hack.

Sometimes they are poked at, spat at, and buffeted before being subjected to other forms of punishment. Many have their throats slit and die slowly for sacrificial purposes, or for " blood paint " to smear fetishes or war drums— while some are speared or shot off-hand. On the other hand, some prisoners are kept to be put to death at the chief's triumph when he returns officially to his people after a successful war. Even children taken in war and slave children are killed off-hand. At a nasty fight not far from where I lived many children were done to death, some speared, others had their brains dashed out against trees or stones. The native idea of war is extermination, and they laugh at white men shooting a man and then carrying him off on a stretcher to a hospital to be nursed and cared for.

Native Courts of Appeal.—(1) *The Poison Cup.*—Natives have queer ideas of justice from our point of view, and very curious tests in order to prove innocence or guilt. One of these is the *poison cup.* The witch doctor prepares gourds full of a powerful poison procured in the forest and called *Mwafi,* and each of the accused must drink it. If the accused drinks and vomits the poison, he is acquitted as innocent. If he dies his guilt is considered proven by the fact of his death. Although there may be faking of the cup for different persons, and undoubtedly there is, the fact remains that some do vomit the poison and are exonerated.

(2) *The boiling pot ordeal* for witchcraft is one that spares few save the old horny-handed and tough-skinned. In this trial a fire is lighted on an ant-heap at the cross-roads, and a long deep pot of water is brought and placed on the fire until the water is boiling. Meanwhile the chief and all the people gather to witness the trial. Those accused, or those who, to prove their innocence, have appealed to the " test," draw near to the pot of boiling water, and the witch doctor, dressed and painted up, sings

and dances and jumps around, and then dramatically drops a small pebble into the deep pot of boiling water. Each of the accused has to plunge the hand in slowly and take out the pebble three times ; after the third time his arm is examined, and if the skin is not burnt or damaged in any way he or she is acquitted ; but if it is in any way burnt or damaged they are considered guilty, condemned, marked with the red chalk, and burned to death. And so with all the accused on trial. Sometimes old people with hardened skins come out unscathed, and this is held up before Europeans as a justification of the boiling-pot ordeal. Sometimes several are thus tried, condemned, and sentenced to death. When they are thus proved guilty and marked with the red chalk (the condemnation mark, as the white chalk is the justification mark) they are hurried away tied up in ropes, amid the jeers and insults of the crowd, who call them all sorts of vile names, spit at them, etc. Firewood is then collected by the public in enormous quantities, the fire is lighted, and the doctor ties the victims to trees round the fire, their faces looking towards the fire. Then the mob perform the death dance around them, chanting weird and gruesome songs, led by the witch doctor, such as :

> " The doctor dons the red paint,
> To-day he's feeding on flesh.
> The lions that hid in the grass patch,
> To-day we've burned to death."

Then the doctor approaches his victims one by one and hacks off an arm which he throws on the fire. He then cuts off another and throws it on the burning pile, the victim looking on and slowly bleeding to death. He next hacks off a leg, then the other leg, then the head and neck, after which the trunk is finally thrown on. This he does with all the victims, meanwhile becoming gory with the blood of the executed. Those present then circle round the fire, singing wild, blood-curdling songs, and often in their mad frenzy cutting each other. When the bodies have been consumed and the fires have burned down, the people scatter to their villages in groups as from war. On one occasion a missionary doctor and myself attempted to save two old women who were tried for witchcraft by the above ordeal, but arrived too late. The fires were still burning though the people had fled, but the smell of burning flesh and the sight of half-burned parts of human bodies were revolting, and we were glad to leave the scene. This happened a mile or so from the station where the missionaries lived.

Trial by Pepper.—In the West Luba country they have a trial by pepper pipe which the accused person to prove his innocence is given to smoke. The pipe is of the usual hubble-bubble type and is filled with tobacco, mixed with red peppers, and other saliva-producing items. He has to smoke an enormous pipeful of this peppery mixture without once spitting, and if he spits he is considered guilty and condemned to death.

In another part an accused person has to swim through a crocodile-infested pool and if he comes out safe it is a proof of his innocence, and that he is therefore under the special protection of the gods who thus justify him publicly.

Burying alive used to be practised at the interment of big chiefs and even small headmen on the plea that they must not be permitted to go to the other world unaccompanied. Chiefs, including Msidi, used to bury men in the ground up to the neck, and dig them out after three days. Kafwimbi, a Luapula chief, and other chiefs, cut off women's breasts for adultery (*vide* Chapter IV). I have heard a native headman (an old friend of mine) tell how Msidi sent him with others to the Luba country to bring back so many human skins. They would attack a village, kill men and flay them, dry the skins in the sun, tie them in a bundle and bring them back to their chief. Some were used for mats, and others were sewn and inflated, and made to stand in the presence of the old ogre.

The Wemba chiefs regularly practised as a punishment gouging or pulling out eyes with fish-hooks, cropping ears, nose, and lips, lopping off hands and toes, and even de-sexing men for immorality. The Wemba are noted for the variety of their mutilation punishments.

Penalty for stealing, loss of fingers.

Attempted murder, loss of both hands.

Adultery, amongst other mutilations, the loss of both eyes.

Lying to a chief, loss of lips.

Betrayal of chief, loss of ears, hand, and foot.

(The last-mentioned crime is a characteristic of Wemba natives, and their name means " the betrayers of their chiefs," and is heard thus : *"Awe mukwai, Ababemba bale-bemba mfumu shyabo,"* adding, *" E Babemba mukwai ! "*)

Sometimes they would tie a man hand and feet and lay him at an ant's hole to be picked to death. Again, they would cut off the eyelids of a man and tie him to a raised frame, face upwards, to expose the lidless eyeballs to the sun. These mutilation punishments were multiplied by every possible device, so that to enumerate all forms of torture and mutilation would be an utter impossibility. As a rule these punishments were only inflicted on criminals as a deterrent against crime, but, sometimes, though not often, vindictiveness or revenge would prompt such cruelty. These mutilated people, many of whom I have seen and know personally, were a walking, living advertise-ment to the power of the king and country's laws, and were meant, most often, to teach that these could not be infringed with impunity.

Often if a big chief discovered a man with the special gift of music, to prevent his ever playing and singing before any other chief he would gouge out his eyes, otherwise mutilate him, and keep him as a court minstrel, for being thus blinded he could not wander far away.

Monstrosities were usually put to death at birth, though cretins, hunchbacks, and otherwise deformed people were permitted to live, and sometimes got the post of court or village jester.

Infanticide is one of the most wicked and inhuman of the African cruel customs. This consists in the putting to death of a baby that cuts the upper incisor teeth before the lower. The cutting of the lower incisors is a great event, and is considered the child's " life justification." A child which cuts its teeth abnormally is a *chinkula*, " unlucky child," and if permitted to live would bring ill-luck on its people and village. A woman who gives birth to a nice healthy baby watches most carefully, as she nurses it, for the first sign of teeth, for the appearance of teeth is the great event in Bantu babyland. Should she wake up one morning to find that her child has cut an upper tooth before a lower, she may hide it for a few days, but soon another upper shows and the mother is heart-broken, for her baby is doomed. She may still try to hide it, but this is nearly impossible, and any attempt to do so rarely succeeds. One day with tears in her eyes she calls her mother and tells her of her misfortune. The mother condoles with her and tells her not to cry ; she tells the elder women and midwives, who console her thus : " Look here, this child is unlucky ; it is unfortunate that it has come into the world, but if it were allowed to live endless harm would result to you and us, so it must die. This is the law of the land. Don't cry, for if you do you will never have another child. Dry your tears and be a brave woman." They then form a little procession and go down to the river with the baby. When they reach the riverside, after again condoling with the mother, they hold up the baby and address it, saying : " Poor little baby, you are a *chinkula*, an unlucky child ; it's a pity you came, but you must go home, much as we should like to keep you. Good-bye, little one, go away." After which they throw it gently into the river where it is soon picked up by a crocodile. They turn again towards the house consoling the mother, and return to the village in procession as they came. When they reach the house they shave the mother's head, wash and anoint her, and give her further advice about crying and fretting, emphasising the fact that she will have no more children if she cries ; and then they leave her, going to their houses. The idea is that if such a child were allowed to live it would turn into a wild beast and prey on the villagers who had failed to smell it out and decree its death.

Koloso executions used to be periodical, when on a fixed day there would be the wholesale burning to death of witches and other criminals who, though sentenced to death, had been kept waiting till others had been brought in from different parts of the country. This was one of the common forms of punishment for adultery with kings' or headmen's wives. A big *koloso* or corral of strong logs was built, say, twenty feet square and twelve feet high. Inside this strong stakes were driven into the ground, to which the guilty pairs were tied, back to back. The whole country gathered and took part in the execution. Firewood was cut and brought and thrown over the walls of the *koloso* until the prisoners were covered and the heap piled high above them. Then, when all was ready, the doctor set a light to it, and began the death-dance round the burning pyre, in which dance and weird accompanying songs the great crowds of people joined. Sometimes before the firewood was brought a young man would manage to free himself and leap over the wall and escape to the country of a neighbouring chief, who, if sufficiently powerful, would refuse to hand him over. Though this happened occasionally by the help of friends, it really happened very rarely, the risk was too great.

CHAPTER VII

The Man from Below

NGANGA, or witch doctor, means the "clever man," the "light-fingered man," the "man who wriggles," but when any one is sick or in trouble and the doctor's services are required, his official title of *Nganga* is not the one commonly used but the homely, eminently descriptive one, thus : " Call ye in the Man from Below " (*Kuteni yamasamba*).

There are various kinds of doctors, with twelve of which I am personally acquainted, and there are higher and lower grades in the profession, but the chief significance of the African fetish doctor is seen in the above name which indicates the leading characteristic of his professional duties. He is a man of the underworld and has to do with the dead, and " dead man's land," from whence come all trouble and disease. The peculiar hang-dog expression of the man, his fierce and implacable resentment of outside interference, his proud, ominous bearing as he swaggers round from village to village with his satellites, all emphasise the fact that he lives in a real underworld of wonder and mystery, the keys of which nether kingdom jingle in his fetish basket in the form of human skulls, bones, hair, finger and toe nails of dead witches and wizards, with every conceivable kind of potent charm. As a qualified practitioner he claims to be, and is, called " the father of fetishcraft," and the initiate he agrees to take along with him, and teach the secret of smelling out witches, and making charms, poisons, and medicines, and who has to undergo a term of one full year's instruction, and initiation, plus many very severe tests, is called " the son of fetish-craft." A fetish doctor in full dress and at work divining, or witch-finding, or carrying out an execution, is the most grotesquely hideous creature imaginable. With great red feather head-dress flapping like some hideous night-bird, painted, bedecked with leopard skins and endless charms rattling round his body, eyelids whitened and grinning like an ogre as he performs the wild death dance, or with hoarse voice calls up the spirits, he is a sight which once seen haunts one always. The sinuous movements of the body as he wriggles, the clutching at the air with his bony fingers as they twist and turn in simulating demon possession, indicate if not an artful, clever rogue and deceiver, certainly a very clever man who personates and is the real recognised ruler of the destinies of Bantuland, and whose name of *Yamasamba*, or *Nganga*, is no haphazard one. To learn the business of fetishcraft, the initiate accompanies the doctor in all his duties, and on all his journeys, carrying his fetish basket and doctor's dress. He arranges the suitable spot for operations, lays out in due order the fetishes and things required for work, and stands by, sometimes shaking a rattle and answering questions, or joining in the doctor's divination questions, songs, and ceremonies, with the interest of his master always in view. Thus he learns the practical and objective part of the business. The doctor also takes him out to the forest and shows him the various roots, barks, and herbs, and instructs him when to collect them, and how to concoct and compound them, and explains to him their several uses and abuses.

The following accounts of the *initiation rites of a young*

doctor and of divination ceremonies were written for me by
an ex-witch doctor :—

A man, in order to receive initation into the business of
fetish doctor, goes to the " father of fetishcraft " and says,
" I want to be a doctor." If the doctor agrees, he says,
" All right, let's go outside the village." They go and,
choosing a suitable spot, they hoe up a little mound.
They place a clay pot on the top of it with some aromatic
plants inside. They then pour water into it, and when
all is mixed the initiate kneels down on the ground and
drinks. Others beat with their village pestles on the ground
as they go round and round the initiate, who thereupon
becomes demon-possessed, and ventriloquises. He strikes
up a little song, singing :

> " A child who asked for a crown,
>   Found it among the departed spirits.
>   Here there must be no crying and tears,
>   Nothing but music and song."

They lead him into the village, where he takes to himself
a new name, saying : " I'm the spirit world, whence the
noises come." Then he listens as though he is listening
to the sound of footsteps, and immediately becomes
demon-possessed again. They then seize him, warn him
not to speak, and put a green leaf on his head. The
following morning they feed him with " hell food "
(a medicine food) in which the eye of a cock fowl is mixed
and make him swallow this. They stand him on a rock,
after which the head fetish doctor takes him away to
the " devil's mound," where he gains his first experience
of the " hell medicine." This is composed of ashes of
burnt witches, etc., and is the medicine which enables
him to obtain intercourse with the demons and departed
spirits, and by which he divines and smells out witches and
wizards. Being given the *bwanga bwa kalunga,* or " hell

medicine," is equivalent to a diploma, so that though he has much to learn still, he is in a position to practise and may take fees.

Initiation of a Nganga ya bwilande, or Spear Doctor (Nganga ya mukove in the Kaonde and N. Luba country). The doctors and people gather and dance and sing while the initiate is placed on a mat in the middle of the chief's compound, and all sing the following song to the music of the drums :—

> " My grown-up daughter
> Has gone to the water.
> On returning to us
> She's a mother of many."

(referring to the *Chisungu*, grown up, or puberty ceremony). As they dance the head doctor springs forward with his spear in his hand, and after making some flourishes, spears the initiate through the chest and kills him (he is supposed to die). The blood is taken as it flows from the spear wound, put into a basin and carried to the hut outside the village to which also the novice's (supposed) dead body is carried. (In this connection read Rider Haggard's story of the Zulu witch, Dr. Indaba nzimbi, who similarly kills Macumazahn in the story of *Allen's Wife*). Only doctors may go there, where the novice is washed with fetish decoctions and made to drink his own blood mixed with other medicines, after which he is trampled on and brought back to life. He is then marked with chalks in many coloured stripes and spots, whitened round the eyes, and decked out in his new doctor's dress, equivalent to cap and gown, and decorated with a set of fetishes to be used in his future work. After this he is led back to the village by the head doctors, and on reaching the drums he springs up and dances his first doctor's dance in full dress. He then takes a new name, saying, " I'm *Kashingu*," i.e. " the spinning top," or some other name considered suitable. He takes his place again on the mat in the middle of the dancing circle, and the people shout and throw him presents of beads, etc. The head doctors then give him his first basket of fetishes with which he has to begin work, learning their uses by accompanying the doctors for a year, during which he may also practise on his own and take fees.

His first (dead) witch case. It happens that a son has a mother who warns him, scolding him, and saying: "Listen to what I say, my boy, and do your duty." The son disrespectfully says to the father, "You shall marry again," at which the mother conceives a grievance at her heart, and after a few days she dies. They bury her in the usual way and return to the village. At the end of a year one of the sons the mother scolded falls sick. They call in a doctor, who divines, and who tells them: "It's the mother you insulted who has caused the sickness, and death will follow." He dies, they mourn for him, and resume normal life. A few days after the remaining child sickens. They call a doctor, who divines, saying: "You insulted your mother, too, and it is she who is killing off the children in this house; neither shall you recover." He also dies. Then they go for the doctor, taking initial fees, and say to him: "We have called you, doctor, to dig up for us the dead, disquieted spirit, which is eating us up." In the morning the doctor and his assistants come with their fetishes and the "hell fetish." On arriving at the house he who carries the divination basket stands till they give him a fee, then he places it on the ground. They make a circle, including the man who has lost the two children and who has asked for the divination. Then the doctor strikes up a little divination song:

> "I am calling, calling, dig me up (dead witch).
> I'm the doctor, that's my business (doctor).
> I'm the demon, homeless, clanless (demon witch).
> I'm the doctor, prosecutor (doctor)."

Next morning they go to where the witch was buried, with guides to lead the way. On arrival the guides point out the place, saying : " She was laid there." The relatives retire, and the doctor strikes up a witch song :

> " O owl that cries in the thicket. Fwi ! Fwi !
> Oh, come and take away my sorrow.
> O demon, to-day I'll take you away, away.
> Come up, come out, I command you."

They sing louder and louder, and dig away with their hoes. As they get down they find some bones, when they strike up a little song :

> " I see a little cute one ;
> Yes, I see a little cute one."   (Repeated.)

They collect firewood and light a fire, and gathering up the bones they throw them on, especially the skull and leg bones. The doctor pierces the skull with an axe and breathes into the opening. When all is burnt up the doctor smears red paint on his body and sings :

> " She's showing her teeth in the skull.
> You weren't burnt in the hole.
> Now you're burnt in the hole,
> You who showed your teeth in the skull."

Having finished burning the bones they take away the charred skull and an old bone, which they carry to the village. While returning home they must not look back. On reaching the village they are welcomed with cheers. Those who went with the doctor may not speak of what they saw and did while they were away, for such would be criminal. On their return they go to the house of the doctor's slave who carried the fetish basket, and sleep there. In the morning fetishes are made from the charred bones and given to the relatives of the deceased as a protection against evil spells. Then the doctor tells them all : " The

FROM " DEAD MAN'S LAND."

A man disguised as a spirit returned from the land of the Dead.

demon witch who was killing off your children, I've got her in my basket. She's gone with the witch doctor. I'm the black stork." He then receives his final fees and departs, dancing as he goes, and singing the following ditty :

> " Where the doctor has gone,
> All sickness has flown."

Twelve kinds of doctors who practise.
(There are besides these many other kinds.)

(1) *Nganga ya mawesa.* Doctor of the boiling pot ordeal.

(2) *Nganga ya chilumbu.* Diviner about sickness and trouble.

(3) *Nganga ya chishimba.* Witch doctor who uses crystal gazing (*ngulu*).

(4) *Nganga ya kapale.* Seed-gourd-rattling doctor and diviner.

(5) *Nganga ya Mupini.* Doctor who divines with axe on a skin.

(6) *Nganga ya kamimbi.* Rain doctor, or the " swallow doctor."

(7) *Nganga ya chipungu.* Pot and basket diviner.

(8) *Nganga ya musashi.* Clairvoyant, who professes to see in a gourd of oil sickness and trouble, etc.

(9) *Nganga ya chikupo.* Doctor who does not divine, but treats those who have already been diagnosed. He has cures for barrenness and serious ailments.

(10) *Nganga ya mukove.* Smeller-out of witches and wizards. His initiation rite has been described. He is called the " spear doctor," and belongs to the Kaonde tribe.

(11) *Buana Mutombo.* Tongues doctor. This is a doctor who is supposed to be able to give a man the power to speak—only during demon-possession—tongues he never knew before, which is only a temporary gift.

(12) *Nganga ya mwafi.* Poison-cup doctor.

Divination, with prayers and promises to spirits in sickness.
If a man becomes sick the people say : " Be sure and call
in the doctor." Then they call the doctor, who drops into
his incantations, saying : " Take him away, O wild fruit
tree. (Of Mr. So-and-so, who does not need to be carried,
you say, he is Mr. So-and-so, who should be carried, i.e.
he's sick). They have broken up his internal organs. It is
he who bears his name who has caused his sickness." (The
one of whom he is the reincarnation).

Spirit, speaking, prescribes remedy : " Let them dig me
out a little boat. Build a spirit temple and put a spirit
gourd inside with idols, and worship my spirit, and the
sickness shall cease at once." Then the sick man says,
addressing the spirit, after hearing the results of divination, " O my guardian spirit, forgive me I pray you, I
beseech you forgive my negligence. All that you ask for I
will attend to, and do at once." When he recovers from
illness he fulfils his promise to the spirit and builds a spirit
hut to his namesake. All bans being removed now, he goes
where he pleases, rubbing some white flour over his body
for joy and gratitude, and is happy.

Patients may call in a doctor to divine about anything.
Recently while I was in the Luba country I sat by a doctor
and watched him while he divined over three different
people who called at his hut one evening. No. 1 had bought
twelve ducks for breeding purposes, and a wild cat broke
into the duck house one night and killed them. He wanted
to know (a) Who caused the cat to attack his particular
ducks, and why. (b) Whether, if he replaced these ducks
by others, he would be successful in the future, and (c)
whether it would be better to drop the matter altogether.

No. 2 was a woman who had been sick and out of sorts
for a long time and she wanted to know the cause of, and the
cure for, her sickness. The divining oracle used was a small

idol six inches long; the thorax was carved out to allow of the doctor and his patient putting each a forefinger through it for the necessary rattling purposes, i.e. in gyrating it round the top of an inverted gourd. The idol wore a string of blue beads round the neck. As the doctor and patient gyrated the idol, at certain points the idol stopped hard and refused to be moved, which was *a call from below.* Then the doctor questioned the answering spirit, and continued interrogating until he got all the information required, and obtained the cure for his patient.

No. 3 was a man, but as it was then midnight and I was sitting by showing rather much interest, the doctor refused to consult and rap further. I bought the oracle idol from him for three francs, and the doctor wanted to know whether I was going to use it for divining purposes among my European friends. When the doctor is called he usually gets a " starter," or initial fee, before he will go into a case. If the case is important, long, and involved, the fees are heavy, but may be paid in instalments stretching over a period of time. If not paid within a certain time the patient is claimed as a slave of the doctor (the word for debtor and slave is the same, *mushya,* and a debtor may be sold as a slave to pay his debts).

Divination on receipt of news of war by a dream. Now it happens that when a chief has slept he dreams of war with a potential successor, and when he wakes out of sleep he says : " Listen, my people, and do not go out to the fields to-day because I have dreamed of war with my successor. War! ah, War! To-day their soldiers are sleeping near here." Then they send a scout to find out, saying, " Go and find where the war party is, and return quickly and tell us." He sets out, discovers where they are, and returns in haste, saying : " Yes, they have arrived and are in camp in the forest not far off." Then the chief goes into his house and brings out a clay pot with water in it, and he holds an Augury stone between his fingers. Then he questions it, saying : " If we shall be defeated please tell us, O our Augury." He then drops it into the water. If it so happens that the Augury stone does not sink to the bottom of the water pot, but floats, then they know they will not be defeated, but conquer. Then they go out and fight till sunset, when they return to their village and sleep. The chief who has attacked them dreams in sleep that he and his people have all been killed. When he awakes out of sleep he calls his people and tells them his dream, saying : " Come here to me and hear how I have slept." They gather and he tells them, saying : " Let's not continue the fighting to-day, for if we fight we shall all be killed. Let's run away," and they take to their heels and clear back home. Those inside the village, on waking up, shout : " Come on, let's out and fight." But there's no reply to their shouting. Then they know that their enemies have gone, they have run away. They shout with joy, saying : " They've run away," and going out to search and failing to find them return to their chief, and putting on the war-paint do a big war dance.

Charms and composition of " hell fetish." Charms are made up of concoctions the ingredients of which are similar to those found in some parts of China. To enumerate the different kinds of charms, and the numerous things for which charms are used, would require a huge volume. Sometimes charms are put inside beetle shells, small buck horns, tortoise shells, tiny gourds or seed pods, lion and leopard claws, birds' bills, etc. Charms are preventive and used as safeguards and luck medicines against all the ills of life. The doctor's fetish basket (*chipe cha fisoko*) contains the most weird and miscellaneous collection of charms, which are supposed to enable the doctor to meet every contingency that may arise. His dress and decorations form another queer miscellany, and he himself, dressed and painted up for work, resembles a sort of walking and dancing Christmas-tree—if you can imagine that—dangling with lions' claws, human skulls and bones, animal and snake skins hung with fetishes of all kinds, and varied fetish horns.

Bwanga bwa kalunga, or the great hell-fetish, by means of which he catches wizards and witches, is made out of a roan antelope horn, moulded round the top with more than a hundred fetish medicines which hold together by means of red clay and the sticky juice of the *mulolo* tree. The outside is decorated with human teeth like bead work, and in the centre is inserted a duiker horn. Some of the medicines used are a small piece of nearly every part of the human body, including hair, heart, finger and toe nails, mandible, skull, etc., heart and claws of the lion and leopard, elephant feet, hippo skin, tortoise-shell, swallow's bill, osprey's eye and vulture's eyebrow, head of a deadly snake, called *ngweshi*, which stands on its tail and springs to strike, heart of python, head of puff adder, sand from footprint of chief, nose of crocodile, fowl's beak, ant-bear claw, sand got from a pounded mountain stone, hair of dead chief, hyena's forehead, head of dogfish, tooth of field rat, scorpion, head of unlucky child, burned honey bee, pounded meteorite, piece of a tree a man committed suicide on, also a bone of his body, a piece of the body of a dead twin child, gall of lizard, soldier ants, etc., etc.

The " hell-fetish " horn is pierced through the middle and set on an iron rod. It is then made to spin, and where it points as it stops spinning is the direction of the witch or wizard, who is promptly pounced on.

Each witch doctor is an expert ventriloquist, which art he uses in calling up the spirits, and speaks and squeaks to them in imitation of the voices of the dead. His wives are many, well fed and chosen from the prettiest. They are also kept well in hand by fear of the poisoned cups of which their master knows so well the many ingredients, and how and when to administer them. His family is well clothed and obedient, for the father is rich, powerful, and prosperous, and a man of importance in the land. The death and burial of a witch doctor is a time of sorrow and much wailing as he is highly respected and greatly feared, besides being known over the length and breadth of the land as *Yamasamba*, " The Man from Below."

Execution of an unqualified doctor. There is a Board composed of the head doctors in each district, and every practitioner must pass through the recognised initiation ceremonies and receive a diploma in the form of a hell-fetish, without which he may not pose as a doctor. Twenty-six years ago a man named Chefye set up as a doctor in the village of Chief Chisunka of the Chishinga country. He professed to have great power in smelling out witches and wizards, and any stooping, doting old man or woman he saw he accused of witchcraft and had them killed. One of his prospective victims denounced him as an impostor, and accused him of lying, divination, and practices, and of practising without official recognition from the Board of head doctors. He was tried by the above chief, found guilty of imposing on the public, and was hacked to pieces and burned to death as a false doctor and as a wizard.

Makandwe, another native in Kazembe's country, also set himself up as a qualified doctor, but was found out and had to flee for his life elsewhere. He escaped the witch's death of burning owing to the European occupation of the country at that time.

CHAPTER VIII
Totemism, Exogamy & Taboo

THERE are four divisions of society recognised throughout Bantu Africa : 1. The tribe. 2. The clan. 3. The family. 4. The individual. Tribal interest ranks first, clan interest second, family interest follows, then last of all and least important comes the interest of the individual. Totemism is exclusively *a clan distinction*, and as there may be many clans in one tribe, so a clan is composed of many families, and each clan is known by its totem animal, bird, insect, vegetable, or mineral.

Just as Kafir Socialism is seen in the life of a Bantu tribe, so in a lesser degree the out-workings of the same socialistic idea of society are seen in the grouping of families who form themselves into clans for social and protective purposes. These clans are each bound by laws whose basic object is to maintain strict exogamous relationships between members of the clans and to lay down which clans may intermarry and which clans may not, with formulated statements and reasons for and against. The maintenance of exogamy is the *raison d'être* of the clan system, for all clansmen and also clanswomen are brothers and sisters. For a man to marry a woman of his own clan is equivalent to a man marrying his sister and vice versa. That is why an African traveller or trader is often nonplussed to understand his carriers meeting brothers and sisters in such distant and different parts of the country. If, e.g., a man of the elephant clan from Nyasaland should meet people of the elephant clan on the West Coast he is bound by clan laws to receive hospitality, is treated as a brother and may claim all the help of which he stands in need. I have seen my carriers meet a man of another caravan westward bound and watched one of them take off his shirt and give it to the needy clansman. " Why do you give away your shirt to a stranger ? " " He's not a stranger, white man, he's my brother." As it had happened again and again I laughed, saying, " Well, boys, you must have a lot of brothers." I did not then understand the totemistic reasons at back of this seeming philanthropy. " He's my brother, she's my sister," explains the clan idea, which is wider than the inner circle of family and blood relationship.

If a man enters into an endogamous relationship prohibited by clan laws he is ostracised and becomes a social outcast, so much so that his own relatives will not visit him in sickness or attend his funeral if he dies. He has committed incest, one of the most abhorred sins from the Bantu view-point. Tattooing the body, cicatrisation, hair-dressing, teeth chipping and filing or extraction have nothing whatever to do with the clan idea, but are exclusively tribal customs. The significance of clan totems is often an enigma to the outside and casual observer. Clan totems are exclusively used to distinguish the hundred and one different clans, and if, as in Europe, the Bantu negroes carried flags, as, e.g., the clans of Scotland used to do, these would bear a lion, buffalo, elephant, bee, ant, anthill, or whatever was the clan totem ; in the same way America flies the eagle, Britain the lion, Canada the maple leaf, Japan the rising sun, and the Chinese Empire the dragon. I have tried to get at the fundamental significance of totems, but as it seems to be a system dating from the remotest antiquity I have not been able to discover the *real reasons* for the original choice of bird, animal, or insect, etc. There has been no new clan started within the memory of the present generation, so that the significance of totems is more or less shrouded in mystery and lies hid under the accretion of ages.

A man of the elephant clan may marry a woman of the clay clan, because the elephant in crossing rivers digs up the clay on the banks with his tusk, and the clay clan uses it for making tobacco pipes, cooking pots, and water jars. The snake, field rat, and grass clans may intermarry, for the snake eats field rats, field rats eat grass, and the clay clan also eats grass. The fish, elephant, clay, grass, tortoise, goat, bird, rain, and a number of other clans may intermarry, but none of these may marry members of the honey bee clan.

The reason given is many hundreds of years old and to the effect that the heads of this clan, when the other clans were attacked and raided, bolted to the Wemba country and hid to save their skins. Prior to European administration, if a man of one of these clans had married a member of a bee clan he would have been killed for entering a clan of cowards. Members of royal clans, as, e.g., the crocodile kings of Wembaland, the dog kings of Lundaland, and the war-drum kings of the Katanga, are not bound by clan laws and may marry women of any clan on the plea that " the king has no prohibitions," corresponding to our " the king can do no wrong."

The elephant is a totem animal and is respected because of its great strength, lots of meat, and valuable ivory. Elephant is the synonym for ivory, and the chief and people are always glad to see ivory come to the kraal— hence the honour of membership in this clan. The lion is taken as a totem because it is strong and fierce and king of the forest. I remember a redeemed slave boy who put his hands over his head and burst out crying because he was chastised for disobedience. He howled : " Oh ! think of my being punished, I who belong to the fierce lion clan." The buffalo is a totem animal because of its great quantity of beef and habit of going in compact herds. The leopard is totemised because of its beautiful skin and ability to defend itself. It is also able to take the offensive and does not hesitate to attack animals bigger than itself.

The crocodile is the favourite totem of some royal clans, e.g., the Wemba in Rhodesia, and the Luena people in Angola. They were originally river people and always filed their teeth fish-shape in imitation of their totem animal. The croc is a great fish-eater, and most Bantus are fond of fish as a diet. I knew a fisherman on the Luapula who took the name of " the enemy of fish," of which he killed and ate large quantities. On one occasion he is reported to have eaten ten large eight-pounder fish, besides a large mess of porridge, and a pot of several gallons of beer as a wash down. He also boasted the name of " Glutton," and for a bet he ate a goat and a pot of porridge and drank a large gourd full of strong beer. He was a crony worthy of the Scottish Rab-Haw ! The eagle clan is proud of its totem bird, and on a member dying he will lament, " Oh ! I, an eagle who have flown so high." As the lion is considered the king of animals so the eagle is looked on as the king of birds. The eagle clan is held in high esteem and to belong to it gives status. The snake is totemised because of its speed and cunning, also owing to its being greatly feared on account of its power to kill an enemy quickly. The African is naturally vindictive and revengeful, and envies, though he fears, the man who successfully deals in black magic. The field rat is a great delicacy and forms a favourite dish of minor venison, and unlike the house rat he is a clean feeder. The ant-hill clan like to build their huts and hamlets near these termitic structures. The wonderful village inside the ant-hill, the security and remarkable building power of the ant, their wisdom, and incidentally their edibility, make their hilly homes worthy to become a totemic distinction. Ant-hill soil is very fertile, having first been filtered through the bodies of the termites, and the clansmen get rich crops from this. The best Katanga and Rhodesian tobacco is grown on these ant-hills. Lake Bangweulu and the Luapula River is the home of the ant-hill clan. The clay clan chose its totem on account of the usefulness of clay. No clay, no tobacco pipes, cooking pots, or water jars. Many Bantu potters make a good living by their pottery, hence the value and necessity of clay. The bee and honey readily suggest the reason for their advancement to a place among the totems. Honey is much prized as a food, from it strong mead is brewed, and the wax is a valuable article of commerce.

Taboos. Throughout Bantuland taboos are innumerable and tie the negro from head to foot on his progress from birth, through life, to death. Tribal taboos are peculiarly interesting because of their antiquity, and the reasons, physical and geographical, at the base of their existence. The Yeke tribe will not eat fish. They say that it is because it is slippery and sickly food, but I think the main reason is to be found in the fact that they were plain dwellers at the north end of Tanganyika, and were compelled to draw their water from wells, rarely seeing a fish or a river; hence they made a virtue out of a necessity. Neither do they eat zebra meat; this custom they may have acquired from the arabised natives with whom they lived and with whom they traded.

The tribal taboos of the Wemba people are (1) Bush-pig; (2) Bushbuck; and (3) the Zebra. These are forbidden to be eaten.

The Lunda tribe have no taboos.

The system of taboos among clans as clans does not exist, and there are no distinctive clan taboos.

Individual taboos are the most numerous, and it is difficult to find a native between the East and West Coasts who has not one or other personal taboo which he regards as vital to his life and well-being. Taboos in Bantu mean " principle," and a " man of no principles " or " an unprincipled man " is called a *mulyelye*, or, " a man who eats anything "—a man without taboos.

If a woman is pregnant and aborts again and again, and abortion becomes a " habit," the doctor is called in. He comes, diagnoses the case, and makes up fetish medicines which he puts into a duiker horn and gives it to her to *be worn round her neck.* Then he imposes the following taboos :

(1) You must not eat mudfish.

(2) You must not drink strong beer.

(3) You must only eat at home.

(4) You must not get fire to light your own from any neighbour's house.

(5) You must not lend your bed or bedding.

(6) You must not lend your baskets to any other woman.

When she gives birth to a child successfully and the baby cuts his first tooth the same family doctor is again called to the house. He comes and examines his patient, then takes her to the river, shaves her head and bathes her. Then she catches a mudfish which she holds in her teeth. It is brought home and cooked, also porridge, and she eats a meal publicly. After this the doctor removes all the previous six taboos and she resumes her normal life and diet.

If a man is accused of sterility his friends go off into the

bush and search for medicines for him of three kinds:
(1) Medicine to drink; (2) medicine to chew; (3) and
medicine to smoke in a pipe. Then two taboos are imposed: (1) Don't eat mudfish. (2) Don't drink strong
beer. If after this treatment his wife subsequently conceives and bears a child the taboos are removed and normal
life is resumed. If a mother is under a number of taboos
the child is similarly tabooed until it cuts its first teeth
and is therefore justified, when normal life is resumed.

Spirit kings and queens (those supposed to be possessed
by the spirits of departed kings and queens) on beginning
their professional life are taken aside by their elders and
instructors, when the imposition of a certain number of
taboos is formally made. These are more severe.

(1) Don't eat mush, or porridge.
(2) Don't drink beer.
(3) Don't eat chicken.
(4) Don't eat mudfish.
(5) Don't eat rabbit.
(6) Don't eat tortoise (some natives are very fond of
tortoise).
(7) Don't eat zebra meat.
(8) Don't eat bushbuck.

These taboos are in force only during ecstatic performances
and when under the influence of demon possession, which
usually lasts five or six days. After this the taboos are removed and normal life is resumed.

A leper who seeks medical help is tabooed as follows:

(1) Don't eat mudfish (natives are very fond of this).
(2) Don't eat bloody meat.
(3) Don't drink strong beer.
(4) Only eat at your own house.
(5) Must not go into the house of another.

Then the doctor gives him medicine to drink. He also gets medicinal leaves and rubs them on the leprous sores, causing a blister. He opens the blister and puts a medicinal paste on the sores; if the medicine " catches," the leper recovers. When he recovers the taboos are removed and he resumes normal life.

If a man contracts syphilis the doctor is called, and among other things he imposes the following four taboos :

(1) Don't eat mudfish.
(2) Don't drink strong beer.
(3) Don't eat chicken.
(4) Don't eat raw meat.

If he recovers his mother goes and digs roots and obtains castor oil. The herbal medicine is powdered and with the oil made into a paste which is rubbed on the body. The mother makes beer and cooks chicken and fresh meat and fish with which he is fed, after which all the taboos are removed.

Hunter's taboos affect also the hunter's wife, and the laws pertaining to success in the chase are numerous and intricate. Inviolate faithfulness of husband and wife during the former's absence in the hunting field is one of the first and most important laws for hunters if they are to have luck. If a woman is unfaithful during her hunter husband's absence, the hunter is exposed to failure, danger from wild animals, and even death. If the elephant charges and the hunter is killed, the woman is tried for murder on the ground of concealed adultery and breaking the taboo, and is at once executed. A young hunter on his first hunt may not eat the game he kills until the older hunter arrives and feeds him with a piece of meat cooked in a medicine. After this he may eat when and where he likes. To give reasons for the hundred and one taboos of Bantu peoples would be as difficult as to provide satisfactory explanations of the Talmud, or the old Levitical laws of Taboo in regard to what may or what may not be eaten (*vide* Leviticus, Chap. XI.) I fancy the initial explanation of this intricate network of Taboo laws is to be found in the undoubted Semitic origin of the Bantu people. When one asks, " Why is so-and-so tabooed ? " the invariable answer one gets is this : " Please, sir, these are our customs," or, " We follow our ancestors' steps." The penalty for breaking a taboo is sickness, and even death, plus the dire displeasure of the spirits and clansmen. A man who would do this is looked on as " void of principle," is despised, called all sorts of vile names, and there are those who would not hesitate to poison or spear him. Very often the sickness on account of which the taboos have been imposed is brought back in a more severe form as the result of breaking them. A man who breaks a taboo, if it becomes publicly known, is branded as a social outcast, just as a man would be among Arabs and Jews who ate pig. These old Bantu laws of Totemism, Exogamy, and Taboo are as old as the Mosaic economy—perhaps older—and strike their roots back thousands of years into the dim, distant history of the world. Even the modern educated Bantu negro is as ignorant of the whence, why, and wherefore of much of these old-world codes as the ordinary modern Jew is of the meaning of the collection of miscellaneous laws found in the Talmud.

CHAPTER IX

Secret Societies & Guilds

BUTWA—A LEADING SECRET SOCIETY IN RHODESIA

THE Batwa people of Lake Bangweulu are one of five Bantu tribes scattered over a large part of Africa and bearing—with phonetic variations—the same name. These Batwa are one of the few Central African tribes about which little or nothing is known. They inhabit the marshes at the south end of the lake and live mainly on fish and antelope flesh. They cultivate the ground around the ant-hills that spring up here and there throughout the marshes, and on other raised patches they grow, at the end of the dry season, meagre crops of cereals and root foods. As they do not produce, however, a tithe of the food necessary for their support they trade their sun-dried fish and smoked antelope flesh with their land neighbours for meal and grain.

As to the other four Batwa tribes, I know nothing at first hand, either of their language or literature. All the information I possess concerning them is of a geographical nature and to the effect that

Batwa No. 1 live in Damaraland.

Batwa No. 2 find their habitat among the swamps of the Kafue River in N.W. Rhodesia.

Batwa No. 3 reside in the Kameruns.

Batwa No. 4 are the pigmies of the Aruwimi forests and swamps on the Upper Congo, while our local friends,

Batwa No. 5, live amongst the marshes at the south end of Lake Bangweulu.

The Bangweulu Batwa, amongst whom I have travelled and worked for about two decades, off and on, form the subject of this chapter. They are primarily a water-people, very timid and conservative, and their full local appellation as a tribe is Batwa-Menda, or the " Water-Beaters," owing to the fact that they spend the greater part of their time in canoes, paddling about among the swamps, fishing and hunting. They are also known locally as the Bana-Nika, which in common parlance signifies " River Children," and their country, if the agglomeration of marshes and ant-hills amongst which they live can be justly denominated a country, is called Manika, or " The Land of Rivers."

Philologically, their language belongs to the Bantu family, and is one of an allied group of fifteen dialects, mutually intelligible, and spoken throughout the greater part of N.E. Rhodesia, part of N.W. Rhodesia, and in the south-eastern corner of the Congo State. Their claim to separate and special consideration here is due to their being the founders and, generally, members of a powerful Secret Society, designated " Butwa." The question whether the society name " Butwa " sprang from the tribal name " Batwa " or vice versa is a moot one, and of no immediate importance. The word " Butwa," etymologically, is made up of two parts, consisting of prefix and stem. The prefix " Bu-" is a qualificative one, and contains the idea of " Society," whereas " -Twa," the stem, is a word in almost universal use throughout the greater part of Central Africa. " -Twa " is the root of the verb *ku-twa*, meaning, primarily, " to pound meal," and secondarily " to pound anything " in a mortar with a pestle—an African custom in vogue since the days of Herodotus. Like most African words, it has its metaphorical as well as its material uses, and is put very *severely* into practice metaphorically if, perchance, a hapless exoteric should venture too near the Butwa temples while a service is being held !

Butwa is an old institution, though different in form from other mysteries. I suggest an alternate etymology which for years has seemed to me the true and possibly the original one, namely, that *Butwa* is derived from the verb *buta* (root *but-*), much used by neighbouring tribes, and meaning " to cover up," " to cover over " (with the idea of hiding) and bears the meaning of the Greek verb *kalypto*. The suffix *wa* indicates the passive voice, and together the root *but-* and the suffix *wa* mean " the hidden thing," " the mystery "; the noun being used in both singular and plural, should be translated here plurally, and signifies " the mysteries," the exact name given to the Greek Eleusinian cult. It is by no means easy, however, to exhume from under the accretion of ages the original significance of such a word.

Butwa is likewise a distinct cult, possessing Initiatory Rites, Ceremonies, and Temple Services, with life secrets imposed at initiation. Its members speak an esoteric language known only to the initiated, and called *Lubendo*. Ability to *Benda* or speak this cryptic speech is looked upon as a sure mark of a member of the Society. This speech finds its counterpart in European argots, and is formed variously: sometimes by transposing the syllables of a common word, e.g. *kasaka* for *kakasa*, meaning " a little foot "; again, by changing an initial letter, e.g. *Temuka* for *Semuka*, " to be demon-possessed," or by introducing an obsolete word, as *Yambe*, an archaic name for " God "; sometimes by a compound metaphorical word such as *Busankabemba*, meaning " The Lake-Sprinkler," which is a secret word for " water."

The female members of *Butwa* form themselves into

singing bands, and to the accompaniment of a native banjo called *Chansa*, peculiar to the cult, they carry on nocturnal concerts which are usually accompanied by wild dancing. Like most Bantu tribes they are *Totemic*, many of them belonging to the ant-hill clan, perhaps most of them. Like most African tribes, also, their *Totemism*, in its main idea, is *exogamic*, and is intended to control marriage relationships outside certain circles to avoid consanguinity. It has nothing whatever to do with worship, as used to be thought.

I shall now proceed to discuss *Butwa* roughly under four heads :

    1. Its Membership.   2. Its Constitution.
    3. Its Aims.   4. Its Influence.

1. The members of this Society are generally found among the water-peoples, though of recent years some land tribes have built Butwa temples, called in Butwa priests, and initiated young and old, establishing lodges over a large part of the adjoining mainland. Its membership is promiscuous, made up of both sexes and all ages. Central and branch lodges are found on both banks of the Southern Chambesi River, that runs into Lake Bangweulu, all round the lake, and on its thirty islands, also among the marshes occupied by the Ba-Unga on the east, and by the Batwa at the south end of the lake and along the entire length of the Luapula-Congo as far as Lake Mweru, on both the British and Belgian sides. The chief Nkuba—originally of Kilwa Island on Lake Mweru—whom I have known intimately for years, is the recognised introducer of *Butwa* throughout these parts, and his name is famous in many a Butwa song. The tribes affected by the cult on North Bangweulu are the Ba-Bisa and Ba-Unga. At the south end and on the western side are the Ba-Twa and Ba-Ushi.

These, with the Ba-Lamba and Ba-Lunda along the Luapula, with the Ba-Shila and a few Ba-Bemba and Ba-Itabwa around Lake Mweru, form the entire Butwa community of these parts.

Lodges with a flourishing membership are to be found some thirty to sixty miles inland from both river and lakes, and everywhere a marked enthusiasm is evidenced for Butwa, while its power is felt in every relationship of life. Many divorces are annually sought and obtained because of the treatment of husband or wife when he or she is a non-member. This is due to the refusal of one or other to join the Society. The non-member has frequently to submit to the insulting language of the other spouse, while the whole Society backs husband or wife in the endeavour of either to convert the obstinate partner. The only possible solution is divorce. Of a husband who resists his wife's entreaties to become a member the following sarcastic ditty is sung:

> *Song of the Obstinate Spouse:* "The husband at home,
> He lies in a heap,
> Like a pig, in a pile."

id est, he sleeps alone while his wife is enjoying herself in the Butwa camp.

Young boys and girls are stripped, at and after initiation, of all sense of shame, and the latter, as will be seen later, are forced to submit to gross indignities. Here also they gain their first lessons in sexual immorality. Even babies are initiated and as they grow up are gradually instructed, until in mature years they become full members, when they are introduced to the whole arcana of Butwa.

2. To speak of the constitution of Butwa I shall have to avail myself of a paper written for me in the native language by an ex-witch doctor. I here give the translation as literally as English will allow.

Initiation ceremonies. Firstly, on initiating people into the Butwa Society, chief's dung is gathered and dog's dung; parings of the feet of the crocodile, the elephant, the armadillo, the tortoise, and the scorpion, besides herbal medicines of various kinds. Pulverised crystal is also added. The whole is then put into a pot with the powdered crystal, and boiled together. When this is done, the first novice is given a drink out of the pot in this manner: He or she is seized hand and foot by the priests and taken inside a hut, where the initiation drink is administered. At this point all strike up a song:

> "Oh, come and drink,
> Ye mother's children, come and drink!
> If any stay away
> He's the child of a slave, let him stay."

Now the pot is passed round and all the initiates drink, whereupon the priest gives each a new name, saying, "Now your name is 'Ferryman.'" They then continue singing and dancing throughout the whole night. Those who have brought their children for initiation cook messes of porridge and chickens, and make beer, with which the feast continues. Thus the night is spent. After a few days have passed and the new moon appears, all—both men and women—become spirit-possessed and speak oracularly. On returning the dishes in which the food for the feast has been brought, the young people beg from those who prepared the feast, while they strike up a song:

> "In the hospitable home
> May there never lack food.
> Ye mothers of the Ferryman
> Bring out your food."

The women give them food and they answer, saying, "I bow the knee to the mothers of Butwa." The women reply, "Arise a perfect Butwa member and look out for scorpions." They now turn about and go back. At this point the Butwa Temple is built and all the members prepare to remove there.

At the cross-roads fetish medicine is laid down and the place is given a name. " This is the Kaminsamanga," is said. The remainder of the food they are eating is thrown down here. Here, also, a bower is made of two saplings, the large ends of which are inserted into the ground, the small ends being bent in towards the centre, where they unite, forming an arch. Each initiate must pass through this arch before entering the temple. On passing through, each hangs his Butwa fetish over the bower as it may not be carried into the temple. Reaching the temple, they strike up a song :

> "Oh, Travellers !
> Oh, Travellers !
> This is the music,
> Oh, listen all."

Leaving the cross-roads they sing another song :

> "No need to point out the path,
> Butwa itself shall lead the way."

" Ad finem, ad templum ingrediens cum initiatis, unus ex eis, sed homo in majestate constitutus (ordinarie unus ex presbyteris) sibi puellam eligit et dicit ' genuflecte, initiate, et medicinam accipe.' Puella consentit et presbyter eam publice polluit, statim omnes praesentes de adulterio conveniunt."

While this is going on, the elder Butwa priestesses bring in beer with cooked porridge and chickens, while a cryptic song is sung which runs thus :

> "Hurrah ! hurrah ! Oh, hurrah, Sir !
> We who give the fetish-horns,
> We twist up your tongue, you are tied.
> Oh, hurrah ! hurrah !"

id est, you are now subject to Butwa secrets and may not speak.

The following day they prepare for the final grand ceremonies of the Butwa festival, when every one is dressed up fantastically and painted with stripes to represent zebras, while the whole camp dances all night. The favourite bird of the Batwa is the crested crane, whose antics and call they imitate in their dances.

At dawn the following day the chief priests and priestesses call the " mothers of the crystal fetish," gather the initiates together, and compound for each a fetish-horn. Some receive two, some three, and even four. Another song is struck up :

> " Be quick and get on the white paint,
> The king's drums are sounding,
> The drums are sounding, sounding,
> Quick and put on the white paint."

All then smear white chalk over their bodies, while the " mothers of the crystal fetish " instruct them, saying, " On no account must you reveal the secrets to the un-initiated. On no account must you speak of the proceedings and of what you have been doing here." Then " the mothers of the Butwa mysteries " bring out articles, including pots of beer, calico, hoes, beads, and other things—the temple initiation fees. Drums strike up boisterously now, and all join in a wild war-dance, while the following song is sung, stooping as they dance to pick up the various things lying all over the ground :

> " Oh! this the place
> Where we pick up the good things " (repeated again and again).

When the dancing is finished, the ceremonies end, and all scatter to their villages.

The priesthood or council of Butwa officers is composed

of five or more elders of each sex, who wear special dress and
bear special names.   Here are a few of the names of both
sexes :

Bainangulu

(Or mothers of the crystal fetish).

Men.	Women.
Katumpa	*Buyamba*
Chimundu	*Katempa*
Luongo	*Ngobola*
Shinini (ya mukulakulu)	*Chabo*
Kasumpa	*Lubuta*

These are looked up to as the organisers and officers of the
cult meetings, and take charge of the initiates, giving the
Chibolo or initiatory drink.   Each of these has his or her
band of initiates, from whom they receive recognised fees
for their services at initiation.   They also claim to possess
magical powers, and terrorise the young members into
obedience by threats of witchcraft which they sometimes
put into practice.   Each *Inangulu* looks on his or her band
of initiates hereafter as his or her " fetish children,"
bana ba bwanga.

3.   The aims of the Butwa in the individual are to
suppress selfishness and to promote social life.   The chief
attractions are dancing, singing, concerts, beer-drinks, and
sexual licence.   *Lubendo*, or the ability to speak the secret
language of Butwa, is, I am told, another much-coveted
acquisition.   From the family standpoint, Butwa cements
members by means of a common tie.   Sometimes a recal-
citrant son or daughter is found who refuses to be initiated.
When such happens, life is made unbearable, and the
stubborn child becomes the subject of mocking jest and
covert raillery in song.

Socially, Butwa resembles a club whose members are

bound by common rules. While services are in progress, processions are the order of each day. To draw water at the river, collect firewood in the forest, all go in procession, singing and dancing as they go. Even going to the bush for necessary purposes, all—men, women, and children—go in procession, and no sense of shame is attached to any necessity, while no privacy is observed or allowed. A man may have sexual intercourse with his mother, sister, his nearest relative, even to his own daughter. However, this licence becomes null and void outside the temple precincts, and immediately after the final ceremony of *Subula*.

Politically, Butwa is a tremendous force to be reckoned with. Its unity gives it power, so that headmen of villages, to safeguard and ingratiate themselves with their people, if not already members, become members on assuming chieftainship.

4. The influence of Butwa from a purely native stand-point is beneficial, with its feasting, drinking, and orgies. Its help in sickness or need, with the prospects of a respect-able funeral and worship after death is much to be desired· On the other hand, looking at it from a Government point of view, Butwa is decidedly and grossly immoral, besides being contrary to good citizenship in any form, e.g., in the year 1909, when the Luapula River had been closed to traffic, owing to sleeping sickness regulations, certain snakes were said to have appeared in some villages on the river-bank. These it was reported were sent by *Songa*, a powerful local deity, who, they said, was very angry because Butwa ceremonies and his worship had fallen into neglect. He ordered them to be revived at once and that all Batwa who wished for a successful harvest must send to him to have their seeds blessed. This order led to the wholesale secret infringement of Government regulations, by chiefs and

people alike. In some places, where they failed to cross the river surreptitiously, they did not cultivate, dreading the *Songa's* curse, and hunger ensued. Butwa is powerful, and a man or woman or child, presuming to change and become a Christian, exposes himself to the dangerous shafts of the whole Butwa fraternity. Non-members are not interfered with, but all members are bound by *the sacred drink* to stand by the rules of the Society, and never, under penalty of death, to divulge its secrets.

A person who has been initiated, " dies Butwa," and is " born again." He is so much *a re-born man* that, on returning to village life, he has to be introduced to his father and mother and relatives, whom he is supposed, and pretends, not to know.

CHAPTER X

Secret Societies & Guilds (*continued*)

SECRET Societies and Guilds permeate the whole fabric of village life. In the last chapter I gave a description in detail of an African secret society with an account of its peculiar significance, and, from material I have gathered, what applies to " Butwa " applies fundamentally and with trivial modification to most other societies. " Bumbuli " is also, or rather used to be, a very powerful society composed of both male and female members. It belongs for the most part to the Luba tribe and was introduced by them into a corner of N. Rhodesia by " Kazembe " and his people, who came originally from the West like the Wemba. Owing to fear of the Government, it is not active in Rhodesia to-day, but is still going strong in the South Luba country and the Katanga. It has temples, with a priesthood, initiatory rites, and ceremonies, with periodical services the same as Butwa. Singing and dancing, with orgies, play a large part in the services, and no outsider may approach the temple precincts while services are in progress. Death is the penalty for divulging the society's secrets. I have seen its activities in the district where I lived many years ago, and only recently have I succeeded in obtaining definite, reliable information, which is as follows :

For initiation purposes a pit some five feet deep, by four feet wide, is dug at the side of the village, and this is covered over by leafy branches in the centre of which a hole is left to introduce the hand and arm of each initiate. A doctor is hidden in the hole who is declared to be a " giant tortoise." Each novice coming forward puts in his or her hand, which is promptly seized and held by the " tortoise." The hand is dragged down bit by bit, and, speaking in a squeaky " spirit voice," the " tortoise " makes each novice confess his or her misdeeds : namely, " witchcraft," " theft," " adultery," etc. The other members gathered round, in jest and song taunt the novices and tease them with sarcastic remarks and wicked imputations, such as :

" Confess your thefts " (*Watanda lwibo*),

" Confess your witchcrafts " (*Watanda buti !*),

—and don't hide anything you have done from the " tortoise in the hole " (*Lolo ñombe*). These confessions are inviolate to the society. Thereupon, the initiate *confesses all*, during which confession he or she is terrified by threats emanating from the unearthly voice in the hole. The initiatory drink is then given, and the initiated person at once " dies Bumbuli," lying on the ground unconscious. To restore " new life " to each, the chief doctor tramps on the head and foot of the initiate, and brings them back to life, giving to each *reborn* person a new name. After this ceremony drums are brought out, and all present perform a war-dance, while the novices stand in the centre, each with a spear in hand. Above is done at the conclusion of the service.

" Kasanshi " or " Buyembe " is another powerful society belonging to the Luba and Western Lake Mweru people, and used to be very active among the hill villages overlooking the lake.

It is the only one I know which has definite cannibal rites and ceremonies. They build their temples in dark forest groves, where they carry out their initiatory rites and ceremonies, with initiation " death drink," after drinking

which they are brought back to life and get new names.
They dig up dead bodies which they cook and eat, with
wild drumming and cannibal orgies. They wear two skins
of the Impala antelope, one in front and one behind.
They dance to the music of long, round drums and rattles.
They practise black magic, and terrorise the districts where
they live. They also have a knowledge of the healing art,
and know many useful drugs with which they practise,
receiving good fees. Their fetishes and medicines are so
numerous that they use exceptionally large baskets called
chipe cha fisoko. When the new moon appears, they
become spirit-possessed, and set off on ghoulish journeys
to dig up dead bodies for their feasts. They have also a
notoriety for stripping recently buried bodies of cloth,
ivory, copper and brass ornaments, and all bodily dress
and decorations. One of these, named Chishishila, who
lived in Kazembe's district (and I am told still lives) is one
of the most notorious of these ghouls, who regularly digs
up and strips newly buried bodies. He was driven out of
the village and lives by himself in the bush now with his
two wives. It is reported that he stripped the body of the
old Kazembe and also of his queen, Ina Kafwaya. He goes
to the graves with his Buyembe fetish and " calls out "
the dead man or woman, after which he strips them of
everything and orders them back to their graves. In
calling them he uses the " Umbilical name " given at
birth. He was found out owing to his having sold, for
beer, etc., the clothes and ornaments of people who were
dead. Many recognised the articles of dress and the decorations formerly worn by relatives who had died. They are
afraid of him, I am told, which is the reason they refuse to
denounce him and his vampire practices. This cannibal
society is strong in the West Mweru district and the neighbouring Itabwa country.

"Bulindu" is another secret society composed exclusively of females. The founder of this society was a chieftainess at the north end of Lake Mweru named Ina-Chituti, and the following story is told which gives its origin and foundation. She had a son named Chituti who was boorish, disrespectful to his parents, and who lost no opportunities to misbehave and insult his elders. The mother warned him again and again, but to no purpose. One day she went on a prolonged visit to friends at the south end of the lake, leaving the boy's uncle in charge. When she returned she found that the uncle had killed her son, skinned him, stretched and dried the skin in the sun, and was using it as a mat to sit on. She was so angry that she planned and founded this society, getting together a number of leading local women to uphold women's mother-rights and to protect themselves from the tyranny of men. This also had its initiation ceremonies and fetish medicine on which the cult was built. This society has also a secret rite which is performed on the initiation of young girls, mildly corresponding to circumcision. The instrument used is the sawlike claw of a large caterpillar. This society is the cause of much divorce, as is Butwa, for the women often spend months away from their homes attending the temple services.

It is exclusively a women's society, and is still powerful throughout the Katanga.

In Bihé, Angola, when I was there, there was in existence a very powerful society of secret service police called "Olongumbu." As far as I know and could learn, their duties were—among others—to warn and, if necessary, punish those who committed any acts contrary to social and tribal custom, or who refused to obey the ordinary constituted authorities. For example, if a man who had been again and again warned by his fellows for reprehensible conduct refused to listen, a complaint was lodged by those concerned before the officers of the Olongumbu cult. These would go to the offender's house at night and call him outside, and if he refused to come they would burst his door open and drag him out and flog him, warning him not to repeat such and such an offence. If the offence was repeated certain Olongumbu police, deputed by their superiors, would again knock him up another night, drag him out of his house, and punish him severely. They were even vested with power to carry out the death penalty. This society was recognised by chiefs and people, and had a wholesome effect in maintaining good behaviour and keeping the people law-abiding. Like other societies it had its abuses.

On the Luapula River and in the Fort Rosebery district of Northern Rhodesia there exists a strong and much-dreaded robber society called Kabwalala. The name is compounded of two parts, *Kabwa*, " a dog," and *Lala*, " to sleep." They claim to possess a potent fetish medicine, which they sprinkle round a village or house before they commence to plunder the owners. The fetish is supposed to drug the dogs and people and send them off to sleep. Hence its name of " Dogs go to sleep." I knew the founder of this society, whose name was *Kunda Shinanga*, " pigeon doctor," and twenty-two years ago he accompanied me out East on the journey referred to in Chapter XXVI. He was a big, ugly, pock-marked fellow, and lazy, and was a member of the Ushi tribe in Rhodesia. It was he who discovered and compounded this sleeping fetish, which is kept in an antelope horn and worn next the body. Years ago a band of six of these attacked a mission station, on which occasion the senior missionary nearly lost his life. It happened in this way. During the dark early hours of the morning they ascended the hill and entered the white men's bedrooms while they were asleep in bed, went through room after room, and carried off in all some six loads of goods. One of the missionaries, awaking out of sleep, in spite of the robbers' fetish, heard a step outside his window and thought it was a hyena. Seizing his rifle and three cartridges he stepped out lightly on to the verandah of his house and hid in the shadow. In a few minutes he saw the figure of a man passing with stealthy motion. He gave the man the usual native challenge, at which he bolted. The European sprang off the verandah after him and fired, shouting, " Stop, or I'll shoot again." The robber, who was naked and oiled and had a big spear in his hand, refused to stop, and continued running. My friend fired again, calling to him to stop, but he kept running. He fired a third time, meaning to wing him, but missed. At this the thief swerved and fell on a heap of stones with the European on top of him. They got into grips, and there was a fierce struggle. The robber shouted, " Let me go, white man, or I'll kill you," and tried to stab him in the back with the spear. The white man got his hands badly cut, and as his strength was nearly gone, he suddenly remembered a native Ju-Jitsu trick, which he performed and doubled the man clean up. He dropped his spear, shouting, " White man, I'm done." The missionary hung on to him till others, who heard the shooting, located them, and rushed to the rescue. The case was tried by a Belgian judge, and the robber got a long term of imprisonment. On the way to undergo his sentence in a Lower Congo prison, he terrified the guards who had charge of him, declaring himself a great wizard, and they let him go. The last word I heard was that he had murdered a man on the Luapula River shortly afterwards. A short time ago, at the police station in Elisabethville, Katanga, I saw a gang of prisoners, and eight or ten

An Elaborate Head-dress of a Girl, Kasongo, Katanga.

A Dancing Demon-possessed Girl of Chilumbu Secret Society.

loads, including tents and travelling equipment. On enquiry I found out that it was a small band of Kabwalala robbers who had plundered a white man's camp, and had been rounded up by the police near Sakania on the Anglo-Belgian border.

Members of all these societies have cryptic signs by which they recognise each other, and a man who, when challenged, fails to give the countersign is put down as a fraud and disowned. They also have a secret language which is only a matter of transposition of letters or syllables. I have heard it spoken and recognised words here and there, though I failed to follow a conversation. These correspond to European argots. Societies like the foregoing represent the bulk of native *society life*, and are a great attraction, as well as being a powerful political factor which can be brought into play at any critical juncture in the life of the tribe.

Every trade and profession has its guild, hunters and fishermen, iron and copper workers, workers in leather and workers in wood, as well as doctors of every branch of fetish-craft and medicine. Musicians, hunters, etc., and even robbers have their protective guilds. Every one of these has for its foundation a particular fetish horn, or set of fetishes, with certain initiation ceremonies and rites. They have their club and temple meetings at specified times, and each has a particular set of rules to govern the relations of members to each other and to uninitiated outsiders. They each have their signs and countersigns by which they know each other, and at initiation each is supplied by the guild officers with a distinct fetish insignia which must be worn at all meetings. The promise of the members to stand by and help each other in need, is as binding as any rule enforced by European friendly societies, to which, in some respects, these African societies correspond. Members must attend and do the honours of the guild at members' funerals, and also attend officially and join in the worship of a defunct member at the spirit temples. *No African dies utterly*, as they express it, *fwililila*, for to the negro death is not annihilation, but a mere continuation chamber in which reincarnation is awaited, and in the interim the living honour the dead by acts of worship. Instrumental music and singing are two of the chief forms of social life indulged in by all secret societies and guilds, and there are sets of songs peculiar to each.

COPPERSMITH'S SONG

" Work and toil, my brother,
　Oh yes, for work is good.
　If it's your own little job, my brother,
　Work, for work is good."

SONG OF THE BLACKSMITH

" I fell at Kampanda River,
　With the metal in my hand,
　While breaking up the iron charms,
　By which I bought my freedom.
　I'm the man who tramps the marshes.
　All chiefs' sons are the same.
　Ivory rings and bracelets
　Belong to the ' grass-clan ' men.

　The Smith, Oh thanks to the Doctor,
　Who helps him in his work.
　He sings the song of plenty,
　With his bins and baskets full,
　With his beer pot never empty,
　And a quiet life on a stool.

　Wealth is not on the surface.
　A lazy man never gets any.
　The blacksmith, with his sledge,
　He hammers out the money."

(Rhodesian Blacksmiths belong to the *Grass Clan*.)

One of the most powerful guilds is that of the Lion Doctor. They claim to have potent fetishes by means of which they can " throw lions " all over the country as an American " throws a gun." They claim also the power of practising lycanthropy, or changing into lions, and they travel all over the forest followed, the natives say and believe, by troops of " dogs," as they call the lions, euphemistically. These lions are said to obey the slightest behest of their " lion masters."

I have known several of these lion experts who, for a certain price, will rid any fellow tribesman or chief of his troublesome enemies. They also claim the power to recall the lions after they have done their work. They profess to have power also to rid a district of lions. (Negro Pied Pipers.)

Lions, of course, must never be called " lions " but " dogs," just as in crossing a river infested with crocodiles they are alluded to as " lizards." The Greeks had this thought in mind when they called the roughest sea beyond the Mediterranean the Euxine, i.e. the sea friendly to strangers.

The paramount chief whose name was Chama and in whose district I lived on Lake Bangweulu was a far-famed lion doctor, and he lived on the edge of a marsh. He was a big, powerful man, with a weird, wicked expression such as one might find in an ancient book of ogres. When at home he disliked the light and usually huddled in dark corners during the day. A local youth whom I knew had been out one day honey-hunting near some of Chama's fenced gardens. The fire he had been using to smoke the bees he left behind, and it caught the dry grass and burnt down the fence of Chama's cornfield. The lad fled and hid in his village. News went round that some one had burned Chama's fence, but the culprit had disappeared. The same night two lions (or what appeared to be two lions) roared till morning round the village where the lad lived. Next day, scared to death, he hastened to Chama's village and confessed his guilt, and had to pay a most extortionate fine that nearly ruined him. Twenty-three miles from there a lion had been giving a lot of trouble, and the suspicion fell on a certain man who claimed powers of lycanthropy. They could not catch him, and the village was in terror of being attacked by this lion whose nocturnal visits and roaring drove everybody indoors after sundown. The local magistrate came to collect taxes in that village and the people told him about it. He decided to sit up and have a pot at the man-eater. He had not long to wait, for after dark the usual lion roaring was heard. He noted the direction from whence the sound came, and seeing a dark form, he fired, and felt assured he had hit it for he heard groans. Next day, however, they traced the blood spoor to a hut, and crouching inside was the man in question with a bullet wound through the leg. On another occasion, with my colleague and some natives, I was walking along the British bank of the Luapula River when we heard what we thought was the roaring of a lion. The boys declared it had caught a bush-pig and was eating it. The grass was long, and in order to see we got on to our men's shoulders, gun in hand. We looked in the direction of the noise, but at first could see nothing. Looking intently we saw a man spring up in a wriggly fashion and then disappear. " Look," said our men, " that is a lion-man and he has just changed back into human form." We shouted, and rushed over, and going round in concentric circles we sought and sought, but could find no man nor the trace of a man or lion either.

Had I been alone I should have said my eyes had deceived me, but there being two of us, Mr. L—— and myself, our eyes certainly did not deceive us. Doubtless it was a native who for some reason or other refused to come to us when we called him, and hid himself, but from the purely native point of view it was certainly a man changing back from lion into human form who was caught in the very act. These lion doctors referred to have a powerful guild and are well known and greatly feared, being mostly big chiefs. The non-man-eating lion is looked on as a reincarnation of a slave, and when a man meets one he falls on his face before it and calls out, " Oh, slave. Oh, slave." Many a native I have known to lose his life as a result of this foolish belief and action, when his spear or gun might have saved him.

The Wemba believe that their chiefs are reincarnated often in the shape of lions and prey on their people from time to time. Such a lion is called a *Chisanguka.*

CHAPTER XI

Native Enterprise & Industry

NATIVE industry and enterprise prove that the Bantus of Bantuland are neither thriftless nor lazy, and use the time, talent, and material at their disposal to both profit and advantage. In the Katanga the Sanga and Yeke tribes who lived in the vicinity of the copper-fields made good use of their opportunities and worked the copper into various articles of trade, with the result that copper in the form of beads, wire, rods, moulds of the shape of a Maltese cross and the letter H, became a regular form of currency for hundreds of miles E., W., N., and S. along the trade routes. The copper was dug out of places where rich deposits lay, and carried in baskets to their small smelting furnaces that had been erected of clay modelled in beehive shape. The copper was built up on the top of a layer of firewood, with charcoal heaped on top of that, and thereafter copper was mixed with further large quantities of charcoal until the furnace was filled. Then after a lot of ceremonies to propitiate the spirits and to ensure success in the work, the firewood was lighted at the bottom, and the fire blown up by means of skin bellows which were inserted in holes round the bottom of the furnace. Holes were also left for air, and, as the furnace was usually built on a high spot in order to ensure a good steady current, at the end of two days the copper was smelted out.

Opposite the little plugged holes round the bottom of

the furnaces were moulds in the sand in the shape of Maltese crosses and of the letter H. The plug being removed from the hole in front of the mould, the molten copper was run in until the mould was full, when the hole was replugged, and the operation repeated as each casting cooled sufficiently to be removed. Some of the copper was sold in blocks, but most of it was used to make hoes and spears, beads, and wire of a dozen different gauges. The finer wire was worked into bracelets and anklets, being strengthened with hair from the tails and manes of the zebra, and when these did not suffice they were mixed with fibre. These bracelets, called *Nsambo*, were sold for two yards of calico per hundred, and the copper crosses, weighing approximately 1½ lbs. each, were sold at one yard of calico each. The hoes used to be hardened for hoeing purposes and would wear out to the tang, but the secret process of hardening the copper died, I believe, with the family who possessed it. Copper spears, axes, and knives were used only for ornament. I have sat for hours watching them dig and smelt the copper, and work it and draw it into wire of many different gauges, some of it fine as hair. Copper was also used for making decorations for spears, guns, and powder horns, fly switches, stools, bark boxes, and idols, and the Fundis were quite adept at it. They also used it for repairing broken leather, horn, and woodwork. While drawing out the copper they always sang, as they did with all their work.

In the Luba country, in the Congo, and in Rhodesia, iron digging, smelting, and smithing was one of the useful trades that brought great benefit to the neighbouring countries and enriched the village blacksmiths. Every man, woman, boy, and girl required a hoe. Some had two and three, hence the demand for this precursor of the plough approximated to the actual adult population of the

country. Then each man and boy required, besides, an
axe, spear, knife, and a supply of arrow heads. All these
increased the value of iron ore, and enhanced the value of
these primitive sons of Tubal Cain. The process of smelting was similar to that used with copper, but instead of the
molten metal being poured into moulds it was taken out
from the furnace in blocks after cooling. These were then
heated by primitive bellows, made of goat or antelope
skins, in a charcoal fire, and held by green bark tongs and
hammered into bars by stone sledge-hammers encased in
skin, on stone anvils. Then these bars were heated white
and shaped into hoes, axes, knives, and arrow points with
primitive hammers, and much care and quite a lot of pride
went in the early days to giving a good finish to each
article. Of course time was no object. The Bantu proverb,
" All hurry, no blessing," corresponding to the Italian one,
" Who goes slowly goes safely," was often quoted by
timeless blacks to hustling whites, and I never forget an
old Luban boy of mine who used continually to remind me,
" God made some of us to go slow, sir."

There is certainly no comparison between the trader's
hoe, axe, and knife sold in stores of to-day and these shapely,
well-finished articles of the Bantu blacksmith's craft.

As in copper and iron, the Africans are certainly not
bad workers *in wood*. I have seen them shape butts for
guns into which the locks were carefully fitted. Much of
the carved work in wood—idols, stools, spear handles,
canoe paddles, with human heads carved at the end of axe
and knife handles, or animal and bird heads—do them much
credit considering the primitive tools they use and the
inartistic environment in which they live. When natives
have been instructed they make fair carpenters and even
cabinet-makers. A number of men work in ivory, and one
comes across all sorts of things carved out of elephant,

A Cotton Spinner.
The thread is woevn into shawls.

Harvest Song and Dance, Katanga.
This is performed by women bearing hoes in their hands.

hippo, and pig tusks. Finger rings, bracelets, war horns, whistles, and well-finished handles for hunting knives are among the productions of the ivory carver's art. I have seen them carve crocodiles, fish, and animals from tusks of ivory, plus serviette rings, vases, etc. I have met a number of native gold and silversmiths, but these have mostly learnt at the coast from Arabs, Indians, or Europeans. A few months ago a native goldsmith from the French Congo asked me for a sovereign and a claw to make a lion claw brooch. He drew me a smart sketch of the design on paper, and after getting the material he disappeared. I have never seen him since. Natives—particularly in towns —are adepts at this part of the business as well as at the other, and past masters in obliterating all trace of their whereabouts when they retire. Many natives were good workers in horn and leather. They never used horn for drinking purposes as we did in Europe, but they make beautifully decorated powder horns. They also make leather belts and engrave them in pretty patterns, also leather pouches for carrying flints, bullets, and fire sticks. Not infrequently a man would have two or three leather pouches attached to his belt. Horns are much used as fetish and medicine holders, and for purposes of cupping, and often these are carved in pretty patterns. Long ago when we ran out of shoes the natives borrowed old pairs, ripped them open, and using them as models, made us serviceable shoes from brayed antelope skins lined with blue calico. These were comfortable, and would wear for three months in constant use. They resembled Boer *veldschoen*. Native blacksmiths have learnt and know every part of a gun, and I have seen them repair broken parts and fashion out at the forge new pieces that would do credit to a European workman. The Arabs always travelled with a number of these handy bush armourers to repair their guns, and when a war was on, the first men requisitioned, who got busy with old guns that had been set aside in peace times, were these Fundis. Cotton used to be more freely cultivated in the interior than to-day. Long ago it was a common sight to see old men and women, and young ones too, spinning cotton at their hut doors or under trees during moments of leisure from other duties. When the cotton, spun into threads, reached a certain number of balls, then some dexterous son-in-law, or failing him, the village weaver, would be employed to weave one or two *matonge* or strong cotton shawls of two or three-coloured patterns, for which he would be paid in chickens or other local currency. These homespun shawls are difficult to obtain to-day owing to cheap calicoes and print cloths brought in by European traders. They were, however, superior, certainly more comfortable, and wore longer than most of the textile material procurable to-day from the stocks of what is called " Kaffir truck." This is another of the many moribund African arts. Natives are expert taxidermists. Few who have travelled on the Cape to Cairo railway through Bechuanaland have failed to be struck with the beautiful carosses (skin rugs) made of brayed buck, monkey, cat, lemur, or skin of the silver jackal, and most travellers buy one or more in passing through. On Lake Bangweulu the Batwa and Baunga make a trade of brayed and decorated black and red Lechwe antelope skins. Patterns are worked on the inside by means of sharp knives, and are decidedly pretty. The native women wear the fur side of the skin next the body, the prettily worked and intricate patterns showing outside. The women are the potters of Bantuland. They dig the clay, puddle it, mix it with powdered potsherds, and work it into a fine mould- able mass. They then take a chunk and work it slowly into shape with the hands. Then they put it over a pot of the kind and pattern required and mould away at it with the fingers, a corn husk, and a small shell. They work it round and round, as they do not use a wheel, and when the outside is well shaped it is left to dry a bit, after which the bottom is made and worked on to the body of the pot or the water jar. When the pot or jar is shaped they work patterns of various kinds round the top and outside on the soft clay. They take great pride in their patterns, and the little girls, who are all keen to learn it, sit by, look on, and watch their mothers at work. Potters get a good price for their pottery. They bake their pots in a simple outside oven, wrapping them all round with firewood and watching the fire closely.

Every native furnishes his house with a bedstead, the pillars of which are sometimes carved with great care, then he requires stools, a fireplace, shelf above to keep fish or meat or other food, besides hanging nets for various sized pots and water jars, and a well-made reed or bamboo door. He also cuts out of solid blocks of wood a mortar and pestle for pounding meal, and gets an upper and nether millstone to grind the small grain. Of course each negro builds his own hut according to the tribal shape and system in vogue, for no man may change the clan custom of house building. Most natives use carved wooden pillows or small blocks of wood as head rests. These are carved to suit the shape of the neck for comfort. There are many native tailors scattered among the rising townlets of Central Africa who have learnt the trade since the advent of Europeans. Apart, however, from these, and long prior to the coming of Europeans, the Luba people made hats, coats, and trousers of woven straw. I have seen Europeans in the bush wearing these hats and trousers and they certainly do credit to the Baluba inventors.

Even in pre-European days they built out their towns in

lines of long streets (*mikensa*). This Luban system has crept into parts of N.E. Rhodesia, and is certainly an improvement on the higgledy-piggledy native village. The Luban system of sanitation (earth closets) is also a vast improvement on what we find in Angola and Rhodesia, where the outside of the entrances and exits to villages are, as a rule, absolutely repulsive.

Mat-weaving from reeds, papyrus grass, and bamboo is one of the most important native industries. A mat is a native bed and chair, and no native travels without his mat, on which he sits during the day and sleeps at night. These are made in many patterns, and sometimes several colours are used. The large Arab floor mats and coloured " prayer mats " I do not include in the above category. Baskets of various kinds are made with and without lids. Long bamboo hampers are made for carrying pots and dried fish, and many Europeans use them as pot-baskets and food boxes on *safari*.

Canoe digging is an occupation that requires experts. Very few natives can dig out and shape a canoe that will lie well on the water and sail easily. The first thing is to seek out a good shapely tree of a wood that does not quickly rot. This is cut down, dug out, and shaped inside and on the exterior. Bow and stern and gunwale are shaped carefully, after which it lies drying for a time. When it has been reduced to its final thickness and shape a fire is lit, water put inside, and the boat is steamed to make it pliable, then it is stretched between the gunwales to open it out. Sticks are then fixed between these to keep it in place until the canoe is seasoned and assumes its final form. Paddles are then made and shaped, and one day the village turns out in gala dress to help to launch their monoxyle. Many songs are sung in praise of the boat, and of the expert boat-builders, and as it enters the water it is, if large, given

a special name. Some canoes are small and intended for
the owner only, whereas there are canoes I have travelled
in that held a hundred men. Bark canoes are made sometimes by hunters to enable them to follow elephant or big
game on the other side of a deep river. I remember once
when out hunting we made a bark canoe in two hours and
launched it. It was used at that ferry for two years afterwards. I had shot a waterbuck which died on the opposite
bank, and it was for that we made the canoe. A big tree
was chosen, ringed a foot from the bottom and twelve
feet above ; the bark was then removed by means of a cut
longitudinally ; the bark cylinder was then laid on the
ground, cut upwards, then a fire was lit at each end. The
ends were bent in and laced up with bark-rope, then after
steaming they were bent upwards, making the bows almost
level with the gunwale, which was made by lacing a split
bamboo outside and inside. The holes were bored by
means of the pointed end of a spear, then laced.

Natives love stock and take great interest in poultry,
goats, sheep, and cattle. They know the value of these,
and will not sell save under the compulsion of necessity.
They make neat dovecotes for pigeons, chicken houses,
goat pens, and cattle kraals. As a rule the foundation horn
or post of these buildings must be laid by a woman who has
borne twins, the idea being fertility. Salt and tobacco are
two of the great industries of Bantuland. From Catumbella River at Lobito Bay to the Lualaba River in the
Katanga, the only salt obtainable is got from the coast,
hence salt is a valuable commodity and article of commerce. With salt one can buy any kind of native produce.
Often when the youngsters came to our camps they were
highly pleased, and their mothers too, when we rubbed a
pinch of salt on the end of their tongue. At the Lualaba
the salt is got by cutting the grass and burning it, taking

the ashes and putting them into earth filters through which water is passed. Then the salt water is boiled until the water evaporates, when the pot is broken, leaving a round block of salt intact. On the Lufira River one finds the famous Mwashia salt pans, which contain pure white salt. This is gathered with shells and piled into heaps, then made into blocks of about 7 to 10 lbs., and these used to be sold at one yard of calico (value 6d.) per block.

Instances of native enterprise are not uncommon. At North Bangweulu a Wemba chief named Fyani Fyani once introduced Lechwe antelopes on the Luena River, where there were none previously, and he also had live fish carried in immense pots of water and let loose on that same river, where to-day fish abound. Kazembe's Luban canal is another instance of native enterprise. A large gang of Luban slaves were used to cut a canal from the Luapula River through the great swamps to his head village at Mwansavombwe. This canal still exists and I have travelled up and down it many times. The Mulenga salt pans are about thirty miles east of Mwashia, and the salt there is in crystals but of a good quality. Going through those salt fields when a wind is blowing is like getting a breeze from the briny, and one has often stood with distended nostrils sniffing the imaginary ozone, and imagining oneself at the seaside. On the east side of Bangweulu there are other salt fields, and round Lake Mweru on the Rhodesian side. The salt there obtained by burning certain grasses and reeds is a potash salt, and not at all usable by Europeans. Natives always speak of anything being " as sweet as salt," and sing a little song,

> " Meat is sweet
> With salt to eat."

Tobacco was formerly used by native travellers as the American Indians in Fenimore Cooper's stories used it. I have seen my men smoke again and again to stave off hunger when food was scarce. Bihéan traders, who only eat once a day, smoke continually. When a man is hungry and cannot get any food he will beg for " a bit of tobacco." The natives cultivate the "weed" largely, and some districts having suitable soil are famous for tobacco, and seem to get large crops. There is one such district near to the Luapula called " Mulangadi." Tobacco is used in three ways—chewing, smoking, and snuffing. Swahili natives chew it, and I fancy they learnt the habit from sailors round the coast. Natives smoke tobacco in various kinds of pipes, but most prefer " the hubble-bubble," a gourd with water in the bowl, on account of the cooling effect of the smoke passing through the water. Very many natives nowadays indulge in snuff, and use it in enormous quantities, applying it to the nose with a small shovel-like spoon. On Lake Bangweulu some put the snuff on a piece of otter skin and rub it over the nostrils. The sneeze is a great thing and supposed to be a sign of exuberant health. Tobacco as smoke or snuff used to be taboo in the time of Msidi at Bunkeya. This is also a great article of commerce and is sold in large plaited rolls, or in blocks. The latter is strong, but the former is mild, and is much used even by tobacco companies in the manufacture of cigarettes. Hemp, or *bhang*, is forbidden by most European governments, but is still cultivated surreptitiously and sold and smoked in secret. Salt and tobacco form an important item in the rationing of the twenty thousand boys employed among the Katanga copper mines and works.

CHAPTER XII

Food & Drink

IF there is a man anywhere who *eats to live*, as the China-
man is reputed to do, he is certainly not to be found
among the Bantu peoples of Africa. The verb
to live, with its many derivatives, is the verb to eat, in
almost all Bantu languages, expressing life, and existence
in every form. " Are you well ? " and " How do you do ? "
in Wemba and other languages means, literally, " Have
you eaten well ? " A native does not say simply " I'm
hungry," but " I'm dying with hunger," and he never eats
satisfactorily if he is not " full up " or, as they say, " tied
up tight." Their views are like those of the little boy
who did not appreciate the Christmas party he was taken
to, " because he did not have that nice sick feeling," or like
the other boy after the children's feast who said, " Mother,
you may lift me, but you mustn't bend me." Whether
in food or drink, " absolutely fu' " describes the negro
ideal of living. In fairness, however, one must give the
other side, and that is that in case of necessity a native
can sit tight without food longer and possibly grumble less
than the average man or woman of European race. The
native is not only a " piggywig " in the matter of food and
drink, but he is also a past master in the art of bluff and
sophistry. He reminds one forcibly of Horne Tooke's
diversions of Purley, where the man on trial for his life
endeavours to play with words and thereby prove that
right may be wrong and therefore wrong can be right by a
process of reasoning. The right hand in Bantu in most

instances, if not in all, is called *the eating hand*, and I
remember once asking a man to hold out his right hand
when to my surprise out shot his left. I said, " No, that's
not your right hand," to which he promptly replied, " Yes,
sir, that is *my* right hand, for it is the hand I use in eating
my food." He was what we would call left-handed. The
meaning we attach to left and right in our language is a
foreign idea to Africans, for his right hand is always his
eating hand (*mulyo* or *kulyo*) and his left hand is his *chipiko*,
or " awkward hand," and neither of them have any association with places such as we attribute to them in English.
He adopts our usage of *left and right* just as he does brown
boots and long trousers. When I have killed several head
of game I have seen my carriers so ill and swollen as the
result of a meat-eating orgie that, next morning, before
they could continue their journey each had to roll his
fellow along the ground and jump up and down on his
stomach, and then come to me begging for a day's rest in
camp to get over the effects of their gluttony. Of course,
to qualify this it would be well to point out that the same
men had not tasted meat for months previously and
possibly were suffering from " meat hunger," for which
they have a particular word—*kashia*. Every Bantu negro
is a farmer and responsible for the cultivation of sufficient
food for the maintenance of himself and his family,
including the little extras for hospitality and some for
emergencies. " No fields no food," and as the song says,
" the only medicine for hunger is hoe medicine," i.e.
cultivation. This is the song they continually poke at
each other when complaints of hunger are made, and
lazy people *pula* or sponge on the thrifty :

> " If you're hungry
> Use your hoe,
> The only drug
> The doctors know."

Much of the modern education given to the native is opportunist and shortsighted. It may be handy and nice to have low-paid native clerks, carpenters, builders, and other tradesmen, but it would be infinitely better for the future of Africa if agricultural officials were sent round the villages, vested with Government authority, to insist on deeper cultivation instead of merely scratching the surface of the soil; also fertilisation instead of changing to new fields every year, and planting only good, fresh seed, instead of sowing the same seed in the same fields year by year as is done with results detrimental to the crops. Well-fenced and more deeply dug fields, better built huts, and sanitation laws enforced, better care of children, sick and aged, better attention to their own village life for the good of all natives and colonists, would result in less outcry against natives taking the bread out of the mouths of Europeans, and fewer problems would exist to perplex statesmen and worry Government officials, to whom those vital native questions are all-important. The native does not only deal in sarcasm and sophistry, but he is a philosopher who carries his philosophy into the region of philology, e.g. *li* is the verb to be, exist; *lia* is the verb to eat; *lima*, the verb to cultivate, and *limuka* means to be shrewd, or wise. Here he argues back that *to be wise* one has to cultivate before one can eat and exist. The radical stem *li* runs through the four verbs.

The natives have quite a number of grain foods, such as mealies, sorghum, millet, birdseed, rice. The maize and sorghum are soaked and husked before being pounded into meal in the wooden mortars with pestles. The smaller grains are ground with millstones set in a clay setting under the verandah near the door of the hut. The meal obtained is used to make *the mush*, which is the staple bread of Bantuland and eaten with one of a number of sauces,

meat, or fish. This is usually well cooked and is very sus-
taining. In the Congo, when white flour ran out, a number
of missionaries and Belgian officials lived on this for many
months. Root foods include cassava, from which starch
is made, and a very popular white meal used exclusively
by some tribes. The root is soaked and sun-dried, pounded,
and sifted to make meal. There are several kinds of cassava
root, but one of these is poisonous until soaked for two or
three days in water to release the hydrocyanic acid contained.
Cassava leaves make a popular spinach, which, mixed
with peanuts, is eaten as a sauce (*munani*=the Scottish
" kitchen "). The natives call this the *all sufficient*, and
say, " We get bread from the root and meat from the
leaves." This spinach is called facetiously " old man's
meat," as it requires no chewing. I had a cook who used
to make a good tapioca from cassava starch, and many
ladies use it for ordinary laundry purposes. Cassava
roots are soaked, sun-dried, and stored away like grain for
future use. Sweet potatoes of many kinds are valued
very highly, and boiled, or roasted in the ashes, are very
nutritious. These are sometimes sliced, dried in the sun,
and preserved for use during the dry season when potatoes
are not procurable. Monkey-nuts have great food value
on account of the large amount of oil that can be extracted.
They are roasted, pounded into a paste, mixed and cooked
with spinach to flavour them. Peanut butter is made from
these, and a very white, good-quality salad oil is also
obtained. Again, a handful of roast peanuts in the pocket
is equivalent to a few cakes of chocolate when travelling.
Good cooking oil is also got by first pounding the nut
coarsely, heating with steam, then pounding, with the
addition of half a cup of boiling water to start the oil.
A white ground bean called *kalanga*, and grown like
peanuts, is greatly appreciated for its nutritive properties.

Edible leaves and fruits are found growing wild everywhere. One we used for soup, several for salads, and a dozen or more were used in the same way as spinaches. A wild mint called *luena* made a good mint sauce for use with mutton. There is a small book illustrating some seventy different edible leaves to be found throughout the Congo. Wild fruits are numerous, and when I built my place on Lake Bangweulu there were eleven kinds of wild fruit growing on the 200 acres of ground we occupied. On account of this I planted three acres of European fruits, all of which, save vines, did well. Europeans remove the flesh from the *fungo* plum and put the dried fruit away in cans. The juice of a red ground fruit—elephants' favourite —preserved and bottled, makes a good, refreshing drink, with the addition of a little sugar. In season, elephants and monkeys, and even small antelopes feed largely on fruit, and one often finds herds of Jumbo feeding in patches of bush where wild fruit is plentiful.

Bread or mush, or mealie pap, as it is called in South Africa, is the staple food of every African. A pot of water is put on the fire and when it begins to boil a little meal is scattered on to the top of the water. When the water bubbles and boils thoroughly, the meal is put in handful by handful and stirred until the porridge reaches a thick mass the consistency of soft bread. It is then removed from the pot with the porridge stick and piled up on a wooden dish, then patted all round until it assumes a circular shape. It is then served as bread, with meat and fish, or spinach, and eaten with the fingers. A piece is nipped off the size of an egg, a dent or " boat " is made with the thumb and this is dipped in the sauce and eaten. This process is repeated during the meal, and any left over is laid aside and eaten between meals or in the morning. It is then toasted on the ashes, or eaten cold, and is called *chimbala*.

Flesh is sometimes stewed, boiled, or roasted on the embers and eaten with mush. The natives prefer their meat *high*, and when they can get them they do it up with pepper and monkey-nut or palm oil. Fish is cooked in various ways. When fresh it is nice grilled on the embers. Sometimes it is boiled with peppers or without. Smoked and dried fish is usually cooked a long time until a brown gravy shows, and of this they are extremely fond. Europeans can rarely eat native dried fish. When salt is obtainable food is highly seasoned, as the natives like to taste the salt. For this reason very few negro cooks are able to season food to suit European taste. Sauces are made from various edible leaves with the addition of fats or oil, pepper or peanuts, when these are obtainable. Fresh-water shrimps, and snails, are a great relish to some tribes, as well as caterpillars, grubs, snakes, and frogs of ever so many kinds, ants, locusts, rats, etc. The man who compared python steaks to salmon chops and fat ants and locusts to shrimps was certainly a connoisseur in the art of "eating black." Still, as natives say, "hunger knows no boundary," and a man's idiosyncrasies are often quite unaccountable.

The subject of cooks, cooking, and the kitchen is one of vital moment to each Bantu black. Every wife is expected to have been trained in the culinary art by her mother and at the village school, and to know something about the numerous and mysterious dishes that make up the essence of life to her husband and his many club friends. To the negro, "to eat is to live," and the married life of a girl who cannot cook will eventually lead to the divorce court, or drive her into the arms of another, who will later on prove equally exacting. A cosy kitchen and a wife who has had a good training in boiling, stewing, and roasting rats, snails, and grubs of many kinds with occasionally meat and fish, usually proves a happy home, if *her tongue is not too long.* Some housewives are dirty and slovenly, while others keep every calabash, pot, and dish in its place, and spotlessly clean. Native cooks are an important item in the African household of officials, missionaries, traders, and travellers, and some of these produce remarkable dishes from local produce, prepared and often served up under circumstances which it is better the master should know nothing about. " Lice and loast beef, sir, with fly pudding " (rice and roast beef and fried pudding) replied a sable cook boy on being interrogated as to dinner, a guest being present. An official I know sent his boy to the local market in a certain cannibal country to buy meat. After dinner, upon enquiry, my friend found out to his horror that he had been eating " black beef "—*nyama ya muntu.* Many instances of this kind occurred in the early days of Congo pioneering. Chipinka, a Bihé lad, was my first cook, and a paragon of cleanliness. He used to spend so much time washing his hands and face that the beans got burned and the food was brought to the table uncooked. Johnny, an ex-slave boy, whom I rescued from slavery many years ago, was certainly one of the best and keenest cooks I ever knew. His rule was never to present the same dish twice during the week. He could cook and prepare the African *nkuku,* " chicken," in a dozen or more different ways. I remember saying to him one day : " Johnny, why did you not serve rice with this meat." " It is not eaten with rice, sir," was his reply. The slave blood of Johnny came to the top, and after many years he became one of the most incorrigible rascals I ever knew, and I had to send him away for his deceit, stealing, and defrauding the natives around my place. The last I heard of him was that he had married a Mashukulumbwe woman, and is now a big chief in that turbulent cattle country. " Always treat your cook as you would your mother," is the African rule, for he has your life in his hands. I knew a cook who was treated harshly by his master—"Too much *shikote*," he said. He therefore decided to poison his boss, and procured the poison from a local witch doctor. One evening separate dishes were being served up at the officers' mess, and this black beauty poisoned his master's dish. The officers dispersed, and Capt. Van den B—— went to his room feeling unwell. In a few minutes he was rolling on the ground with excruciating internal pain. Luckily, at the same moment, a black sergeant was walking past the huts where the officers' native servants lived, and heard a noise in the cook's dwelling. The cook was dancing and singing and shouting loudly : "Master will be dead to-morrow, and I shall get no more *shikote*." The sergeant thereupon suspected something and, bursting into the hut, seized the boy by the shoulders and ran him up to the Chef de Poste. Meanwhile, the latter was writhing in pain on the ground, and on the sergeant's story being told an emetic was administered at once, and the life of Capt. V. d. B. was luckily saved. The cook was tried by court martial, sentenced to death, and shot at the native market the following Sunday morning. I visited the cook the day before execution and he confessed frankly what he had done, and why.

Natives eat only one solid meal a day under ordinary circumstances, and few native women would consent to cook oftener. This used to be the Medo-Persic law of the Bantus, but civilisation has swept this law into the waste-paper basket of the past, and, in towns, a native likes his three meals per diem the same as his *Bwana*. Of course, he would indulge in snacks in the form of a chunk of roast cassava, or potato, or a handful of peanuts between one evening's supper and the next. Again, he would indulge in a pull at the gourd pipe, or a pinch of snuff.

Geophagy, or eating earth, is indulged in by children and by pregnant women. The latter say that they eat earth only during and after quickening owing to its quieting internal effect.

It is no meaningless alliteration to speak of " the Boozy Bantu," whose love of beer can only compare with the Scotchman's *reputed* love of whisky and the Dutchman's pençhant for gin. Drink beer, think beer, and one might add truthfully, *stink beer*, for a beery nigger can be smelt many yards off. Here are the names of ten kinds of beer :

(1) Maize beer (*katata*).
(2) Sorghum beer (*bwalwa*).
(3) Millet beer (*chimpumu*).
(4) Early millet (*mwangwe*).
(5) Red millet (*sonkwe*).
(6) Birdseed beer (*bwalubedi*).
(7) Palm wine, tapped from oil-palm fronds (*malefu*).
(8) Palm wine, tapped from raffia palm (*fibale*).
(9) Honey beer (*mbote*).
(10) Unalcoholic beer (*munkoyo*).

Grain for beer is soaked in pots, covered, and kept warm until it sprouts. It is then sun-dried and ground and the beer is made from the malted grain thus ground. Palm beers are got by tapping the oil-palm fronds, and the raffia. The temperance beer called *munkoyo* is made from a root which tastes like hops and is mixed with meal and made in the ordinary way. The strongest of these drinks is the palm wine from the raffia, though the other is also strong, particularly when left a day or two. Honey beer, too, if left, becomes powerfully intoxicating. The weakest beer is *munkoyo*, and is unintoxicating. The favourite means of poisoning is to doctor the beer cup of the intended victim. More people die in Africa by means of poisoned beer than

Home Scene in Bantuland.

Malting Grain for Beer.

by anything else. This has given rise to the expression
" There's bones in the beer," and is one of the strongest
arguments against beer drinks. When a man becomes
beery he gets first quarrelsome, and then sleepy, and is
thus more at the mercy of an enemy, potential or actual.
More adultery, murders, and wars have sprung from beer
drinking than from any other cause. " Beer is not mad,
but mad is he who drinks it," runs the Luban proverb.
Bwalwa, " beer," means literally *cause of war*. *Ku-lwa*
means " to fight," and *Bwa* is the prefix signifying cause of.
Thus *Bwalwa*, " beer," cause of war, fighting. *Kachasa*
is a strong whisky made from beer in two native pots
joined together by a gun barrel which is inserted in both
pots, and a gentle fire kept burning underneath. One
pot is full of beer, and the other empty, and into this the
alcohol percolates through the gun barrel. I have seen
officials when cut off from Europe make this and drink it ;
also European hunters in the bush. The above is the reason
why native Christian communities will not play at moderate
drinking of beer, but go in for *total prohibition*. They know
better than white people their own weakness, and certainly
ought to be allowed their own form of legislation in this
matter. There are gluttons and drunkards, and among
most tribes are to be found men who boast of their capacity
to eat and drink more than their fellows. One of my best
headmen was an awful drunkard and used to go *literally mad*,
and it was due to a drunken mad fit caused by beer that he
was killed by his wife. In my early days I used him as
interpreter, but he told such lies (like most interpreters)
that I was compelled to dispense with his services. " Why
did you tell that chief and his people that I was a fighting
white man and had guns to carry and kill at an impossible
distance ? " " Well, sir," with head hanging down,
" I'm sorry, but if I had told them what you asked me to

say they would have despised us and robbed the caravan."
"*Traduttori Tradittori*" is an Italian aphorism that
fits here.

Kanwa, "mouth," means "the drinker," in the ver-
nacular, or "he who drinks," from the prefix *ka*, "he,"
and *nwa*, the verb to drink. The native is childlike, and
is still at the dawn of self-consciousness, the awaking of the
ego. He does not realise that "this is I." He talks to his
arm, or leg, or head, or feet, as he does to a bird, or buck,
or bush. The body is *mubili*, "the two-divisioned one."
Two eyes, ears, arms, cheeks, nostrils, legs, etc.

The head is—"the apex," *Mutwi*.

The eyes are—"the gazers," *Mense*.

The ears are—"the sharpers," *Matwi*.

The nostrils are—"the perceivers," *Myona*.

The mouth is—"he who drinks," *Kanwa*.

The feet are—"the trampers," *Makasa*.

He has been for so many centuries a mere cog in the
tribal machine, a slave, that the idea of individualism and
freedom is a thing to be shunned. He is a socialist to the
bone, a member of a great responsible society called a tribe.
Natives are extremists, and either eat too much when they
can get it, drink too much, and dress immoderately, or
starve and go naked. Our civilisation has been too hurried,
and caught the negro for the nonce, napping, for here in
the interior of Bantuland he is still rubbing his eyes, yawn-
ing, and stretching himself, while muttering like a man in
a dream : "What is it all about?" He still has a vague,
unformulated notion in the back of his head that the white
man will yet go away and leave him at peace to go his own
ways and do his own sweet will. He would rather a thousand times have the old palmy days with their own rule of
black tyrants, mutilations, and slavery, than all the unsought
blessings of our—to him—doubtful civilisation.

CHAPTER XIII
Native Dress & Habits

DECORATION rather than dress seems to have been the primeval idea of all primitive peoples. To prove this one has only to glance at photos of a dozen native tribes on the equator who go absolutely naked, or of the South Sea Islanders. The custom of hair-dressing, teeth chipping and filing, with tattooing and cicatrisation—three important bodily forms of decoration in vogue among savage peoples—is much more intricate and highly developed among tribes who go absolutely naked than among people who have adopted dress of various fashions. Among a few tribes who despised, and some who yet despise, clothing as effeminate are the Konde people of Nyasaland, the Mashukulumbwe of Northern Rhodesia, with the Fans, Dinkas, and many other equatorial tribes. Other Africans call them " the go-nakeds " (*Chenda bwamba*). An infinite number and variety of hair-dressing styles obtain all over Bantuland, including the use of made-up tails and wigs, plus imitative hair-dresses representing animal horns, including the buffalo horn head-dress worn by the chief Kazembe, which is imposing and only worn on state occasions. At such official functions he also wears lion manes round his arms, and woven bead puttees round the legs, also facial head decorations. Native women are very proud and vain in the matter of personal appearance, and this is seen perhaps more conspicuously in the matter of " coiffure." I have seen chiefs' wives and big ladies spend five to ten days over a "coiffure," and this represented work of at least six or more hours a day. It is very noticeable that the nearer one approaches to the coast and civilisation the less imposing and fewer one finds the styles of head-dressing and decoration, and the greater tendency there is among men and women to adopt European customs in the matter of dress and habits. I have made a list of ten different styles of head-dressing, including wigs and pleated tails :

(1) *Mapango*, " the buffalo horn head-dress worn by the chief Kazembe."

(2) *Kapompo*, " is a bunch of hair in the shape of a big bun worn by the same chief at the back of the head."

(3) *Nkoka*, " is the hair pleated from front to back in long straight lines."

(4) *Tukamenye*, " is a Wemba style of head-dressing, fuzzy and bunchy, and plastered with oil and red dye."

(5) *Tusula*, " are wigs made out of beaten bark cloth soaked in oil and red dye, with holes bored through them, through which are passed small strings knotted inside to prevent coming out, while the inside of the wig is lined with a soft skin. These are worn also for baldness."

(6) *Misishi ya Nsupa*, " is a wig made of a gourd, over which wax is laid and pleats of hair stuck round upon the stiff wax to resemble a wig."

(7) *Buyange*, " are long pleated tails of hair and other material oiled up and powdered and hang down head and neck."

(8) *Ndobo*, " fish-hook style of head-dressing, and is made so that each hook of hair hooks on to the other with hook side up and is plastered with castor oil and camwood powder."

(9) *Kashinga*, " is a circular style of head-dress made by dressing a circle round the outer edge of hair, and working

in concentric circles towards the centre. It is stiffened with castor oil and red powder."

(10) *Tuminankula*, " is the hair pleated, each pleat half an inch long and straight. It is tied round with other hairs and the ends are singed off even with a small firestick. Peanut oil is squirted and poured over from the hair-dresser's mouth, after which camwood powder is applied for stiffening."

N.B.—There are other hair-dressing styles in vogue among the tribes between Angola and Rhodesia, with wigs, tails, chignons, aureoles, etc. The hairdresser is called *Mulushi wa misishi* and *Kaluka wa musishi*.

Neck decorations are popular with women, and take the form of brass and copper wire collars. The wire, which is softened first by heat, is twisted round the neck by the coppersmith, or an expert, into the shape desired. This is often regulated by the amount of wire possessed. If the woman is wealthy the neck is covered, then the coils are continued until the collar lies on the shoulders three inches from the neck. Some women wear woven bead collars of pretty patterns of many-coloured beads, which—unlike the wire collar—may be removed at pleasure and changed for other patterns. Some merely wear necklaces of whatever kind of bead happens to be in fashion at the time. Traders are often left with stocks of unsold beads owing to the quickly fluctuating fashions of the black Bantu beauties. I knew a European who had boxes of a bead that, as the fashion had changed, went out of favour and the beads became dead stock in his store. One day he called on the queen of the country and gave her a bunch of these out-of-fashion beads with a present for her trouble in wearing them. In a few days the beads came back into fashion again, and my friend quickly disposed of his whole stock at good prices.

Arms and legs also receive a certain amount of attention
long before the waist is attended to or the laws of decorum
fulfilled by these sable sons and daughters of Eden. Ear
and nose sticks and rings of beads, metal, or ivory are used,
while by some a heavy disc is inserted to distend the lips
and gives that duckbill-like appearance adopted by the
women of certain tribes. I was told that the women did
this to make themselves ugly in the sight of the Arab slave-
traders, who preferred pretty women, as they brought better
prices. Finger rings of metal and ivory are worn. Bracelets
of brass, copper, and iron, strengthened with zebra hair or
fibre, are also much worn, and women are to be found with
four hundred to five hundred of these round their arms or
legs at one time. Some like heavy ornaments, as it gives
them a slow walk and stately appearance. Armlets of brass
and copper five-sixteenths of an inch thick are twisted
round the wrist, and wound up the forearm spirally, almost
to the elbow. These are much coveted by women, and
though heavy and awkward are worn daily for years. Some
women also decorate the upper part of the arm in a similar
manner. The lower extremities are treated in the same way
as the upper, and often the weight of brass and copper wire
round the legs is enormous. This tends to a slow, stately walk
which, among the natives, is considered a mark of superior
birth and breeding. *Muntu wa mutende* is a slow person,
and is also a person of a gentle, superior type. The hustling,
hurrying European from a native point of view is considered a low-type person, for speed and hustle is looked on
as the special mark of slave blood. I have seen some women
wear toe rings, but these are not at all common.

Next and last come body and trunk decorations. This
is the last step in decoration and ornament, and usually
from this the first step towards dress begins. At first,
women usually wear a girdle of beads round the waist, and

when dress fashion develops and clothing comes into vogue the girdle becomes the central and permanent part of a woman's wardrobe. When a married woman dies, her sister who takes her place as inherited wife is said " to inherit the belt." Men wear as a rule a rough leather waistbelt long before they think of covering their nakedness. Hunters wear rings of ivory on arms and legs for each elephant or buffalo killed ; but generally speaking the only bodily decorations worn by men are fetish ornaments of various kinds attached to arm, leg, neck, or waist by a string or thong.

Now we come to the question of tattooing and cicatrisation, practised all over Bantu Africa. Each of these marks or designs branded on the body has, as a rule, some special secret significance. It is also a sure sign of tribal origin and a means of identity. It has a tendency to promote union among all with similar markings, because in every instance they must belong to the same tribe. Again, it binds a man to his tribe for life, because if he should run away and join an enemy tribe his tribal marks would betray him, and probably sooner or later cost him his life. This custom Herodotus describes as one of the characteristic features of the Thracians and Scythians, and to this may possibly be traced the origin of heraldry. Absurd as it may seem the conventional emblems in use at the present day, and the devices which are used on note-paper and carriage panels, owe their distant origin to the indelible tribal marks which were cut and punctured on the skin of our early ancestors. In cicatrisation the skin is sometimes pulled up by a pair of crude forceps, and then cut with a native razor, as is seen very uniquely on the Bangala and Basoko people of the equator. The cicatrices raised are more like scars, blackened and rendered permanent by the rubbing in of charcoal, mixed with burnt *libamba* grass. The Wemba tattoo tribal marks consist in a vertical line down the middle of the forehead which ends between the eyebrows, and is called *mutoso*, and a crossbar on either side of the face called *mimbuli*. There is also a vertical marking from the nape of the neck half-way down the spine, which is the most common. The arms of a Wemba hunter are usually tattooed to indicate the number of elephants or big game he has failed to kill, for these tattoo marks all represent the elephant medicine rubbed in to give him success, and not the number of animals killed, i.e. each time he fails he has to have recourse to fresh medicine and have them tattooed in. Boys and girls are usually tattooed about the age of puberty, seldom before. The women are tattooed elaborately over the abdomen, and I am told that these are merely meant for beauty and appearance. These tattoos are called *Nsangwa*, and the principal one, which extends to the umbilical cord, is called *Mukomango*. The Yeke tribes of Katanga tattoo on each side, over the abdomen, four rows of tattoo marks, called " fishbones," which they resemble. They also make similar markings on each side from each breast to the shoulder. All men, women, grown-up boys and girls are thus tattooed. Each tribe has its special tattoo markings, the details of which are so elaborate and meticulous that for a full description, with drawings and explanation of their significance, not one but several very large books would be required.

Filumba, or " tribal pride of ancestry," is the only answer I can get as to the reason for tattooing. The original meaning of the pattern tattooed lies buried, like much else in Bantuland, under the accretion of centuries. These Bantu peoples are worthy of interest, because of their being the only existing modern witnesses of primitive humanity as it existed thousands of years ago, after it had extricated itself from the swaddling clothes of pure animality. In these Bantu

HAIR DRESSING.

A native hairdresser at work in a palm village, Lubaland. Twelve different styles of coiffeures are used.

peoples there remains the only hope, ere civilisation floods the earth, of finding out the secrets of life lived by the world's earliest inhabitants. Here is a field where one may expect at any time the re-discovery and re-emergence of a lost world.

Dental decoration is another of the primitive customs which pervaded Africa, and one that is perhaps more wrapped up in mystery than either hair-dressing or tribal tattooing. Teeth to the savage are what the knife and the mincing machine are to a civilised man and woman. Life and death depend on dentition, according to tribal law, to break which brings misery, disaster, and ill-luck to all concerned (see Chapter XVI). Radiating from the baby's first tooth are dental customs which are both numerous and curious. Most fishing tribes, or " water children " as they call themselves, chip and grind their teeth in imitation of fish, which disproves the old dental theory that once the enamel is destroyed the teeth decay. Wemba, Twa, Unga, Shila, Luena, and many other tribes file their teeth thus to sharp points as described, and so do most fishing-folk. Some tribes like the Luba, Lunda, and Mambwe knock out two, and sometimes four, of their lower incisors. Some tribes file the teeth in serrated fashion. The Yeke, Nyam-wezi, and Swahili tribes do not practise teeth deformation in any form. Mashukulumbwe knock out all the upper and lower incisor teeth. The Baila of N. Rhodesia knock out the two central lower incisors and file the two upper central incisors into an inverted V shape. No special dental deformation can be described as the hall-mark of one particular tribe, for the matter of teeth decoration is often left to the discretion or the individual taste of the man or woman. This may, however, be due to a tendency to tribal slackness owing to more civilised natives poking fun at them for their " crocodile teeth," etc. I asked a man

once, " Why do you chip and file your teeth ? " He
answered thus : " If my teeth were allowed to grow any
way they would grow out of mouth and eat my ears off."
The reasons I have heard given in regard to nudity are also
equally primitive : " Why should we cover our bodies ?
We have no diseases to hide. We were born naked, and
why should we dress ? " Also the eternal African answer
to most questions : " It's our custom handed down from
our forefathers, and we won't leave it." Dress has its
inception among primitive peoples in (a) a desire to cover
the genital organs for comfort and protection, and (b)
later on a sense of shame (nsoni) which is not, however,
highly developed among the interior tribes. Men and
women often bathe openly in the rivers and pools, and
fishermen, hunters, and blacksmiths often go about their
work naked to the blast.

The first stage of dress allowance is very limited, and
always and everywhere associated with a desire, on the part
of the women, to cover mere nakedness. Eventually the
belt or cord and a two-inch bark rag or strip of skin gives
place to something bigger, which gradually goes on increasing until you get the full-dressed and *the finished*
(European!) *article*. In the matter of dress, woman's first
concern is to pass a strip of fibre, or grass or bark cloth,
under the armpits to keep the breasts from dangling, for,
after the birth of the first child, they become extraordinarily
broad and long. Later on, the size of the band increases
until, after touch with civilising influences, it becomes a
full-blown under-garment. A mission lady was once so
shocked to see women come to her house with uncovered
breasts that she made a rule that no woman with breasts
uncovered should ever approach her dwelling. The first
woman who showed face after this was promptly sent off
to cover her breasts. She went outside and returned in

a few minutes with her breasts covered by the small cloth that she always wore round her waist, which left her otherwise naked. The lady never repeated her rule, and after that she allowed the women round her place to make haste slowly in the matter of dress.

The Luena women wear skin aprons of slit skin, four inches wide and a few inches long, which are worn in front and a strip of skin behind. This is kept in place by a belt. The Luba women wear short grass skirts about ten inches wide. The Katanga women to-day, with the women of the Lunda and Wemba tribes, wear as a rule full dress from under the armpits to the feet. These are often two yards square. Batwa, Baunga, and Bisa women on Bangweulu wear decorated skin shawls of Lechwe, or plain ones of Sititunga, antelopes. They also wear sheep skins, which, when cleaned and dressed, look decent and are certainly more comfortable than trade calico. Men wear two cat skins, one in front and one behind, and sometimes otter skin. Nyasaland women make very pretty aprons of woven bead-work, with bead girdles, necklaces, bracelets, and other adornments, and are quite expert in this though they are very loth to sell the same to admiring Europeans. Bark cloth, shawls, and blankets are made from the bark stripped from several kinds of trees, principally the Mutaba tree, which is planted as a shade tree round villages and also makes a beautiful green avenue. We had one such at the Government station at Fort Rosebery, N. Rhodesia. They strip a piece of bark a yard or more in width, then, after knocking off the outer bark, beat it out with a wooden mallet scored on the face with criss-cross lines. The bark is thus reduced by hammering, and teased to an equal thickness. These pieces are then sewn together until the requisite size is obtained, after which they are oiled all over and rubbed with red dye, and with fibre thread are sewn and decorated in pretty seams and patterns. Several dyes are used which are made from berries, roots, and flowers. A red dye is got from the bean of the Usishi tree, and the cloth is frequently boiled in camwood. A khaki dye is made from the bark of two different trees called Mubaba and Namwenshi. The Lubans and many Congo tribes are expert in making fibre cloth of various kinds, and a strong, useful grass cloth also which they weave by hand. These they cut up, and make into trousers, coats, hats, and skirts. In fact, Lubans long before the arrival of Europeans had actually adopted styles of dress and building and other European habits, with towns laid out in streets, and up-to-date sanitary arrangements were also in operation. Last comes the European trader with all his bric-a-brac from Brummagem, now summed up under the obnoxious title of " Kaffir truck." With cheap calicoes, blankets, clothes, Africa is at last emerging from her Eden-like simplicity in the matter of dress and habits. Some of the trade calicoes and clothes are good, wearable, and quite substantial, while there is much that is poor, full of starch, and after the first shower of rain leaves the wearer less covered than he was with fibre, grass, bark cloth, or skins. Headgear used to be worn in the form of skin caps, or head-dresses of various kinds decorated with gaudy feathers, or cleverly constructed wigs. To-day the hat, called *chapeo* (from the Portuguese), is worn in the form of straw, broad-brimmed felt, policeman's helmet, or the bowler; or, as at the coast, a stovepipe edition. I have seen an old native trader coming up from the coast with frock coat and trousers, boots over his shoulders, and three silk hats on his apex. By Rugarugas and German East African natives the turban is used, and out East the red Morocco fez cap is worn, also a white embroidered cap is worn by the Swahilis and Zanzibaris.

Footgear used to be worn in the form of skin sandals fastened at the toe and round the ankle. These were made from zebra, waterbuck, and other big fauna skins, and were much worn by native travellers and hunters. To-day clogs, and hobnailed, black, and brown boots, and even kid, are much in evidence, and worn by a quarter of the natives round mining towns. The imitative tendency in the Bantu is a potent factor in the transformation of the dress and habits of a people who thirty years ago only concerned themselves about body decoration as seen in the elaborate head-dresses, tattooing, and teeth chipping and filing already described. As in their language and languages, their government and social system, their laws and regulations, their system of building construction, and their religion, so in the sartorial art the Bantus are quickly copying the fashions of Europe. Their languages are dying, their arts and manufactures, industries and enterprises, are all in the same moribund condition, so that in a few decades the African will be living as artificial a life as the modern civilised peoples of Europe. Whether it is for better or for worse remains to be seen. *Nous verrons !*

CHAPTER XIV

Courtship & Marriage

HERE I translate and transcribe the formal ceremonies associated with courtship and marriage as written out for me some years ago by a Wemba man in his own native idiom ; merely a simple statement on the subject, and void of decorative detail.

" If a man wants to marry a woman he first of all looks out a suitable person himself, or on enquiry hears through others of a likely partner. Then he asks if she is unspoken for, and if she is free from any taint of disease, acquired or inherited. All the villagers where she lives say, ' No, she is clean, gentle, and is a careful and modest person, she has no bad manners, and is not long tongued.' Then he sends his go-between, saying, ' Go and ask her if she is willing to marry me, and hear what she says.' Then the marriage go-between reaches the girl's home and calls for the girl, saying, ' I have a message for you, lady. My companion sent me to deliver it. He says, " I love that woman and want to marry her " ; this is the message I have come to deliver.' Then the girl consents, saying, ' Whoever refused an offer of marriage ? I think two are better than one if the two are mutually agreed.' The marriage go-between returns and says, ' Yes, she is agreeable.' In the evening he who wants to marry goes on a visit himself. He says to the girl, ' I want you to be my wife.' The girl answers, ' Yes, sir. I agree, provided you love me truly.' The man

replies, ' Yes, truly, lady, and no lie. I love you.' Then the
girl agrees, saying, ' All right, then, if you love me, but
remember I do not want to be a polygamous wife, for
polygamy is not good for a woman.' The man answers,
' No, I shall never marry another. I only want to marry
you.' The girl consents again, saying, ' All right, let us
marry.' Then the man sends his go-between to the mother
and aunts. The go-between says, ' I have been sent with
this message from my friend to you ladies. He says, " I
want to marry your daughter." The mother and aunts say,
' That's all right, we are quite pleased. The chief thing
is that they should care for each other, and that he work for
his wife. Also, he should respect his marriage relations
and help them and clothe them as becomes a son-in-law.'
Then the prospective mother-in-law enquires, ' What is
his clan ? ' Then the go-between replies, ' He belongs to
the field rat clan.' Then the go-between takes the message
back to his friend, saying, ' Yes. The mother and aunts
agree ; it's all right.' Then the prospective son-in-law
sends a request for tobacco, and the prospective mother-
in-law sends the tobacco asked for, which is a sign of agreement. (Native women ask for tobacco when they offer
themselves to men, and this custom is prevalent all over
the Katanga and Rhodesia). Then the young man knows
that they have accepted him to marry their daughter.
From now on he may begin to court the girl with the
parents' permission. When the prospective son-in-law
his finished his courtship he gets together a marriage
present. He hands it to the go-between, saying, ' Go and
arrange all the business concerning the marriage.' Then
the go-between takes the marriage dowry to the prospective
mother-in-law, saying, ' See, we have brought the dowry.'
The prospective mother-in-law says, ' All right, sit down,
sir.' They say, ' Let's call the girl that she be present at

the arrangements for her marriage.' Then they call the
girl, and the mother strikes up a little song :

> 'Oh I'm so happy, happy.
> I'm so pleased and happy,'

and she adds, 'Yes, Mr. Go-between, what I'm saying is
absolutely true. I like my prospective son-in-law. Go
straight and tell him that from me.' The go-between
then asks, ' Now, what about the marriage-day and arrangements ? ' The prospective mother-in-law says, ' But the
things for the wedding feast have not yet been got together.
We shall sleep and wake over to-morrow, and then the day
after shall be the wedding-day.' Then the girl's marriage
relations announce the matter publicly to the whole village.
When the prospective son-in-law arrives he greets them
and they give him some beads and a bracelet, and later
an arrow which is to pierce any seducer of his wife. When
he is satisfied he returns to the village in the evening and
says, ' Let them bring me my wife now.' Then on taking
her away from the mother's house they first give the girl
a string of beads and a hoe. She is carried on the back of a
strong woman (her wedding coach) as it is not considered
dignified for her to walk. She must pretend to be very
reluctant to leave her mother's roof and her maiden liberties.
At this point the crowd of women guests present strike up
a little song, the words of which are :

> 'Oh night-jar, oh little bird,
> Your long, lovely feathers have grown.
> Your time has come, your year of love.
> Oh night-jar, oh little bird.'

Then the men pay up a girdle of pretty beads to the
bride's party, on receiving which they strike up the following
song :

> ' Bring me a hammer,
> To smash the hyena.

CONGO CHIEF AND HEAD WIFE.

The Chief is on the left, and one of his Councillors, in a white helmet, is on the right. Both
are wearing leopard skins, while the wife is adorned with beads and ivory bracelets.

Let's break his bones,
And his wife's bones too.
She also is a hyena,
Let's break her bones.'

Then the women draw near and strike up another little
song :
    'The wild cat's skin dress,
    They are calling and calling for.
    I'm dragging, dragging her.
    We're bringing her, bringing her.'

They give the women a belt of beads, and the men sing
again :
    'My oil-palm tree,
    Does it refuse to bear fruit.
    Oh there's no nuts on it,
    We can't wait all night.   (At the door of the house.)
    We're hungry now.
    Oh bring us the fruitful palm tree.'

The women then knock at the man's door and they sing a
little song :
    'The crowns have stuck to the spirit stone.
    Oh who shall take them out alone?'

"The men then pay up a hoe, and the bride and bridegroom are put to bed and then left alone. (Wedded and
bedded according to old Scotch custom). In the morning
the elder women come and fetch them out and instruct
them in their duties thus : ' Now, my children, know only
each other, you woman your husband, and you man your
wife. You are married now. See, man, that you have
only eyes for your wife and don't be all eyes for other
women.' Then the elder women rise and strike up another
little song, thus :
    'A young bride is proud, is proud,
    And on the marriage bed she's proud.
    We dance at your wedding, little bride,
    Though we don't know the man you've married.'

Further instructions are given by one and another, thus :
' In a house there can't be two lions. See to it, girl, that
you listen to and obey your husband in all things and be a
good wife.' Then the official marriage is over and the guests
all scatter. When the marriage company has gone the
mother-in-law brings food to the bride and bridegroom,
singing a little song :

> ' Ding-dong, we bring good food.
> Nothing pleases the bridegroom.
> The feast is spread, he's got no eyes—
> No eyes or thought save for his bride.'

They put the food down at the house and the bridegroom
calls the go-between and the principal elders to come and
share the feast. Returning the empty dishes the men
put a new hoe and dress or nice cloths into them—a present
for the women-folk. The bridegroom pays the go-between
his fees, after which the marriage is over and the ceremonies are ended."

The basis and starting-point of all society upon which
depends the family, the clan, the tribe, and the individual,
is found in the bi-sexual couple, man and wife. In Rhodesia
and a great part of the Katanga the courtship and marriage
customs are much alike, so that one may generalise and yet
be true to type. Boys' and girls' rites, e.g. circumcision
and puberty ceremonies, are more or less considered as
leading up to marriage and the consequent tribal con-
tinuity, and hence are not out of place here. Circumcision for boys, though practised by the Luba, Lunda,
and Luena tribes, is not in vogue throughout Southern
Katanga or Northern Rhodesia. There are a number of
secret societies where boys are initiated and learn much
regarding their future duties, but the main lessons taught
by natives at puberty are reserved for the girls. When a
young girl discovers that she has attained puberty, she

runs into the forest and hides herself until, as a rule, she is discovered by some one, who rushes back to the village, saying, " I have discovered a *Chisungu* girl." She is then sought for by the elder women who have to do with the *Chisungu* or puberty ceremonies, and after ceremonial purification is brought back in the evening to her hut in the village. When the usual period of a few days have elapsed she is allowed to do odd jobs about the house. During the initiation period, which lasts for at least a month, the girl may not leave her hut save in the company of elder women. Drumming and singing and general rejoicing is kept up during the initiation month and no male is allowed to enter the initiation hut where the girl is confined save a *shimpundu*, or father of twins. (In laying the foundations of pigeon houses, chicken houses or goat pens, or anything for breeding purposes a similar favourable concession is made to either a father or a mother of twin children. It is supposed to have a beneficial or prolific effect. There is a native woman I know who has had twins three times, and she is in great demand for laying the foundations of pigeon and chicken houses, goat and sheep pens, and even a cattle kraal.) At these puberty ceremonies the girls are instructed in the ordinary facts and duties of life, and they are very roughly handled by these primitive teachers of savage life and morals. They are made to do all sorts of absurd things to prove that they are fit to enter the society of grown-ups. Sometimes a basket of tiny bird-seed grain is poured out on the ground, and they are made to pick it up, replacing every grain, and during the process songs inculcating thrift and the value of food are dinned into their ears. The girl is taken by the women elders inside a hut called *Mbusa* and shown all sorts of weird things, which are pointed out and explained to her so that she shall not enter this new state of life " in blissful ignorance." She has to pass through many other rites and ceremonies which are supposed to prepare her for her future life as a wife and mother, and at the conclusion of this puberty initiation she is considered as grown up and marriageable.

Sometimes the girl is matched and sometimes married before puberty, when a ceremony constituting marriage is gone through with much solemnity and ceremonial, just as in the case of an ordinary *bwinga*, or marriage ceremony. Under these circumstances I have heard a man proudly say of his wife, " Did we not grow up together ? Did I not see her through her puberty ceremonies ? Are we not just twin children ? " I have seen some happy native couples who have married very young and gone through life together until death parted them. In polygamy such a woman usually becomes the head wife. Though the *Chisungu* wife has high status, the real ceremonial wife is the *Ina bwinga*, or " married mother," as she is called, for whom all the sacred tribal marriage rites were solemnised in the presence of the spirits living and dead. She is the real *mukolo*, or head wife, who gets all the praise in song, and presents in kind. She and only she knows her lord and master, his strength and weakness. Then there is the commercially acquired wife, a free woman and the eligible daughter of some local somebody, who if virtue and beauty count for anything may eventually oust her predecessors, and get the coveted headwife's place. Fourthly, there used to be the slave wife, who had merely a marketable value, and who could, with her children, be sold to pay a debt or to fill the family purse. These slave wives were often exchanged or sold.

The system of wife inheritance is one that involves many complications and much trouble. For example, if a man loses his wife by death he sends a messenger with a big present representing what is called "the death dues," or rather, part thereof, for the first "death payment" is a mere instalment to notify, and many an unfortunate widower has been ruined in an endeavour to satisfy the greed, and appease the sham wrath, of his dead wife's relatives. If the notification parcel (representing the black-edged card) is too small, the relations send it back, saying, "Our sister cannot be dead, or a suitable announcement would have reached us." Therefore, to notify a dead wife's relations, if numerous, is a serious and expensive preliminary. Again, the *malilo*, or "wake," may not commence until the dead woman's nearest relatives arrive, hence the delay due to haggling over the preliminary notification. Then before they can bring a sister to take the dead woman's place with the husband the man has to pay and pay, and to get together enough he has to borrow, and often he is left with debts that will keep him down for years to come. If the nearest sister is married then the next is called, and if she is too young, as in a case I knew years ago, they have to provide a slave woman or hire a woman to take the place until the young sister is grown up. If there are no unmarried sisters then a married sister must spend a night or more with the widower "to take the death away from his body." This may, and does often, lead to trouble and even divorce.

Divorce may be sought and obtained for a number of reasons, barrenness being the most common. I have known a husband and wife accusing each other and bickering over no children until the woman appealed to be given as a temporary wife to a man who had already a large family. This was done, and the woman gave birth to a healthy baby boy. The man was jeered at as the cause, and, strange to say, he married a widow with a family of three, by whom he also had several children.

Incompatibility of temper is one of the causes of frequent

divorce, and I have known a woman who, to get rid of a man she disliked, plagued his life and pursued him like a fury from day to day. She eventually tore his clothing from his body and acted in a nameless way such as is common in Central Africa. Frequent adultery is often a common cause of divorce, though ordinarily this crime can be settled by a money payment to the injured husband. Sometimes the man kills the woman, and sometimes kills the guilty pair. I knew a man at Johnston Falls, where I lived, whose wife had gone repeatedly after other men. He followed his wife to the field one day, killed her there, and cut her into pieces. He fled, but was followed by the woman's brother, who killed him in a thicket.

Jealousy causes endless trouble, and often leads to separation and to divorce after long years of a happily married life. Sometimes a headwife will threaten a husband with desertion unless he puts away So-and-so—some young wife of whom she is jealous—and often the man obeys, as he cannot afford to part with the wife of his youth and all the associations, though he can easily obtain another young wife to fill the place of the inferior woman. Sometimes the husband fails to clothe and provide for his wife, and his mother-in-law, and to help in the gardens, and the mother-in-law, after frequently warning the son-in-law, takes the girl away, restores the dowry paid, and marries her daughter to a wealthier or more industrious suitor. This was not easily done in the old days, but now the transition to European law has brought about a laxity of application in the more stern and rigorous native laws and their code of morals.

CHAPTER XV

Polygamy & Polyandry

MONOGAMY, according to the generally accepted Bantu view-point, is a practice in vogue only among civilised people and poor blacks. The natives aver that our civilisation being based upon Christianity and the Bible, we, to be true to our teaching, must keep to the one man one woman view of marriage and society. In Africa a native accepts and adheres to monogamy because of poverty, laziness, or inability to work for and support more than one woman. On the other hand, polygamists are usually hard workers and aristocrats ; men who by virtue of hard work and royal blood are able to work for and support a number of wives. In other words, where a savage state of society obtains polygamists are, as a rule, the best type of men and the most staunch upholders of tribal life and customs. Of course, polygamists' families being large they have greater interests at stake ; more to gain and lose. Polygamy, why ? is a question that is easily asked but, to be fair to polygamists, it takes a lot of answering. Polygamy at its lowest estimate is by no means an easy outlet and argument for the satisfaction of lust. The propagation of the species and the consequent increase of population, with the upbuilding of a society that shall be held together by laws equally binding, coupled with the protection and mutual benefits derived therefrom is, I think, one of the chief native arguments for polygamy. Sometimes war is the cause, for, by the killing off of males, there is a superfluity of females, and to prevent promiscuous concubinage these are given to the warriors as slave wives, by which means the population is multiplied and the country enriched. Sometimes women are to blame, for I have heard native women again and again advocating polygamy and almost forcing—at any rate coaxing—their husbands to marry more and more wives. If the husband inconsiderately brings friends frequently for dinner and is fond of entertaining, the burden of all this falls, not on the husband but on the wife. If she is a monogamous wife she has all the water and firewood to get. She must mill sufficient meal and cook and prepare and entertain as becomes a good wife. If, on the other hand, the same man is a polygamist the work is divided up and each of the wives takes her turn at preparing the food and entertaining the guests. Therefore from the housewife's point of view polygamy is easier on the woman. There are, on the other hand, many women who object to a polygamous marriage and who prefer to be the only wife. With the break-up of tribal power, with slavery, and with native wars women are not so numerous, and many men are settling down to a monogamous state by sheer force of circumstances. Women, too, in Katanga, Angola, and Rhodesia are more and more insisting on monogamy and equal rights, and European law upholds them. Of course the period of pregnancy and maternal duties necessitates—according to native law—the woman living apart from the husband, and this enforced abstinence has been held up by many as a sound and irrefutable argument against monogamy. Some friends of missions, from motives of sympathy with missionaries and their work on the West Coast, propounded what was facetiously called "the feeding bottle theory." I think, however, that the question of polygamy with many other difficult questions will, from the negro view-point, be settled in time as African civilisation advances, just as such questions were

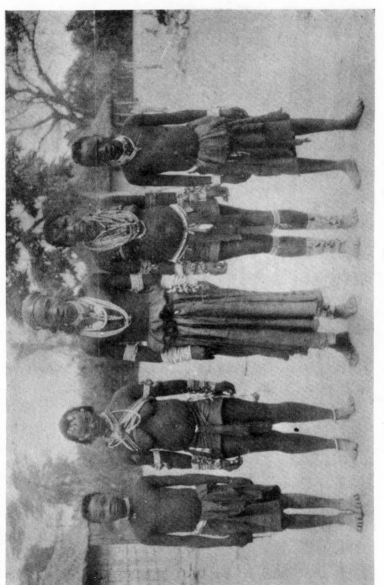

A Paramount Chief with his Two Wives and Two Sons.

settled by Britons in early days when polyandry obtained, and it was the custom for one woman to be wife to all the brothers in the family. To put the clock back, Briton and Bantu had much in common both as to laws, customs, and the moral code. Jerome tells of the cannibalism of the early Britons amongst whom he lived, who were no whit behind the cannibals of the Congo. Does polygamy produce better and bigger families? I think that this question will require a lot of settling, and by experts in eugenics rather than by the ordinary observer from ordinary points of view. I should say that polygamy does produce bigger families, all things being equal, but as to their being better families, i.e. physically, mentally, and every other way, I do not for a moment believe that this is so. I have seen a monogamous wife with a family of ten, and I have seen a large number of barren polygamous wives.

Where the matriarchal system prevails and children belong to the mother, barrenness is looked on as a curse, whereas with the prevalence of the patriarchal system means are often used to prevent the birth of children. The natives have long been in possession of medicines which seem permanently to kill all fertility, and many chiefs' polygamous wives have sought to, and do, prevent families by these known means, preferring to have children by means of slave women whom they give to their husbands for this purpose, as they profess to dislike and object to the inconvenience of childbirth. Of course the children of a polygamous marriage lack the opportunity of training and care that is usually bestowed on the fewer children resulting from a monogamous marriage. One of the chief arguments I have seen adduced against polygamy is the fact that owing to jealousies many polygamists are poisoned by their polygamous wives, who complain of neglect. I have known many instances of this, and one in particular where the one wife, out of jealousy, poisoned the other's child and was hanged for murder in the Congo. The usual way to avenge supposed insults was to make beer and invite the spouse to drink, he being handed a poisoned cup. The explanation given in extenuation is, " Well, if I am killed for it I have the satisfaction of depriving my enemy of his caresses, for I shall have killed him." Native men usually know the evils and jealousies resulting from polygamy, and are as a rule careful to try and avoid giving offence to the lesser wives, by sharing their favours all round.

The puzzle of the polygamous family tree is a by no means easily solved or soluble one. To get up towards a twentieth wife with her family and to find and define relationships between family No. 20 and family No. 2, or with the other eighteen families, would take a specially developed mathematical mind and an intimate lifelong residence among polygamous natives, plus a congenital knowledge of their language and system, such as one finds sometimes in European children born and brought up in the country. Native women are very thin-skinned and sensitive. I remember being roused up one morning in Bihé by an awful hubbub, as though some one were being murdered near my house. I ran out in my pyjamas expecting to see some one speared or hacked to pieces with an axe. Instead I saw a native woman with her hands clasped around her head. She was crying, and the big tears were coursing down her cheeks as she ran along the road. "What is it, woman?" I asked. "Oh," she said, "my husband spoke roughly to me and I'm going home to my mother" (*veyange wamopia. Ngenda ku mai*).

I remember a young fellow returning from the mines with clothes and money he had brought affectionately back for his young wife whom he had left behind. She, however, had heard during his absence that he was dead and had married another. The youth was so broken that he ran off to the forest and committed suicide by hanging himself to the branch of a tree, where he was found dead the following day.

Polyandry as practised among the Indian hill tribes was practised among the Scots in North Britain in Jerome's day, and is common, in some form or other, among many Central African tribes at the present day. Among the Wemba and tribes in Northern Rhodesia it is only permitted to the *Inamfumu*, or " mother of kings," who can choose any man that takes her fancy ; she also chooses her own consort after the consummation of puberty ceremony, leads him to the royal hut, and if no children result, can put him away and choose another, and yet others. The most striking instance of tribal polyandry is practised by the Luena of Angola, and I believe that the neighbouring Lunda tribe also practise it. Evidences of the general practice of polyandry by Luena women is seen everywhere and they have an intricate and secret code of assignation signals by which any woman may call to her any man she may choose *pro tem.* Young boys are used by these women as " go-betweens," and thus as they grow up they drift into the universally recognised practices of their elders.

The queen of the whole tribe was a woman of remarkable ability and personal character named Nya-Katolo. The history of her springing into power, conquering the country she occupied, and subjugating the surrounding tribes is very interesting reading. About fifty years ago she lived on the Luena River. For the purpose of conquest she got together an army and fought her way through the countries intervening between the Luena River and the Kavungu stream. She scattered every force that opposed her and established villages at the head of which she put women chiefs. She eventually reached the Kavungu stream, where she built her capital, and from there sent out war parties and broke up the then waning power of Matiamvo. Her warriors returned from these raiding expeditions laden with booty and slaves, and these were sold to Bihéans for guns, gunpowder, and trade goods, by which she maintained her prestige and extended her boundaries, as well as paying her soldiers and clothing her people. She instituted a system of women chiefs all over the countries she conquered, who were tributary to her and sent in regular caravans of tribute each new moon. These women chiefs put in charge of villages were not chosen haphazard, mere nondescripts from anywhere, but carefully selected ladies of strong personality, many of whom were well fitted for the posts of headwomen and chieftainesses. At the capital and at many centres where trading caravans from the coast or the interior halted to buy food and replenish their meal bags the female prerogative was utilised, and these chieftainesses used to send their women-folk with men bullies to entice native traders with the ultimate object of robbing them. Immediately the women entered the trader's hut a man who was lying in wait pounced on the unsuspecting native trader and accused him of robbing him of his wife. Thereupon he was robbed, and I have seen such unwary men stripped of all they possessed, having to return to their country semi-naked.

The Luena tribe is one of the most debased and immoral I have seen and a tribe of regular highway robbers, who used to attack and plunder caravans, holding guns at their victims' heads and making them literally " stand and deliver." With my caravan I was attacked on four occasions by armed bands of local Luenas while passing peacefully through their country, and we were plundered.

Mahanga was one of Msidi's queens, a tall, handsome Luban woman with arms and legs encircled in ivory, and head stylishly coiffured by her many maids. The chief made her his *mugodi* or " head wife." Though of chiefly lineage, she was caught in a raid by one of Msidi's war parties and carried back a prisoner to his capital. Her beauty captivated the old roué king and he installed her as one of his chief queens, giving her almost unlimited powers of which she was not slow to avail herself. After Msidi's death she was inherited by his son and successor, Mukanda Bantu, whose wife she became and bore him two sons. She was certainly a remarkable woman of powerful personality ; an Amazon who led her regiment to battle in person, and I have seen her perform a war-dance with a pile of over twenty heads in front of her. She had her own following of men and women and about a dozen maids who regularly waited on her. Her word was law, and I might say she was the most feared woman in the Katanga. She was a notorious poisoner and the name of " witch " from the Bantu standpoint applied to her if such could be applied to any African. She was such a notorious poisoner that she never ate food outside her own house. At a school distribution of prizes I remember asking her to join in the feast, and the look of refusal she gave me I am not likely to forget. Said she : " I never eat outside my own house." My excuse for introducing her here is that she was a notorious polyandrist whose lovers were legion, and woe betide the hapless man to whom she took a dislike. I remember distinctly one occasion where three men were knocked on the head, sacked, and thrown to the crocs in the Lufira River by her orders. She said they insulted her. After Msidi II died she retired with her son to the home of her youth in Lubaland. This son, named Mafinge, is one of the most powerful chiefs on the Lualaba River, and like his mother one of the most arrant rogues to be found anywhere in Africa. Mahanga means " the

persecutor," and Mafinge means "the man of curses."
No misnomers !

The third of the trio of polyandrous queens was Ina-
Kafwaya of Kazembe's Lunda people in North-East
Rhodesia. She was the leading lady in the Lunda country
along the Luapula River, and a photo of her appears in
Dr. Livingstone's *Last Journals.* Last time I saw her she
must have been well over a hundred years old. Nya-Katolo,
queen of the Ba-Luena of Portuguese Angola, Mahanga,
Msidi's handsome Zenobia of Katanga, and Ina-Kafwaya,
queen of the Eastern Lunda tribe of North-East Rhodesia,
were certainly from every point of view three of the most
remarkable women I have seen or heard of in Central Africa.
Their names are immortalised in scores of songs of love
and war, and they are not likely to sink into historic oblivion
for another fifty years or more.

I cannot finish this chapter of polygamy and polyandry
without referring and paying a just tribute to the brave
polygamous wives of the Yeke chief Chamunda of Katanga.
He was sent north by Msidi to make war on the people of
Chona in the Luba country and bring back slaves. The
fighting was in full swing when Chamunda got a bullet
that smashed his leg, and he would have been killed but
for the plucky and dashing rescue of his wives. Some of
them carried him off the field of battle, while others faced
the foe and kept firing until the safety of their lord and
master was assured. He bore about on his body until his
death, some years ago, the mark and lameness got in that
memorable Luban battle in Chona's country, a reminder
of the debt that he owed to his brave *bachima*, which he
never failed to hold up to the itinerant missionaries who
occasionally visited his village as a feather in the cap of
polygamy.

CHAPTER XVI

Bantu Children

THE birth of a baby is one of the great events in the life of every Bantu village, and the status of a woman is enhanced according to the size of her family, the potential commercial value of which is considered a great asset. The public annunciation of coming maternity is always made the occasion of great rejoicing, but the coming of a new baby into the kraal is hailed with gun-firing, feasting, and giving of presents. Baby-birth is the big event in African village life. Granted the safe arrival of baby and the safety of the mother, who must be greeted after delivery with the words : " Are you saved ? " the question of next importance, asked and answered, is : " Is it a boy or a girl ? " The answer to this question in a land void of mock modesty is as crude as nude, for the baby is held up to public view to show its sex—male or female. One hears much of the custom in Oriental countries of giving a special welcome to a boy because of his future commercial value as a trader, workman, or soldier, whereas we are told that female children are not wanted. In Bantuland, where the matriarchal system prevails, this is certainly not so, for the little girl is as warmly welcomed as a potential household help and mother, who by marriage will bring sons-in-law to the kraal. These will fish and hunt and hoe for the marriage relations.

A baby girl is spoken of as a " little wife for somebody," and a boy as a " little husband." In fact, the baby girl is often betrothed shortly after birth, yes, and oftener a betrothal is made long before the baby sees the light of day. When the baby is born, if parturition is difficult, and often before, a doctor is called, who divines and tells them that it is a dead relative who is being reincarnated, and his or her name is given to the child. If the birth is easy, and the baby gives no trouble, it is often looked on, not as a case of reincarnation, but as an ordinary birth, and the family come together to discuss a suitable name for their new-born. If the child is born on a Friday or Saturday it is called Friday or Saturday. If any event takes place, or a white man passes through the kraal at the time, it is called after the event or the white man. Thus a baby may be called Locust, Snake, Smallpox, or Elephant, Smith, Brown, or Jones. If it is a light-coloured child it may be called White, if dark it may be called Black. Hence a trader, or traveller, or Government official who moves about among the villages, may find a dozen different kraals all over the country where his name is bandied about. The " baby name " is only used temporarily, though it is retained permanently and is called " the umbilical name." By means of this name one can trace a thief who passes muster, otherwise, under a dozen aliases. Like the Arabs the Bantu children take the father's or family name. Thus, if a child's name is Sunday—having been born on that day —and the father's name is Market, the child is known as Sunday Market. Or, for the same reason, if the child's name is Saturday, and the father's name is Morning, the child is known by the name of Saturday Morning. Or if the child has slept much after birth and has earned the name of Sleepy, while the father's name is Sam, the child is called Sleepy Sam, and so on.

Every baby at birth must receive a little first fetish, called *Musamfu*. This is made from a piece of reed about one inch long, which is hollowed out inside, and a piece of the father's or mother's hair inserted into it. It is then perforated, a string passed through the hole, and passed round the child's left arm to protect it from evil influences. Baby must be made hardy, hence no dress allowance is made. The little boy has a thread passed round his waist, and the little girl the same, but she also has in addition a small piece of bark cloth two inches wide hung down in front like a doll's apron. Thus exposed to the weather the mortality among Bantu babies is appalling. Missionaries, to encourage dress, often give warm garments to babies, as " birth presents." By and by baby develops bronchitis, or other trouble, and the missionary is called in to help, when he finds to his disgust that the little garment has been carefully folded and laid aside, whereas the child has been exposed to cold and wind and rain.

If a child cuts its lower incisors first it is a " lucky child," and receives life's justification mark—the white chalk. If other teeth sprout first the child is " unlucky," and condemned to be thrown into the river.

When baby begins to speak or sprawl, all the aunts and uncles take great interest in their growing nephew or niece, and nothing pleases them better than to be allowed to hold or dandle it as it tries to say words or take a few first steps. " Mamma," the great world-word for mother, is usually the first word a black baby lisps, and very often it is the last word a dying native man or woman utters. In joy or sorrow, peace or war, this is one of the great words one hears continually used. The first decoration of a child is usually a bead bracelet, or necklace, whereas the first dress for a boy consists in a small goatskin, simulating a pair of trousers, and called *tunsudi* ; that of a girl is a small piece of bark cloth, skin, or calico worn in front and behind. As a boy grows up he is initiated by his elders into the useful art of trapping young birds and rats, and catching fish for the pot. He learns from A to Z how to make traps and snares of all kinds, and rarely fails to bring home a few rats or a string of fish, a partridge or guinea-fowl, or even a small antelope for the sundown supper—the meal of the day. He also learns to dig up fibre, spin string, and make with his own hands a serviceable, small fishing net which he has already become proficient in using.

The difficulty in native schools is to get these boys to attend regularly, for they delight in playing truant as much as any English boy. I remember a number of these boys playing truant, which was a bad example, as the school had an average attendance of two hundred scholars. We eventually pitted our wits against theirs, and after a long chase rounded them up in the river, returning from their expedition—a band of real Huck Finns, with strings of rats, fresh fish, birds (dead and alive), nests of eggs, and a quantity of caterpillars and other tasty grubs. They were marched back to school with their trophies, and lined up in front of the others, to the uproarious merriment of their schoolmates, who, in their hearts, lionised and envied them.

Then the boys learn to work, and trade, or they may help in digging out a canoe, or building a new hut, or fencing the fields, or sowing seed, or selling meat or fish or other products. Thus, in the company and under the eye of the elders, they learn the facts and arts of life, which soon they will begin to practise on their own. The girl, meanwhile, helps to nurse baby, or following her mother, will help her in the household or other duties which are considered exclusively women's work. She may learn pottery, mat-weaving, basket-making, spinning cotton, or a dozen other things that girls do, and thus she grows up, as does the boy, to the early years of adolescence, when she is put through the ceremonies prescribed by law and custom for her sex.

Savage children are full of fun and are up to all sorts of mischief and games. They are fond of playing " See-Saw," and driving a peg in the stump of a big tree about three feet high, they cut a hole out of the centre of another log and place it on the peg. A boy then gets on each end, and they swing up and down, much as children do in other lands, but with this difference : that they also swing round as well. They sing while they swing, and shout to each other, and often one tries to swing the other off to increase the fun. *Kampwe* is another game they play. One boy gets hold of a live and supple branch of a tree and swings at the end of it ; the others push him and swing him higher and harder, and he must hold on and not fall. They sing as they swing him roughly :

> " Swing, sing, swing.
> Hang on to the branch.
> Look out ! If you fall,
> Your mother's a witch."

If the boy lets go and falls they beat him and call him " the son of a witch," when a free fight ensues between the boy's chums and rivals.

" Shooting the Pumpkin " is a favourite game. A pumpkin is thrown along the ground, and as it rolls they follow it with their toy bows and sharpened reed arrows, and shoot into it. I have seen the pumpkin stuck with arrows like a pin-cushion. Boys become very adept at this kind of archery, and learn thus to shoot at moving targets. Later, they practise on birds and game with great success. They play the same game throwing spears instead of shooting arrows. They make pop-guns from grass stalks called *mpolo*, which is the name of the game. They cut these green,

about three feet long, and tie them in bunches, and then
they go to a rock alongside which they light a fire. They
insert the end of the grass stalks in the fire, and then
extract them hot, one at a time. They raise and strike the
burnt end sharply on the rock, which causes an explosion
like a young cannon. In the season when the grass is
ripe they often carry on this pop-gun game for hours at
a time.

Fita is a war game, a kind of *kriegspiel* played by boys
with rival camps, and regiments officered by the local
Huck Finns and Tom Sawyers. The parties each form
camps, and build their huts at a distance from each other.
Then they draw up in line as warriors, and when the war
whoop is sounded they rush with mimic guns and spears
and bows and arrows and fight a mimic battle. They often
get serious, and there is a lot of lively horseplay, and when
one party is considered beaten they retire with yells of
defiance. The victors set up a shout, do a war-dance, and
sing boisterously to announce their victory.

Girls dance in a ring, taking hands, and sing as they circle
round, just as girls do at home :

" Play, play, play,
All the day.
That's our work
For this year."

This game is called after the first word in the song,
Sampala.

Diavolo is played by boys with great dexterity. The game
dies out from time to time and again breaks out afresh,
when boys may be seen everywhere in the villages throwing
their " diavolo," which they call *shingwa*.

Mupila, a ball game, is also played by boys and young
men, and they put tremendous energy into it, sweating in

the hot sun. One strikes the ball hard on the ground, and as it rebounds they all jump and clap their hands, after which each springs into the air to catch the returning ball. A boy may not catch it until he has first jumped and clapped his hands together.

Kafifi, or " Blind Man's Buff," is a game which causes roars of laughter. The boy's eyes are covered, and he is chased and poked at by the others, who go as near him as they dare, and shout, " Catch me if you can."

Top Spinning is another favourite game, and is played with the hard seeds of the mahogany tree found in the pods, or others similar. The rule is that several spin at a time in a hollowed-out, smooth circle, and try to knock out each other's " man." The game is called *Mpeta*. Bantu children make most of their own toys, save some few made for them by father and mother, or an uncle or aunt. Boys make their toy bows and arrows, toy guns and spears, toy hoops and all the paraphernalia of child's play life. In making these they show an ingenuity born of necessity that knows no law. In their ante-puberty years they often surpass in inventive genius the young folk of more favoured toy-shop lands. I have seen them with most cleverly made toy cycles and motor cycles (imitated), motor cars, trains, and two-funnelled steamers with small fires burning in an empty sardine tin in imitation of the real thing. They often steal their mother's clay used for pottery work, and model elephants, hippos, and all sorts of animals, wild and domestic. Girls make some of their dolls out of corn cobs, with clay heads, and beads for eyes and mouths. They wrap them up in bark cloth, and carry them about pick-a-back as the mothers do their babies. They nurse them and talk to them, and call them " my baby," and give them little pet names. When a little girl dies, her sister inherits her doll, but, if she has no sisters living, the dead child's doll is ceremoniously buried in the grave beside her. They like to play at housekeeping, and make their own little sets of furniture. The girls are proud of their good looks, and very jealous, whereas the boys swagger and boast to others of their strength and speed. They also indulge in wrestling, racing, and canoe-paddling contests.

CHAPTER XVII

Surprise Stories

THE following folk-lore stories will help to reflect the mentality of the Bantu peoples. They are in common use, but have never, so far as I know, appeared in print.

HUMP NAVEL AND THE WITCH

An old witch woman had been killing large numbers of people in the villages, and in one of these about that time a woman gave birth to a baby with a hump navel. The boy grew up and one day the mother took him to the cave where the old witch woman lived, and laying him at the mouth of the cave she went off to the forest to gather mushrooms. While looking about for mushrooms she met the old witch woman, who killed her and ate her. Then the sun went down and darkness fell, and the child thought to himself: " Where has mother gone ? " Then the child set off to look for his mother, and finding her footmarks, he followed them until he reached the spot where his mother had been caught and killed. He went into the bush and cut a tree and let it fall exactly at the spot where his mother had been killed, and running behind a clump of trees holding his father's spear tight in his hand, he hid himself. The witch soon returned, and, looking down, said : " Who put that tree in the path ? There was no tree there when I went away." Thereupon the boy sprang out and stabbed her with his father's spear and killed her. Then he cut her stomach open, which was full of live people she had swallowed, and these commenced to shout and dance, and the people in the villages far and near on hearing the noise rushed to the spot. The mother of Hump Navel, springing out from the witch's belly, shouted: "That's my boy, that's my boy." The people all fell on their faces and, clapping their hands in gratitude, shouted aloud: "He's our chief, he's our chief now, for he saved us from the wicked old witch woman," and that was how Hump Navel became their chief.

"A hump-navel child is a child of play,
He sleeps by night and thinks by day."

The Chief who Killed his Counsellors

A big chief was persuaded by his head wife to kill all his counsellors, "for," said she, " it is they who are bewitching and killing the people in your town, with their knowledge of black magic." The king issued a proclamation throughout his country to call all the people and headmen together. One boy had heard of the plot and was determined to save his father, and so warned him, saying: "Come, father, follow me, and I will hide you safely in a cave." He took his father secretly and hid him in a cave, rolling a big stone to the mouth of it, and carried him food there from day to day. When his people and counsellors gathered, the chief addressed them and said: "I don't want any more counsellors for they are killing my people; I only want boys." Therefore he killed all his elders and counsellors.

Shortly after this event the chief was lying asleep under a tree when a great python came and coiled himself round the chief's body and neck, and pointed his fangs at his eyes. The people rushed about saying: "What shall we do? A deadly snake has coiled itself round our chief. If we spear it we may kill the chief." No one knew how to save the chief, and the python, meanwhile, was tightening his coils and slowly crushing him to death. The boy remembered his father, and ran away secretly to the cave and told him. "All right," said the father, "that's not difficult. Go, my son, with a hoe and dig up a big field rat, tie it to the end of a string and dangle it in front of the python's eyes. He will gradually let go his hold of the chief, uncoil himself, and follow the live rat on the string." The boy caught a rat and tied it to a string and did as his father told him. And so when the python saw the live rat he uncoiled himself from the chief's neck. The boy went farther back with the rat, and the snake followed, gradually uncoiling himself from the chief's body and legs until the chief was free. The people then killed the python, and their chief was saved. The chief then called the boy into a hut and said : "Tell me, boy, where you got that wisdom." At first he refused, and said: "No, chief, it's my own idea." The chief said : "No, but you must have hid your father somewhere. Tell me, and I will give you one of my daughters to be your wife and you shall be my son-in-law." On being assured he went to the cave and called his father, who came, and the chief was so pleased that he gave him an important chieftainship and his daughter in marriage, besides loading him with many presents. This is the story of the chief who took his wife's advice and killed his counsellors.

The Hare, the Lion, and the Earless Boy

A famine broke out all over the land, and the people all died off save one woman who was about to give birth to a baby. She said to herself : "I'm off elsewhere, for I don't want to give birth to my child in a foodless village full of dead people." She went away, and finding a mountain climbed to the top and made a bower, where her baby was born—a fine, big boy. She went off from time to time to get mushrooms, which she cooked and ate. Each time she went she said to her boy, warning him : " Play on the top of the hill and see you don't go down below." One day a hare came up the hill, and seeing the boy, said : " Oh, I'm so glad to see you, I hope you are well, little nephew." Then the mother brought cooked mushrooms which they all ate, and afterwards the hare and the boy played on the hill-top. Each day the hare went home at sundown. One day, when the mother was away gathering mushrooms, the hare said : " Come, nephew, and let us play on the side of the hill ; there's flowers and lots of nice things." They went and played and then returned for food. At sundown the hare went off as usual. Next day the mother went off early to gather mushrooms. The hare came and said to the boy : " Let's go down the hill to-day." " Oh, no," said the boy, " I can't do that, for mother told me not to." " Oh," said the hare, " it's all right, we can be back before mother's return." And they went. They got to the bottom of the hill and began to play, when a lion appeared and caught the boy and killed him. The lion went off for a stroll, leaving the hare to cook the meat. The hare quickly cut off the ears, cooked and ate them while the lion was away. When the lion returned he said : " I'm hungry, bring the food." He looked through the meat, but could find no ears. " What have you done with the ears, hare ? " said the lion. " Oh," replied the hare, " that boy had no ears." " Oh, you lie, little animal," said the lion. " All animals and human beings have ears." " All right, listen," said the hare, and he called to the mother on the hill-top, who was crying like to break her heart for her lost boy, " I say, woman, had your boy any ears ? " " No," answered the mother, " he had no ears,

for if he had he would have listened to me and not
disobeyed, leaving me childless." This is the story of the
boy who had no ears.

The Man who Hunted with the Devil

A man went out to dig a game-pit at the edge of his
field in the forest. He dug'and dug longways of the fence
until the pit was deep enough. Then he looked at it and
thought : " How can game be caught in a pit dug the
wrong way ? " As he was talking to himself the devil
appeared and greeted him. Looking at the newly dug pit
the devil began to laugh, saying : " Whoever saw a man
dig a game-pit that way ? it's all wrong. You won't catch
any game in that. Look here," said the devil, " I'll help
you, and together we'll catch lots of game. Get a hold of
a corner of the pit and I'll take the opposite corner and
we'll turn the pit right round." They did so and fixed it
up nicely. " Now," said the devil, " I don't eat beef, but
I want the liver, the heart, and the kidneys for my trouble."
" Agreed," said the hunter, and he went home to sleep.
Next day he returned to the pit in the early morning and
found a roan antelope caught. The devil appeared, saying :
" Success, friend ! " (*Bambeni*). " Yes," said he, " we've
caught a roan antelope." Said the man : " I'm off to the
village to get help to carry the meat home." " What ? "
said the devil. " Who helped you with the pit ? Wasn't it I ?
Come, come, give me the liver, heart, and kidneys, as agreed."
The devil then caught the antelope by the tail and the
man caught it by the legs, and they dragged it out of the
pit and the devil got his titbits. The man returned to his
village and said : " I've caught a roan in the trap, but it's
got no liver, heart, or kidneys." " No," said the chief,
" you're mistaken." They went, however, and cut up the

meat and brought it home, but the liver, etc., were missing. Next day the hunter went back and found an eland in his pit. The devil again put in an appearance and demanded his share. " No," said the hunter, " I got into trouble last time and I must not do it again." " Oh," said the devil, " did your friends help you to fix your pit ? Wasn't it I ? " So he gave him the heart, liver, and kidneys. He went to the village and told the chief and people again, and the chief was very angry, saying : " You lie : you've eaten them yourself in the forest." He protested, but they only laughed at him. They went and cut up the meat and brought it home, when the chief was very angry. Next morning he went off to his game-pit early and found a buffalo caught. The devil, who was waiting in hiding behind a tree, again appeared and claimed his share as before. " Oh," said the man, " you'll have me killed this time." The devil said : " All right, when your chief and people come I shall refer the case to them for decision." So he gave him his share. The hunter returned with the same story as before. The people threatened to kill him, and he confessed that he had hunted with the devil, who had helped him to straighten his game-pit, which accounted for his success and the price he had to pay. The chief and people went with him this time, and on arrival at the pit, the devil, who was hiding, came out and stated his case to the chief and people. He told how he helped the man and of the agreement to pay him heart, liver, and kidneys as the price of his help. " Now," said the devil to the hunter, " if you want to be rid of me, pay me for your slander and my share in the work of fixing the game-pit." The chief justified the devil and condemned the hunter to pay up a heavy fine. The devil then left, and the people cut up the buffalo and carried the meat home to their village. This is the story of the man who hunted with the devil.

The Bushman, or, You'll always Remember Me

A hunter went out one day and shot a sable antelope. The people came and helped him to cut it up and carry it home and were very happy over the meat, singing and dancing. Another day he killed an eland, and the chief and people were delighted at the large quantities of meat being brought home. Another day the hunter wandered all day through the forest, but had no luck. Suddenly, on returning home, he saw vultures and knew there was a dead antelope near. He went into the thicket and found a dead bull hartebeest. He had an axe and no knife, and wondered how he could cut up so much meat without a knife. He heard a noise of a man cutting a wild plum tree for the fruit. He called: " Come, friend, and help me, I've picked up a dead hartebeest." The hunter borrowed his knife and cut up the meat, and they slept all night in a hut they built close by. In the morning the hunter cut a pole and tied the meat to it and was about to return home. The bushman whose knife he borrowed said: " Is that how you treat me for my help which you sought ? " " Oh no," said the hunter, " the meat is mine ; I found it, not you." " All right," said the bushman, " but you'll always remember me and think of me from now." When he reached the first river he laid down his load to rest and drink. But he couldn't forget the bushman and his words. He went on till he reached a second river and laid down his load to rest and drink, but he couldn't get rid of the thought of the bushman and his words : " you'll remember me." Finally he reached the village and the people greeted him with shouts of welcome. They cooked meat and food and laid it at the door of the hut where he had gone to rest. He tried to eat, but couldn't, for thinking of the bushman and his last words : " you'll remember

me." Day after day his appetite failed and he grew thin
and emaciated. The chief asked him the cause of his illness, and he told him of his experience with and unfair
treatment of the bushman. " Well," said the chief, " you
were in the wrong and acted unjustly. Go now and take
seven hoes with you as a present, confess your wrong to
him and pay him up." He took the hoes and a present
besides, searched for the bushman and found him. " Ho,
friend," he said, " I wronged you and have come to pay
you for the wrong I did you in not giving you a share of
the meat for the loan of your knife." The bushman
received it and said : " All right, your appetite will come
back. Go home and live prosperously." This is the story
of the hunter who wronged the bushman and what he
suffered.

The Mother and the Fairy Nursemaid
(Nsambu ya chibanda)

An orphan girl was married as a polygamous wife and
had a young baby to nurse. The husband cultivated a field
of millet for her and fenced it to keep out the pigs, and
when the grain was ripe she took her baby with her to the
field to harvest her crop. She found it difficult to nurse
the baby and cut the grain at the same time, and she sat
down to cry : " Oh, that I had a mother or sister to help
me." Suddenly there appeared a wicked fairy, who said
to her : " Poor child, you've got no mother to help you.
I'll help you and nurse the baby for you while you cut
your grain." The fairy took her baby away and nursed
it and brought it back in the evening. The girl took her
child on her back, a basket of grain on her head, and went
off home. The second day she did the same and the
fairy mother came as before and nursed her baby, walking
round the forest with it. The third day the grain was

nearly all harvested, and the wicked fairy turned up, but though she did not show it she was angry at not receiving any remuneration for the previous two days' work. She took the child, however, but when she got outside the fence she cut its head off and laid it down at the entrance to the field, hiding the remainder of the child's body.

The mother finished her work and called to the fairy to bring her child, but no answer came. She called and called : " My child, oh my child, where have they taken you ? " She looked but could not find it and prepared to return home. On leaving her field she found her baby's head lying in the gateway. She took it up tenderly and carried it, crying all the way home. When she reached her house her husband said : " Where's the baby ? "   " Oh," she said, " I put it under a tree and while I was working some wild beast killed it, and I found its head in the entrance to the field."   " Why did you not look after the child ? " said the father ; " this is all your fault ; let's go now to the field and search for the body."   On the way to the field the wicked fairy appeared with the child's body wrapped in a skin and hid under her arm, and said : " What are you looking for ? "   They replied : " Our baby."   She then produced the body, which they recognised.   " Let's go to the chief," said the wicked fairy, " and put the matter before the court."   They did so, and each told their story. The chief gave verdict that the fairy was justified, because the woman attempted to defraud her of the lawful wages due.   This is the story of the mother and the fairy nurse.

The Man who Hid the Honey
(Kaonde country)

A long time ago a man and woman married and five children were born to them. A famine broke out in their district, and as no food was procurable the father went off to the forest and found a hollow tree with honey.

He dug it out with his axe, and bringing it home hid it in a pot. He went out at night and dug a deep hole in the ash-pit and hid the pot of honey there. He inserted a long reed in the pot, which projected a little bit above the ground, and levelling it all round with ashes he went away. Each day when he was hungry he came and sucked at the reed, and one day his children saw him do this. " What are you doing, father ? " they asked. " Oh, I'm eating ashes, my children, I'm so hungry." The boys were astonished at their father, and struck up a little song :

> " Father's eating ashes,
> Hunger makes him mad.
> Father's eating ashes,
> Hunger is so bad."

One day the elder son watched the father go to the forest to hunt for honey. He ran to the ash-heap, and taking the reed in his mouth he sucked, and was surprised to get mouthfuls of nice sweet honey. He sucked till he almost burst, and then he went and told his mother and the others and they all came and sucked till they emptied the pot. They filled it up with water and ashes and re-placed the reed. The father came back, saying : " Oh, I'm so hungry, children, I'm off to eat ashes. Come and sing to me, my children." They went and struck up their little song to father :

> " Father's eating ashes,
> Hunger makes him mad.
> Father's eating ashes,
> Hunger is so bad."

Immediately he got mouthful after mouthful of ashes, which made him angry. He raked aside the ashes and found the honey pot had been emptied during his absence, and filled with ashes and water. " Why did you do this ? " said the infuriated father. " Oh, we only followed your example, dad."

The father was so ashamed at his selfishness, and at being found out by his wife and children, that he went and hid himself. This is the story of the selfish man who hid the honey.

THE MAGIC MAT

About a hundred years ago there lived a chief named Munkombwe, who belonged to the pottery clan and who was a famous elephant hunter and soldier. The village where he lived was on the south bank of the Kalunguizi River in North-East Rhodesia. He was reputed to be in possession of a magic mat which he jealously guarded and only used for crossing rivers and swamps. When he went to war or returned with spoil he always crossed the river on his mat. When he went elephant-hunting in the Mweru marsh or returned with trophies of the chase he spread his mat at the river ferry and crossed quickly and safely while others had to wait for canoes. When he died his mat disappeared and his two successors knew nothing of its whereabouts. This is the story of the magic mat.

CHAPTER XVIII
Hunting & Fishing

AMONG the primitive peoples of Bantuland Hunting and Fishing developed under the lash of necessity's stern law and not from any sentimental idea known as " love of sport." Men attacked elephant, buffalo, lion, etc., in simple obedience to the primal law of self-preservation, or to provide food for themselves and families. They did not hesitate to run up to within three yards of a bull, elephant, or buffalo and drive a heavy spear into the great brute's vulnerable part at real personal risk of life and limb. *Fighting* was the common word used for attacking big game with primitive weapons, and the hunter who came safely back from the chase was welcomed as a hero returning from war by the men and women of his kraal, with clapping of hands and songs, war-paint and feathers. Many a time I have heard this expression used by a returning hunter, *twalwa nabo*, i.e. " we fought them," meaning elephants, buffalo, or lions, or any dangerous game. As a rule these negro Nimrods are modest men who rarely sing their own praises or speak even of tight corners they have been in, until pressed or persuaded to recount their experiences by Europeans eager to hear. I have heard a man tell how he fought lion, leopard, or crocodile, without the least thought of vanity or desire to draw attention to himself. I have heard a man tell how he was tossed into a tree by a charging buffalo, or caught up by an elephant and hurled into the air, or thrown along the ground, and how he narrowly escaped death, at the same time showing the scars as though it were a matter of everyday occurrence. Though the impelling and initial law of the chase is stark necessity, I have seen and known many a famous black hunter with the true sportsman instinct very highly developed, and the love of sport as strongly in evidence as among the best hunters of the white race. I have hunted many times with Msidi II and many other hunter chiefs, and headmen of the interior, and I have found very few to whom the title of "good sport" and "jolly good fellow" could not be truthfully applied. I do not refer to the ordinary rank and file of white men's followers, but to native and professional big-game hunters, who have been tested and proved again and again, and whose pluck and sang-froid in an ugly corner left very little to be desired.

On the other hand, more than once I have known white men come swaggering back laden with a caravan of ivory which they claimed as having fallen to their guns, and have heard them tell stories of charging and furious elephants, when I knew that these same Jumbos had been shot by natives with the white men's guns, while the latter were safely seated in their tents drinking tea. I have also seen white men return from a journey with record horns and unique big-game heads and heard them tell how they shot them, and in the evening passing casually through the camp I have heard the same man's cook tell his chums with a twinkle in his eye where his master bought them, and how many yards of calico they cost. I have seen a photo of a white man, gun in hand, in hunting costume standing hunter-like alongside two dead lions poisoned with strychnine. It is a common thing to-day in the Congo and Angola for white traders to take out an elephant licence and employ natives to do the hunting and killing and taking of risk, while they claim the credit and the tusks.

There used to be tribes who distinguished themselves as elephant hunters and had always large quantities of ivory to sell. The Sanga, Lamba, Luba, and Wemba were four such tribes among whom were large numbers of famous elephant hunters. These usually had a society, or guild, with initiation rites and ceremonies, and laws and regulations that had to be obeyed under pain of expulsion.

There used to be great tribal hunts, too, when hundreds of elephants would be driven into a cul-de-sac of the river and speared. Sometimes they would be driven into swamps, where they would stick fast in the mud, and the hunters would go round and finish them off at leisure. At other times great spears were set in the path of a herd of elephants, and the big bull in front would step on a stick cunningly covered, releasing the spear above, which would, thus released, plunge itself into the neck of the great brute, which would stagger along and die of its wound in a short time, or be attacked and finished by the hunters who followed the blood spoor. Sir S. Baker tells how the Abyssinians would hamstring elephants with sharp swords and afterwards kill them by hand. Of course many hunters were annually killed in those days when weapons of high velocity and precision were unknown. Even with flint-locks and percussion cap guns, natives are frequently killed. On the other hand, I have known a native hunter who shot his three elephants a day, and during his life he must certainly have slain hundreds of elephants. On approaching a herd he would scatter his fetish medicine, then picking out the big bulls, would proceed to shoot elephant after elephant. He died only recently. His name was Mutwila, brother of Mpande, chief of the Basanga.

I have never shot or seen a rhino, though natives sometimes come across them and shoot them. The rule is, I am told, that when the rhino dung is intact he is not far away and usually returns to scatter it. The hunter, arriving and seeing this, hides in a tree near by, and when the rhino puts in an appearance to scatter his dung prior to departure, the hunter gets his chance. The rhino has an ugly habit of charging through a passing caravan, greatly to the annoyance and amusement of travellers.

On the Luapula, where I lived many years, buffalo were plentiful and natives used to drive them into the river and chase and kill them in canoes with long spears. I have seen native hunters again and again follow wounded buffalo into long grass or into dense bush or thickets. The native is very daring and does not hesitate to run big risks when bent on killing buffalo. I have seen a native hunter chased by a charging, wounded buffalo, which I killed at a few yards with my 400° express rifle. As stated in my chapter on sport and travel, buffalo is the most dangerous of all game. Sometimes they fall into deep game-pits and are easily despatched, and sometimes they are killed by poisoned arrows, in which case the hunter has to get very near so that the arrow penetrates deeply.

Eland are often caught and killed in game-pits dug along the field fences, where they come and destroy large quantities of food in the native gardens and break up the fencing. A herd of eland can ruin a native family in one night. Why governments put them in the elephant category I do not know, unless it is to increase revenue. Among big game the eland is the native's great enemy. For two years I had to buy a £25 licence for game as eland was the only game meat near my place, and I had to furnish food for a large camp. The native loves hippo-hunting with harpoons, and goes at it with great zest. Many natives used to lose their lives annually in hippo hunts. They also set heavy hafted spears for them in the paths where they left the river to feed at night. Hippo are valued for their meat, fat, and hides which are used for whips, while their tusks used to be sold to Arabs to make handles for their swords and daggers. Arabs give a good price for hippo ivory.

Otter hunting and trapping is carried on about Lake Bangweulu, where thousands are trapped and speared annually. I used to buy these long ago at 4d. each, and to-day they sell locally at 3s. 6d. per pelt. They are very plentiful among the swamps round the lake and on the Luapula River, and the natives are very fond of their flesh.

On Lake Bangweulu great tribal battues take place every year, when the grass is burned off and thousands of black and red Lechwe antelopes, besides Sititunga antelopes and otters, are killed. They hunt these among the swamps in canoes or on the islands with spears and bows and arrows, in the use of which they are particularly dexterous. They also use long nets and packs of fierce dogs. They delight in these cynegetics and are wonderfully attached to their wild dogs, and are rarely to be seen without them. The flesh of the game is dried and sold to the people of the mainland; and beautiful shawls are made from the skins, which are well brayed and worked into pretty patterns. These are in great demand and most Baunga and Batwa women wear them as dresses or use them to carry their babies pick-a-back.

Some of these hunter tribes are expert at imitating bird and animal calls. I have watched them bring birds and animals to within a few yards of them by the perfect way in which they imitated the bird or buck. It is quite pathetic to watch the way a duiker antelope or reed buck will come trustingly to within observation distance before discovering its mistake. Guinea-fowl, partridge, and duck do the same. They sometimes use reeds or leaves or horns as calls for bird and buck, and with these clever imitations they decoy them to perfection. The natives make powerful bows and strong steel-pointed arrows, some of which can pierce the thick hide of a buffalo. I have seen them shoot and kill with the first arrow, and some are expert archers. Formerly they used these in war, and do still in some parts. They often poison their arrow-points, which are also frequently barbed, and death ensues in a very short time from tetanus. Lieut. Hankinnson, a Belgian officer, was killed in the early years by a poisoned arrow. Spears are much used, the biggest of which is the elephant spear ; it is some eight feet long, the haft about two inches thick, and has a powerful blade. Guns are much in evidence in Angola and throughout the Congo, but in North-East Rhodesia these are forbidden save to a few natives who are known to have no criminal record. Chiefs, however, are usually allowed one gun each to kill game for themselves and their people. In Angola and the Congo the flint lock and cap gun are too dangerously common, and ammunition can be too easily obtained by anybody at traders' stores, hence natives hunt and kill more game to-day than in the early days. In the Katanga many natives do a regular trade in game meat at the mines and in the towns along the railway.

Game-pits are often dug in the game tracks and I once picked up a nice pair of tusks in one where an elephant had met an untimely end. Hippo pits are cleverly constructed, and are very dangerously hidden ; I nearly lost my life once in one of these at the south bend of the Luapula River. They are big, and deep, and covered over with light saplings, leaves, and earth, which make them difficult of detection from the surrounding ground. Eland, roan, sable, and hartebeeste antelopes are often trapped in these, and my boys once got a lion in one of them near to my cattle pen. Pigs, small antelopes, guinea-fowls, and partridges are caught by means of snares set in the path. They are cleverly constructed, of various kinds, and rarely fail.

I have seen pig and antelopes caught and struggling in these.

Nets are used for duiker and small antelopes, also for Lechwe and Sititunga. These are stretched across the forest or swamp, and half a dozen or more are caught at a time. The net is made of strong, thick cord, is set, and held in position by long forked sticks stuck in the ground. When all is ready the chief gives the word and the bush is beaten and the game are, with great noise and lullilooing, driven to the nets, where they are caught and afterwards killed. There is a recognised native close and open season. When the grass is long in the rutting season hunters rarely go after game. When the grass is burnt the call to hunt sounds all over the land and, day after day, hunters go out with gun, spear, bows and arrows, nets and dogs, and hunt from sunrise to sunset. Sometimes the hunters camp in the forest where game is plentiful, and kill and smoke the meat of a number of animals before deciding to return home.

There is a distinct class of hunter chiefs throughout the country who, by virtue of their prowess on the hunting field, have gathered together a following of natives, and have been given chieftainships by the lord paramount.

These chiefs are looked down on by others as upstarts with no legal claim, though they are held in respect by many on account of the ivory and meat with which they supply the tribal larders. I know a large number of these whose only claim to chieftainship is based on the gun. They are usually fine fellows, head and shoulders above the ordinary type, in brain, brawn, and good breeding. Kasangu, a Yeke elephant hunter of repute, told me of an experience he had that nearly cost him his life. He was after a bull elephant which he had singled out as a big tusker when to his surprise a lion sprang on Jumbo before his very eyes.

A MASKED DEVIL-DOCTOR.
HEADDRESS OF LUBAN CHIEF.

HEAD OF A 21-LB. TIGER FISH.
HEADDRESS OF NATIVE WOMAN.

He rushed up, and seeing the fierce fight between these two forest giants, he shot the lion, which turned round and attacked him, and afterward followed on and shot the elephant. He eventually lost his foot and died on Lake Mweru, hugging his old elephant gun. Mulevi, an elephant hunter who lived on the Luapula River, killed enormous quantities of game. Suspicions having been aroused, one day he was followed, no shots being heard—and he returned to report having killed five head of game. Whispering went round the village that he practised lycanthropy, and that when he reached the buck he changed into a lion and pulled down as many as he wanted. He was tried for hunting by sorcery, and, with his nephew Kalaba who accompanied him, was sentenced to death by Chief Mulundu (at whose capital I lived) and burned as a game-wizard.

Fishing is carried on in a larger variety of ways than in Europe. A fisherman is also called a hunter. Blacksmiths forge hooks of all sizes. I have seen scores of children in canoes on Lake Bangweulu fishing for carp and other fish with small barbless hooks. Larger hooks are used for *monde*, a kind of cod, some of which weigh from 40 to 80 lbs. Sometimes a number of hooks are fastened to long lines and left overnight, attached to a big float, when many fish are caught. Bamboo rods are used to angle only small fish. Many natives are quite expert at angling. Nets are made from fibre collected in various parts of the country. They spin it into cord, make it up into balls, then weave their nets with meshes of different size. Trammel lines are used top and bottom, with pith floats and stone sinkers. Little boys make small nets and their elders make longer and larger ones. Sometimes a party of fishermen form a combine, join their nets, and stretch them across the river at a place where fish is plentiful. They then draw the net round in a circle towards the shore, enclose it, and haul it up. They empty out the fish, which is shared alike by all the partners. They dry their nets in the sun, but have no system of barking. Long spears and forks like a trident are used to spear big fish, at which fish spearing the natives are very skilful. In the marshes where fish abound, but where nets and hooks are useless, they paddle their canoes through the reeds and use their spears. Large and small basket traps are used all over Africa, and these are made of reeds and bamboos. Some of these are six to nine feet long, conical-shaped, with a cleverly constructed entrance that is self-setting, closing as the fish go in. I have watched them on the Luapula take out hundreds of pounds of fish in a very short time. They sometimes make weirs and insert their basket fish traps at the openings intentionally left for the purpose. All other parts are closed up with stones and clods. Diving for fish was resorted to at Johnston Falls by men called divers (*mwibilishi*), who could remain a long time under water. They told me that if a croc approached when they were fishing at the bottom among rocks, they held out to him a fish, and if he took it it was safe to continue, but if he refused to take it they got up to their canoes on the surface as quickly as possible. They used spears under water and fastened the fish caught to a cord tied round the waist so as not to hamper their movements. *Buba*, or fish poison (of which there are five kinds), is much used to kill fish in pools. The plant is grown by natives and the flowers and leaves are powdered, carried in baskets, and scattered over the pools. The fish turn up their bellies and are gathered by the fishing folk quickly. Fish poison seems to have a narcotic effect, for sometimes the fish recover and escape. During the rains fish used to come up the river to spawn. During the night they would enter small streams and scatter over the flooded plains.

The natives in the morning promptly dammed the

streams at the mouth, and when the water went back, the fish were left high and dry on the plains—which I have seen in the season literally white with fish. Tons of fish were thus caught, killed, and smoked annually, and the fisher-folk did good business in bartering with their land neighbours. Several European traders are now established near there, and send tons of these smoked fish (and also fresh) into Elisabethville by motor lorry. Fishermen fish during the day, but the best fishing is usually done at night. They place a bunch of dry inflammable firewood (*mwenge*) at the bow of the boat to attract the fish, and they then drive them to their nets by beating the water with their paddles as they approach the nets in a semicircle. I have gone out fishing with natives at night but found the mosquitoes bad. Tiger fish, when caught, are knocked on the head as they give a dangerous bite. I have the names of forty different kinds of fish found in Lake Bangweulu and the Luapula River. Crocs and otters account for large numbers of fish, so do ospreys, cormorants, and divers, and the little energetic kingfishers. Fish, if small, are prepared by sun-drying, if large by means of smoking over slow fires. For sun-drying the fish are spread out on mats or over the grass thatch of the hut. For smoking purposes stands are made of forked sticks and cross-pieces, and the fish are laid out on these, while the fire is kept going underneath. They are not so particular in the choice of wood for smoking purposes as in Europe, hence the coarse smell and taste, and the fact that few Europeans can eat fish so preserved.

Fishing tribes like the Bashila, Batwa, and Baunga, as well as the Angola fishing tribes, are despised by landsmen and called "water-beaters." Fishing people, when they travel or visit other tribes, always deny their fisher origin, and insist, somewhat facetiously, that they have never heard of or even seen a fish. To some tribes, like the Yeke, fish is taboo.

When the Shila fishermen go after cod on Lake Mweru they fish *in puris naturalibus*, and they have a peculiar cursing ceremony. When they reach mid-lake they drop a big stone at the stern and another at the stem as anchors. They then tie a hooked fishing-line to each hand and one to each foot, four in all. Then the fisherman commences to curse the dead who have been drowned, eaten by crocs, lions, leopards, or murdered in any way. He curses thus : " Listen, all ye dead people. I've come. I'm here. Now's your chance. Up and kill me, or eat me if you like ; I fear none." He then throws red powder on the water, which is a fighting challenge to the spirits. The more fish he catches the louder his oaths and curses, until he eventually hoists his two stone anchors and paddles off home with his catch.

CHAPTER XIX

Study of Language

LANGUAGE is said by one to be given us " to conceal our thoughts " ; by another it is described as " a habit of uttering sounds to represent ideas " ; and by a third, " a method of conveying our thoughts by signs and symbols." As a boy I remember witnessing a play called *The Dumb Man of Manchester*, in which the said mute had been witness of a murder and was brought into court to give evidence. His dumb description of the murder and the events leading up to it so impressed me visually that I never even thought of it in spoken form. Years later, on Lake Mweru in the Congo, I remember seeing a crowd of natives held spellbound by a deaf and dumb Luban lad who was describing with inimitable gesture a journey from which he had just returned. He spoke by signs for an hour with the most impassioned eloquence, and described mimetically his being called up for the journey, his parting from his friends, his being given a load to carry, his being scolded for coming into camp late, and eventually, amid roars of laughter, he demonstrated how he had been laid down and got many cuts with the hippo whip because he failed to understand what had been expected of him.

Many theories of the origin of language have existed from time immemorial, but I think the onomatopœic theory of language suggests itself as aboriginal, for one finds not only a *certain number* of true onomatopœias, but a clearly defined system in vogue that points conclusively to the onomatopœic origin. Call this the "bow-wow" theory of language if you please, as was sneeringly done by a learned professor once, but the fact remains and one has seen its method of working during an extended and intimate study of sixty different African dialects. The story of Psammeticus, an Egyptian king, who was curious to find out the world's first language, recounts that he cut out the tongues of two shepherds, in whose care a child was placed, and they were put in a hut removed from human dwellings to find out the first word the child would speak. They reported that it said *bekos*, the Greek word for "bread," hence the accepted theory that Greek was first spoken. A witty Englishman, on hearing this, said : "No, the child was only asking for its breakfast ! "

That man was created with a perfected form of speech I do not believe, although I certainly think that mankind was created with the speech faculty, the potential gift of language, just as he was given arms to work with and legs to walk, and that these had to be developed by use. The chief *raison d'être* of language is, I presume, to make ourselves understood and therefore, whether by gesture or by audible speech we attain this end, our medium is language.

There is nothing so discouraging and mystifying to a beginner desirous of acquiring a working knowledge of another tongue than to be confronted, at the outset, with a mass of rules such as one finds in most modern grammars. Why is it, and how, that an ordinary African, brought into contact with European civilisation for the first time, picks up a conversational acquaintance with any form of English, French, Portuguese, Spanish, and even Dutch and German, quicker than we acquire his lingo ? I think the main reason behind this phenomenon is that he endeavours to learn our language much as a child learns to speak. He adopts the natural, the mimetic, method, whereas we employ the unnatural, the visualising, method. " L'oreille faut la pratique aussi bien que la langue " (the ear must have practice as well as the tongue), said a great actor and author on one occasion. The man in question was a linguistic prodigy, who spoke, wrote, and acted fluently in most European languages and several Oriental. He might have added—" et l'œil aussi." Ear and eye as well as tongue require to be trained. Apropos, Emerson says :

> " I heard the throstle sing his song,
> Sitting at dawn on the alder bough.
> I brought him home in his nest at even.
> He sings the song, but it pleases not now,
> For I did not bring home the earth and the sky—
> He sang to my ear, they sang to my eye."

The psychological methods of sequence adopted and taught by François Gouin, the Berlitz, and " Methode directe " schools in teaching languages I have used again and again with marked success. The rule of language teaching and acquisition should be : language first, grammar after. As a French professor of languages put it : " Il faut apprendre la grammaire par la langue, et non pas la langue par la grammaire " (one must learn grammar by means of language and not language by means of grammar).

In each of the world's great speech families, and in their subdivisions, we find race characteristics evolved by environment and embalmed in language just as we find in different dialects, e.g. why does an Englishman speak of " being born with a silver spoon in his mouth " ; a Frenchman of " being born with hair dressed " ; and an Italian of " being born clothed " ; and a German of " being careful in the choice of parents "? The thought is the same in every instance, but the mode of expression or idiom is different, indicating a pronounced racial characteristic. A negro once said to me on comparing African poverty and misery with European wealth and comfort, " But, sir, ye are God's firstborn," which is the Bantu equivalent to the " silver spoon."

Language rhythm or melody is also an important factor with each tribe, and the man who hopes to speak " like a native " to natives must master this important item which differs with every dialect just as there is said to be a different timbre in the vocal chords of each race. I have seen a European who was invisible to his hearers mistaken for a native owing to his having acquired the native language rhythm to such perfection, whereas on the other hand I have met men who never lost the rhythm of their own *patois*, and who spoke Bantu with a Scotch, American, or Belgian accent. In 1903 I lived with the veteran missionary, Dr. Laws, in Nyasaland, for two months. The Staff was Scotch and mostly Aberdonian, and the thing that struck me in this great Native Institute was that natives who came from many different tribes to receive their education, adopted a Scotch accent in speaking their own dialects. I have seen the same thing on American mission stations in Angola, mission boys speaking Umbundu with an American twang. This is due to the African's irrepressible tendency to use mimetic methods.

Many of us are acquainted with the mission boy in Africa who, when asked by his master a certain word in his language, replied, " Is it a verb or a noun, sir ? " The ordinary native knows nothing whatever of grammar, and to him a word is that which expresses some concrete idea. His system of punctuation, too, is vocal and requires a trained ear. It is very nice, and even gratifying, to our amour-propre to have learnt the whole orthography, etymology, and syntax of a language before opening our mouths to speak in a foreign tongue, but from a practical point of view it is certainly better to put into immediate use whatever little we know until we have learnt more. Foreigners do not generally laugh at our mistakes, but, as a rule, show a sympathetic appreciation of our efforts to use their language.

Bantu is possibly the most easily learnt and spoken, and, being the Italian among the Oriental speech families, is the most musical and euphonious. European children born in Africa pick up the native dialect long before they speak their mother tongue, and during the first years of my children's lives my wife and I always spoke to them in the native tongue. Bantu languages are more speedily acquired than European. A knowledge of any one Bantu language provides a key to 276 known languages, which represent fifty millions of people inhabiting a third part of the African continent.

In my long and extended studies of comparative Bantu languages, there is one thing that has constantly forced itself upon my notice, and that is the fact of the self-determination of language groups. Each group represents a distinct geographical area, and possesses a central or leading language around which constellate a circle of cognate dialects.

Between Lobito Bay and Lake Nyasa a definite language group boundary meets us approximately every 150 to 200 miles, viz. :

1. Between the Quanza River and Catumbella, Umbundu is spoken with a group of *patois*.

2. Between the Quanza River and the Kasai River the Chokwe language obtains with its *patois* group.

3. Between the Kasai and Lufupa Rivers, the Luena language is paramount with its dialect group.

4. Between the Lufupa and Lualaba Rivers a form of Lunda is in use with its many dialects.

5. In Katanga between the Lualaba and Luapula Rivers the South Luba language prevails, which has a large group of dialects.

6. Between the Luapula and the Loangwa Rivers, Wemba is the commonly accepted medium of speech. Wemba has fifteen dialects, viz. Bemba, Bisa, Ushi, Twa, Unga, Senga, Lala, Lamba, Lunda, Lungu, Tabwa, Shila, Kunda, Wiwa, Nanwanga.

7. Between the Loangwa River and Lake Nyasa, the Ngoni and Chinyanja languages prevail with their dialect groups.

Each of these dialects, taken on an actual average, contains a proportion of at least 75 per cent words common to the group.

As a result of Government, Mining, and Commerce, there have sprung into existence all over Africa a large number of Linguæ Francæ or trade languages, the three leading of which are :

1. Arabic—Northern Africa.
2. Swahili—Central Africa.
3. Kitchen Kaffir—South Africa.

Again, in every colony or large district of a colony there are to be found more circumscribed Linguæ Francæ, e.g. :

1. Chinyanja—Nyasaland.
2. Wemba—N.E. Rhodesia.
3. Sekololo—N.W. Rhodesia.
4. Tebele—S. Rhodesia.
5. Umbundu—Angola.
6. Fiote—Lower Congo.
7. Chimoyo—Central Congo.

8. Bangala—Upper Congo.
9. Kitchen Swahili—Katanga.
10. Kitchen Hausa—Nigeria.

White men learning a Bantu language often make ridiculous mistakes, some silly, but others more serious, e.g. a doctor who had a riding-ox and who wanted his servant to fetch it, said, to the amusement of a group of bystanders, " I'm an ox," while another man who wanted the native name for an axe held up one before a native, saying, " What do you call this ? " " What do you say ? " replied the boy ; and " What do you say " was entered in the notebook as the name for an axe. A lady who was perplexed to find that there was no native word for " half " got a potato, and cutting it in two held up the half potato in her hand, asking her cook-boy the word for " half." " *Nachimona* " (" I see it ") replied the 'boy, and " I see it " became her word for " half," despite explanations to the contrary. In Cust's *Book of Modern Languages of Africa* we find the " Kaya " tribe referred to, " Kaya " being the equivalent for " I don't know." In another book on Nyasaland, we read of the " Kaya " tree. The white men obviously asked the name of the local tribe and of the tree, and were answered by the word " Kaya," meaning " I don't know " ; hence the mistake.

To learn a Bantu language is by no means the most difficult of tasks if we use the natural method, that which a child employs in acquiring its mother tongue. It seems incredible, but one can see at any time in Elisabethville, a native employed as interpreter between a Belgian and a Britisher, neither of whom knows the other's language, the medium used being either Kitchen Kaffir or Kitchen Swahili. I have seen the same thing in the early days between a British and a Belgian official on Lake Mweru, and we used to laugh over the joke of a nigger interpreting between two Europeans. I am pleased to say that to-day most Belgian officials speak English and most English officials speak French, and both, to qualify, have to pass an examination in a native language, which indicates greater care in the choice of men to fill Government posts, and higher standards of efficiency. In the old days, Government billets went a-begging, and any man who was around trading or shooting elephants was sure of a job. To-day, men are carefully chosen and trained. Whether as Government official, trader, or missionary, a successful career in Africa depends, and will in the future more and more depend, on a knowledge of the native languages.

Preconceived ideas of natives and their languages must be dropped by us and we must remember that *Africa is a new world,* and as the Romans used to say, " Semper aliquid novum ex Africa." New tribes and new languages are daily coming to light and bringing with them new responsibilities to the European.

Not only the languages, but a knowledge of the Customs, Laws, etc., is desirable and essential. The story is told of a young Government official appointed to an important post in the interior. He had great ideas about giving the people " good old British justice," as he called it. When he arrived at his post he was waited on by a deputation of chiefs, and at the interview he said, " I'm going to kick out all your native laws and give you good old British justice." One of the chiefs, who was spokesman, replied, " Sir, one of our laws forbids a man to marry his own sister. Is that law to become null and void ? " Africans are not out-and-out fools, nor wholly stupid, nor are all their laws altogether bad.

To become proficient in our knowledge of the natives, their customs, laws, and the whole political and social system, and so save ourselves and those who succeed us

endless trouble, worry, and even war, there is one way, and
that is, to get hold of at least *one* of the 276 languages of
Bantuland ; the one spoken in that particular part of the
continent where one lives. The importance of learning
at least one native language well is being more and more
recognised by European Governments. There are sufficient
books obtainable on African problems and languages, so
that ignorance of the African and his language in this
twentieth century, instead of being a mark of superior
civilisation, has become a mark of neglected or defective
education, and involves, on the part of the European, gross
culpability.

CHAPTER XX

Language & Languages

THE African language problem is beginning at last to find its solution as the result of the conscientious, plodding studies of men of various nationalities and professions in many parts of the continent.

The 1913 *Language Map of Africa,* by Bernard Struck, shows six linguistic families with languages and dialects, as follows :

1.	Semitic ..	10 Languages,	12 dialects			
2.	Hamitic ..	47	„	71	„	including
3.	Hottentot —		—			
4.	Bantu	182	„	119	„	
5.	Sudanese..	264	„	114	„	
6.	Bushman..	11	„	3	„	
		514		319		

As Hottentot and Bushman are believed to be allied genetically to the Hamitic family, only four families remain, viz.

1. Semitic.
2. Hamitic.
3. Bantu.
4. Sudanese (Negro).

Semitic, to all intents and purposes, means, with the possible exception of ancient Ethiopic and Amharic of Abyssinia, Arabic, which was introduced from the East and dates from the Mahommedan invasion between A.D. 640 and A.D. 711. Thus we are left with only three African families to account for :

1. Hamitic.
2. Sudanese (Negro).
3. Bantu.

Numerically the Sudanese family preponderates, though geographically Bantu represents the greater land area in Africa.

The Bantu family of languages is now known to have originated from the fusion of the Hamitic and Sudanese elements, which explains their Northern origin and the Migration Legend common throughout Bantu Africa.

A copy of a colossal work on the Comparative Study of Bantu and Semi-Bantu Languages (Oxford, 1919), by Sir H. H. Johnston, just to hand, shows " Illustrative Vocabularies of 276 Bantu and 24 Semi-Bantu languages and dialects." These, in the author's words, prove that " the political importance of the Bantu languages in the future will be as great as the political importance of the Indian vernaculars."

Bantu languages and dialects number approximately 366 (plus eighty-seven semi-Bantu). The former are spoken by fifty millions of negroes. The boundaries between languages and dialects have been, until now, more or less arbitrary, but these are being gradually determined and fixed by the modern crystallising process of the Press. In this respect missionaries have been the pioneers, and now not only in mission fields, but also in mining and industrial centres, native newspapers are being edited, printed, and distributed in the vernaculars, under the supervision of educated Bantus. In one field where five different translations of the New Testament existed, all the missionary societies—save one—appointed a representative committee of their best linguists to hammer out a " Union Version " to be used by all. This language-fixing principle is at work all over Bantu Africa.

Hitherto each leading language representing a group of dialects was that employed by the paramount people of the country. Sometimes, as in Nyasaland, the language was named after the country, e.g. Chinyanja—the lake-language spoken by the people round the Lake. At other times it was named after the conquered people if the tribe was large and had a history, e.g. Chiluba, used in Katanga prior to the advent of Europeans. In Katanga a bastard form of Swahili, which was introduced by Arabs, is in use. Bemba or Wemba of N.E. Rhodesia bears the hall-mark of the warlike Awemba, and is spoken with variations by sixteen tribes. Hence their saying, " *Awe mukwai, i Chibemba chabembakana konse*," meaning, " The Bemba language has become current all over." The Bemba came originally from Lubaland in the Congo, and one finds in their language and customs many traces of their Luban origin. The Luba language contains many customs and words of purely Semitic extraction, e.g. *mema*, their word for " water." This is, excepting the final vowel of the word used for euphony, Arabic and Hebrew. *Tohu* and *Tuhu*, used interchangeably all over Lubaland, bear the meaning attached to the word in the Hebrew story of creation in Genesis i. *Tohu wa bohu* (" without form and void "). From Congoland to Nyasaland the name for God is *Lesa*. This also is of purely Semitic origin and corresponds to the Jewish name *El-Shaddai* (" God Almighty "). So *Bene* or *Bena*, which means " people of " (*Bene Israel*=people of Israel). It is thus used by the people of Lubaland, Bembaland, and other adjacent countries.

Luba has more dialects than any other language I know.

AN ANTHILL AS A DWELLING.

Some idea of the enormous amount of work expended by the indefatigable little workers may be gathered from the fact that the mound can be hollowed out to form a substantial dwelling for human beings.

Bemba represents fifteen, all of which have at least 75 per cent of words exactly alike. One is also struck with the variations of rhythm employed, and other peculiarities. A nice Swahili speaker invariably lisps. A Bemba man uses lallation, and a seemingly excessive use of the letter " F," which has given rise to the verb *Ku-Fyaula*, just as in French we use *Zezayer* of a man who uses " Z " for " S."

A Sanga man rolls his " R's " like the " Northern Farmer." A Henga man uses frequent gutturals and aspirates, and a Lunda man seems to be for ever talking through his nose. The " social shout " of the " noisy negro," complained of by Mary Kingsley, is an outstanding feature of all Bantus, and a Congolese native, on returning from Belgium, declared that " white men all whispered."

There are three lengths of vowel-sound, e.g. long, medial, and short, found in Bantu vowels, which correspond to Italian. The difference between " gathering grubs for food," " smoking tobacco," and " worshipping God," can only be determined by the three lengths of the vowel " E." So with the other four vowel sounds. Vowel and consonantal harmony is also a feature of Bantu. Nasalisation is important, and is seen, among other things, in the first person singular of all verbs. In fact, one must, without fail, denasalise letters to get to the root-meanings of all words.

THE DEFINITE ARTICLE IN BANTU. The employment of the article in Bantu languages has long been considered a moot question, though it has been the subject of much heated discussion. It is, therefore, with a certain amount of reluctance that I write, with a request for patience on the part of those who may only be acquainted with one or two Bantu dialects, and therefore be over-hasty in prejudging the merits of the case.

That there are two distinct sections of the one great

family of languages marked as Arthrous and Anarthrous seems to some of us a fact now beyond dispute. In these we have a definite precedent or example in the Latin and Greek languages; the former, like the African division represented by Swahili, Nyanja, Yao, Luba, Luvale, and many Congo languages, illustrates the Anarthrous Bantu; the latter, which is highly Arthrous, is seen in Zulu, Kaffir, Suto, Pondo, Swazi, Herero, and the Mbundu languages of Angola, plus Bemba and its dialects. Though the modern leading Latin languages, viz. Italian, French, Spanish, and Portuguese, possess both the Definite and the Indefinite Article in both genders and numbers, we know that these have departed from the parent stem, and only the modern Greek has retained its pristine purity in respect to the article. From analogy it would seem quite conceivable that Bantu languages should also have undergone as a result of attrition or natural development similar changes of expansion or contraction and that Bantu should be subject to the general philological rules that govern other languages, as well also as have a history of its own.

Now, to look at the North, whence Bantu originally sprang, we see that both Hebrew and the Arabic languages have no indefinite article, and that the definite article in Hebrew—*ha-ha* and in Arabic *el* or *al*—is as in Bantu prefixed to the word and is the same in both genders and numbers (the difference being that in Hebrew a strong *daghesh* is employed). We can quite understand how that by laws of expansion and contraction—and for lack of literature—the initial vowel article developed or was dropped altogether. That the " classifier " or noun prefix of Bantu was originally a noun, first generic, then specific, is well known; that the demonstrative pronoun is also the definite article in non-initial-vowel Bantu we have long known; but that this initial or incipient vowel is the definite article and the characteristic of a division of the Bantu languages we only now venture to assert after long study of the subject. Whether on the West Coast, in the South, up the East Coast, or in the far Interior, there is no question as to the existence of the initial-vowel-Bantu and non-initial-vowel Bantu as two distinct divisions, and that these represent Arthrous and Anarthrous Bantu. Looking over a number of Bantu grammars representing the philology of East, West, South, and Central Africa, we see what writers have to say on the subject of the Article in Bantu :

1. Heli Chatelain, author of a valuable grammar of Kimbundu, the language of Angola on the West Coast (written in Portuguese), as also the author of other works on Bantu, says : " O artigo definido o serve para ambos os generos e numeros " (the definite article serves for both genders and numbers), " and is seen in the incipient vowel O of the prefix in the singular and A in the plural."

2. Padre Ernesto le Comte, R.C. missionary in the province of Benguella (Lobito Bay), in his *Methodo Partico da lingua Bundu*, also pronounces the incipient vowel element to be a definite article.

3. F. S. Arnot, who came to the country about forty-three years ago, says in his Umbundu grammar (the language of Bihé and the trade tongue), " in the case of nouns denoting species, the initial O may be regarded as a sort of Definite Article."

4. Dr. Wesley Stover, of Bailundu, Bihé, also writes in his Umbundu grammar, page 11 : " The substantive pre-formative consists as we have seen of the derivative prefix preceded by the Demonstrative Article O which is equiva-lent to the generic definite article."

5. Bishop Steere, in his Swahili handbook, page 4, says : " There is nothing corresponding to the English definite

article, the word when standing alone implying the indefinite article, while the definite article can in many cases be expressed by the use and arrangement of the pronouns, but still must often be left unexpressed."

Note.—As Nyanja, Yao, Chewa, and other languages round Nyasaland and Eastward do not possess the initial vowel element it is only natural and appropriate that any reference to the existence of a definite article should be wanting.

6. Going South, we find one of the earliest Bantu philologists, Rev. J. L. Dohne, writing in his introduction to a Zulu-Kaffir dictionary that the " first member initial vowel of the incipient element has the force of an Indefinite Article."

7. Dr. Bleek, the father of Comparative Bantu, also regards the prefix as consisting of two parts, the first of which, the *initial vowel*, he regards as an article.

8. So, Father Torrend, who probably knows more Bantu languages than any living man, both theoretically and orally, in his Xosa-Kaffir grammar, makes two articles, one simple or vowel as the initial U in *Umfana* (" boy ") and the consonantal, as M, the other or second part of the prefix in *Umfana*. Also in his larger comparative grammar, a colossal work written later, he says : " In Kafir the Article both Definite and Indefinite is U, I, or A, according as the Classifier following it—expressed or understood— contains U, I, or A." Torrend represents our opinion entirely as to the Article Definite or Indefinite, and his wide knowledge of Bantu makes his opinion of great value.

On the other hand, Bishop Colenso, Grout, and Berthoud, of the Swiss Mission, Delagoa Bay, are all of the opposite opinion.

9. D. Crawford, Luanza, as the result of close study of many Bantu languages, both East, West, South, and in

Central Africa, is of opinion that the demonstrative pronoun is the Definite Article in Bantu, and so uses it in his
valuable translation of the Luba New Testament. As
there is no incipient vowel in Luba and the Demonstrative
is undoubtedly so used this rule of the Demonstrative
supplying the place of the Definite Article certainly
applies to Luba and those other Bantu languages that do
not possess the incipient vowel element, or Bantu Definite
Article.

Now to come to Bemba, not to speak of the many others
where the incipient vowel exists which is equal to a definite
article and is so used—*please note*, that the incipient vowel
is in every case the allied vowel of the classifier and is in
reality an abbreviated demonstrative, e.g.

> *U-muntu*—the person (Definite).
> *A-bantu*—the people   „
> *Mu-ntu*—a person (Indefinite).
> *Ba-ntu*—people   „

Here we have an example of the use of Definite and
Indefinite Article.

Uyu is the demonstrative singular and *Ava* the plural of
above class and mean That and Those, thus *Uyu muntu*,
" that man," and, *Ava bantu*, " those people," become

> *U-muntu*—the man.   *A-bantu*—the people.
> *Mu-ntu*—a man.   *Ba-ntu*—men, people.

This seems to be the working theory of the abbreviated
demonstrative or Definite Article of what may be called
the Anarthrous Division of the Bantu language.

A Short Introduction to the Study of a Bantu Language

Any person learning one of the 276 known Bantu languages has a key to all. If necessary this could be proved
by producing a table of a dozen types of Bantu, including

Umbundu, Luena, Luba, Bemba, Nyanja, Zulu, Suto, Swahili, Luganda, Nyamwesi, besides Congo dialects, if space permitted.

These, however, are easily accessible to those interested in African languages.

There is no question about the inherent simplicity of Bantu speech. To learners, however, the chief difficulty that exists between Bantu and our own language is found in its entire dissimilarity of construction.

Bantu is an alliterative family of languages and this alliteration is seen in the Noun Class system with its tendency to govern the various parts of speech. In other words, alliteration, or the recurrence of the initial vowel throughout the sentence, is its distinguishing feature.

The wide range of usefulness and potent influence of Bantu is becoming daily more apparent to all classes of Europeans whose calling in Africa involves contact with natives. The hundreds of tribes occupying fully two-thirds of the African continent, that part which extends from Cape Town, north to the Niger and between the Atlantic and the Indian Oceans, use Bantu speech in one or other of its forms.

To show the simplicity of Bantu, take the following examples in Bemba, one of an allied group of fifteen dialects spoken with local variations and mutually intelligible throughout the greater part of Northern Rhodesia and the south-east corner of the Congo State.

WEMBA

Wemba Alphabet Abbreviated

The vowels have actually three degrees of length—(1) Short; (2) Medial; (3) Long, but the ordinary five vowel-sounds common to Italian serve for most purposes.

A like " a " in father
E „ " a " „ fate
I „ " ee " „ feet
O „ " o " „ hope
U „ " oo " „ foot

The consonants are almost the same as in English, except that C and H are only used in the combination CH for the " ch " sound in " Chip."

G is only used as in Go, never as J.
S „ „ „ „ So, „ Z.
Y „ „ „ a consonant or semi-vowel, and never as in Any.
N with the nasal mark resembles the first NG in Singing.
B is sounded slightly like BW, and some prefer a W for this un-European sound. It is really a bi-labial V.

N.B.—Both Bemba and Wemba are written. The other letters require no comment in this short article.

THE NOUN.—The Noun has nine classes which undergo changes according to the initial syllable which, for convenience, is called the Classifier or Prefix. The final and unchangeable part is called the Stem. We give the working of the Class System in the first three classes, which are the most important.

Class I.—Sing. : *Muntu*—a person
        Plur. : *Bantu* —people
Class 2.—Sing. : *Muti* —a tree
        Plur. : *Miti* —trees
Class 3.—Sing. : *Chintu*—a thing
        Plur. : *Fintu* —things

From the above it will be seen that the noun changes in its initial syllable to form its plural number, at the beginning, and not at the end, of a word, as with us, thus :

	Classifier.	Stem.	English.
Class 1.—Sing. :	Mu	-ntu	a person
Plur. :	Ba	-ntu	people
Class 2.—Sing. :	Mu	-ti	a tree
Plur. :	Mi	-ti	trees
Class 3.—Sing. :	Chi	-ntu	a thing
Plur. :	Fi	-ntu	things

The first is the personal class, and includes all persons and personifications, the initial syllable " mu- " being the Classifier and " ntu " the Stem. Only the Prefix changes from " mu " to " ba," e.g. *Muntu*, a person ; *Bantu*, people.

The second class has the same Classifier in the singular, but changes in the plural to " mi," e.g. :

Muti—a tree

Miti—trees, the Impersonal Class

The third is the Neuter Class, and embraces all words beginning with " chi." These take " fi " in the plural. Hence *Chintu*, a thing, becomes *Fintu*, things.

PRONOUNS.—The principal pronouns for use with verbs are of two kinds, Conjunctive and Disjunctive.

CONJUNCTIVE

Singular.	Plural.
N—I	*Tu* —we
U—thou	*Mu*—you
A—he or she	*Ba* —they

DISJUNCTIVE OR EMPHATIC

Singular.	Plural.
Ine —I	*Ifwe* —we
Iwe—thou	*Imwe*—you
Uyu—he or she	*Aba* —they

Then we have the Possessive Pronouns, which require the appropriate Sentence Prefix.

POSSESSIVE

Singular.	Plural.
-Andi —mine	*-Esu* —our
-Obe —thine	*-Enu*—your
-Akwe—his	*-Abo*—their

VERBS.—Most verbs end in the letter A, and are composed of two parts, Root and Stem. *Only the Stem Vowel changes,* e.g. :

Root.	Stem.	
End	*-a*	*Enda* —go
Mon	*-a*	*Mona* —see
Tet	*-a*	*Teta* —cut
Lim	*-a*	*Lima* —cultivate
Ishib	*-a*	*Ishiba*—know
Is	*-a*	*Isa* —come
Let	*-a*	*Leta* —bring and so on.

The Verb Stem is equal to the Imperative Singular, e.g. : *enda*—go thou ; *ishiba*—know thou. *Ku*, prefixed to the Verb Stem, gives the Infinitive, which is also the Verbal Noun, e.g. *Kwenda*—to go ; *kuenda*—going.

Herewith three Verb Tenses :

1. SIMPLE PRESENT TENSE, formed by prefixing the Conjunctive Pronoun to the Verb.

Singular.

Nteta muti	—I cut a tree
Umona muntu	—You see a man
Aenda kubomba	—He goes to work

Plural.

Tulima libala	—We dig a field
Muishiba fintu	—You know things
Balwa bukali	—They fight fiercely

2. SIMPLE PAST TENSE, formed by the insertion of " a " between the Conjunctive Pronoun and the Verb Stem.

Singular.

Nateta muti —I cut a tree
Wamona muntu—You saw a man
Aenda kubomba—He went to work

Plural.

Twalima mabala—We dig fields
Mwaishiba fintu—You knew things
Balwa chibi —They fought hard

3. SIMPLE FUTURE TENSE, formed by the insertion of the infix particle *ka* between the Conjunctive Pronoun and Verb Stem.

Singular.

Nkateta muti —I shall cut a tree
Ukamona bantu —You shall see people
Akenda kubomba—He will go to work

Plural.

Tukalima libala —We shall dig a field
Mukaishiba fintu—You will know things
Bakalwa bukali —They will fight fiercely

ADJECTIVES.—These are formed variously, but we shall take the simple form and work with a few pure adjectives. It will have to be remembered that these have no use apart from the noun they qualify; e.g. :

Suma—good
Bi —bad
Tali —long
Ipi —short
Nono —little
Kulu —big

Alliteration will be seen in operation in its most elementary form here.

EXAMPLES

Class 1.—Sing. : *Muntu Musuma*—a good person
Plur. : *Bantu babi* —bad people
Class 2.—Sing. : *Muti utali* —a high tall tree
Plur. : *Miti ipi* —short trees
Class 3.—Sing. : *Chintu chikulu* —a big thing
Plur. : *Fintu finono* —little things

In the first and third classes the Classifier is added to the Adjective to give them their full value, while in class two only the vowel of the Classifier alliterates.

Again, to show further alliteration, let us take the Possessive Pronoun, with Noun and Adjective, e.g. :

Muntu wandi musuma—My good man
Bantu bobe babi —Thy bad people
Muti wakwe utali —His tall tree
Miti yesu ipi —Our short trees
Chintu chenu chinono —Your little thing
Fintu fyabo fikulu —Their big things

Note that only the initial vowel alliterates with the Possessive Pronoun in the Singular of class one and plural of class two. All the others take the full prefix.

I shall now give a full alliterative sentence to show the position of Adjective, Pronoun, Verb, and Noun.

Singular.

Muntu wandi musuma ulima, libala
Man—of me—of good—he digs—a field — English literal
My good man he cultivates a field translation.

Plural.

Bantu bobe babi bateta miti itali
People—of thee—of bad—they cut—trees—of height English
Thy bad people cut tall trees literally.

PREPOSITIONS.—The almost universally used Prepositions are :

	Pa	Ku	Mu
and mean :	At	To	In

e.g. :

Pa ñanda	—at the house
Ku ñanda	—to the house
Mu ñanda	—in the house
Ali pa ñanda	—He is at the house
Aenda ku ñanda	—He goes to the house
Aingila mu ñanda	—He enters in the house

These represent the Classifier of the ninth class of Nouns, called the *Locative Class*, also by suffixing the particle *No* to these three forms, the Adverbs here, hereabout, and in here, are built with many others, e.g. :

Pano	—here
Kuno	—hereabout
Muno	—in here

Ndi pano pa ñanda	—I am here at the house
Aisa kuno ku ñanda	—He came here to the house
Baingila muno mu mushi	—They entered into the village

The most convenient and useful source of Preposition is found in what is called the Relative Stem of Verbs. This Stem contains every possible Relative Preposition in use. It means : for, against, on behalf of, in the name of, for the sake of, etc., etc., e.g. :

Kulwa	—to fight
Kulwila	—to fight for
Kulwila ñanda na bana	—to fight for home and children
Kwenda	—to go
Kwendela	—to go against

Kwendela bantu babi	—to go against bad people
Kuima	—to stand
Kwiminina	—to stand up for
Kwiminina buloloke na chine	—to stand up for right- eousness and truth
Kwikala	—to sit, to live
Kwikalila	—to live for
Kwikalila masange	—to live for pleasure
Ku sosa	—to speak
Kusosela	—to speak on behalf of
Kusosela balanda	—to speak on behalf of the poor
Ku enda	—to go
Kwendela	—to go in the name of
Kwendela shikulu	—to go in the master's name

ADVERBS.—These can be, variously, Prepositions, according to the structure of the sentence. Vide Preposition, e.g. :

Pano—here	*Apa*—there
Muno—in here	*Umu*—in there
Palya—yonder	
Mulya—in yonder	

Like the Preposition, so the bulk of Adverbs are made from one of the eight Verb Stems, called the *Intensive Stem*, which conveys every adverbial idea of thoroughness or intensiveness suggested by the Verb, e.g. :

Ku lima	—to dig
Kulimishya	—to dig thoroughly
Ku enda	—to go
Kwendeshya	—to go quickly
Ku teta	—to cut
Kuteteshya	—to cut up in bits

Ku mona —to see
Kumoneshya —to see well
Kuishiba —to know
Kwishibishya—to know fully

etc., etc., through all the Verbs.

CONJUNCTIONS.—These are simple and easily learned.

Na —and, with
Kabil —also
Mwandi—but
Lelo —now, to-day

e.g. :

Iwe na Ine twaishiba fintu
You and I we know things.

Twenda na bantu besu
We go with our people.

Kabili alwa na bantu bakwe
He also fights with or against his people.

Basosa Chibemba chibi mwandi baishiba bwino
They speak Bemba badly, but they know it well.

INTERJECTIONS.—These are mostly onomatopoeic, and the theory of the origin of Bantu as living speech is that it was interjectional, i.e. all words, nouns, verbs, etc., were originally Interjections, of which the Noun Prefixes are the only remaining vestiges of proof.

CHAPTER XXI

Bantu Literature

BANTU literature, though so little known, is nevertheless of paramount importance to an understanding of the races that inhabit Bantuland because it furnishes us with the only existing key that can open to us the whole arcana of Bantu life and history in its fourfold aspect : the *Individual*, the *Family*, the *Clan*, and the *Tribe*. Native doctors, diviners, medicine men, musicians, poets, orators, with instructors and instructresses of secret societies, guilds, and clubs, or schools, which the young boys and girls have to attend, and where instruction is liberally given in the science of esoteric anthropology, are the recognised repositories of Bantu literature, and it is to them we must go in order to learn and record what may be gathered on this subject. Circumcision camps for boys, and *Mbusa* temples for girls who have attained puberty, are found to be the only places where the young folk of Bantuland receive a public education. This education, though primitive and crude, and distinctly immoral looked at from the European standpoint, is certainly very much better than no education at all. Of all the above authorities on Bantu literature the doctor comes first and foremost, for practically all the business of life must be brought to him and pass through his hands. He is the representative of the spirits of the departed and the recognised and only medium between the living and the dead. The following items have been gleaned from everyday life, and most of them taken down first hand from native doctors and diviners.

DIVINATION OVER A SICK CHILD. A man once had a child who was sick. The child became dangerously ill. The husband called his wife and said to her : " Why is it our child is sick like this ? " The wife answered him saying : " All that is the doctor's business." The husband rose and went off to fetch the doctor. On reaching the doctor's house he sat down. He said to the doctor : " Sir, please come and divine for me about the sickness of my child." The doctor said : " Good, but first give me the initial fee." On receiving the initial fee he went at once. They then brought him a mat, with which he covered the divining instruments. He then began divining and questioning the spirits, saying : " If it's you, dead spirit, who have caused the sickness of this child, who are you ? Are you the uncle after whom the child is named, whose body is in the cold ground ? " The spirit answered saying : " Don't mention my name, please." The oracle then refused to give further answers, so the doctor rapped again, and said : " Is it the child's dead grandmother who has caused this sickness ? " The oracle again refused, saying : " No, it is the paternal grandfather." He says : " Bring me a beer offering and decorate my spirit hut." They did so and the divination held fast.

The doctor went out of the house and the woman remained with her husband. She said to him : " Have you heard what the doctor says, my husband ? Your guardian spirit has brought this sickness on the child, so, bless us." Then the father turned and said to the sick child : " Oh, I'm so sorry, my child, I beg your pardon. I bless you," and he spat some beer of blessing all over the ground, saying : " That's because I mentioned your maternal uncle, that's the reason," and he blessed the child again, squirting beer all over it. Then the doctor came and said : " Give me my fees, I have divined. My name is the fighter of demons " (*kalwa fibanda*).

DIVINING CAUSE OF CHILD'S DEATH. A wife and husband live together and a child is born. The child one day becomes sick and dies. They mourn. After a few days have passed they say : " Call in a diviner." The diviner comes and drops into his incantations at once and tells the parents the result, thus : " The child in the grave says : ' Let father pay up my mother,' " .that is to say, let them straighten out matters at home between themselves. " If father refuses, saying, ' I shall not pay up,' then let him get out of our home. If he refuses to get out I will come and kill mother." The parents talk together and say, " We accept the decision : now there only remains to pay mother." The doctor says to the woman, " If finally he refuses to do this you must separate." The doctor then says, " I have divined, sir," and leaves.

DIVINATION OVER UNBORN CHILD. Now when a woman becomes pregnant and the pregnancy is far advanced, if on the day of giving birth parturition is difficult, those present say : " Let's call in the doctor." The doctor comes and drops into his divination and gives the " divined-about ones " the result. The doctor says, " The cause is due to the paternal grandmother," who answered saying, " It is I who am now being reincarnated," and on saying so the divination held fast. The doctor says to the pregnant woman : " Tell me everything and keep nothing back." She then, to save her life (lest she die in childbirth), confesses any unfaithfulness and anything wrong she may have done, and then says, " I understand that it is the paternal grandmother who is coming to be born." The doctor then says, " All is right now. I have divined, sirs." The woman thereupon commences to give birth, while those present sing : " Come gently, gently out of the womb. Oh, my good spirit, we shall make you a present of a young chicken that you may follow on nicely." The child is safely born and the matter ends.

REINCARNATION AND GIVING NAMES. When a woman becomes pregnant a public announcement is made. On the day of announcement she says to herself : " You must avoid being seen in public places now your pregnancy is far advanced." They divine and the divination says, " It is your brother who died who is coming back to be reborn in you." When he is just born she tells those present, and he receives the dead brother's name. In the womb is the place where the name is given. He is accordingly called by the dead uncle's name.

DIVINATION OVER IMPENDING ABORTION. When a woman is pregnant and the pregnancy is advanced, and after a time the womb prolapses and she becomes very ill, all the midwives say : " Let's call in a doctor to find out the cause of this illness and womb prolapse." One of the mothers present (only mothers are allowed to be present at the birth of a child) takes " initial fees " for the doctor in her hand and goes to call him. She addresses the doctor thus : " Sir, please divine about our sick daughter, for since becoming pregnant she has not been strong." The doctor goes and carries with him a fetish, and a small pot in readiness, and on arrival he says, " Give me a mat that I may get on with my divining." They bring him a mat and spread it on the ground. He covers the divination instruments and spits a blessing all over them. Then he divines thus : " If, O dead spirit, you are an uncle who has caused this person's sickness, tell us." The oracle replies, " No." He continues questioning the departed spirit thus : " If you are a brother who has caused this sickness, tell us." The oracle answers, " No " (the

doctor ventriloquises, talking to the spirit), " I called you
' father ' in order that you might give me the right
medicine, not to revile and insult you. Some alternative
medicines, please. Oh, bless here and get on the top of
death so that the mother's children shall get on the top
of the child who shall then descend." (This refers to a
certain practice adopted by African midwives.) At this
point the doctor declares, " It is the uncle who is the
cause, saying, ' I shall be born in her who has womb prolapse. If you spit a blessing on her she will then give birth
without trouble.' " (Every difficult case of birth is supposed to be a case of reincarnation.) The doctor then
finishes and says, " I have divined, sirs." " All right,"
answer those present. Then he says as he leaves, " Come
out gently from the womb, O good reincarnated spirit.
We are all your servants and breathe a blessing for your
recovery." Immediately the child is born it gets its name.

QUEEN OR KING OF THE SPIRIT CHIEFS. A person falls
asleep and during the night a demon enters his body. He
burns up bed and bedding and roars like a lion. He talks
like a ventriloquist and jumps in the air, catching hold of
the roof of the hut. The people gather round and sing :

> " Come and carry my little stool,
> O child of my mother, come.
> They who come from afar like me
> Should be carried pick-a-back."

Those standing outside the house take up the song. They
then go inside the hut and clothe him. He then comes
out, having taken a new name, saying : " I am Chikonwe.
I have come to put an end to the smallpox and plagues, and
forbid these to kill any more people." Then he dances
and sings all the evening. He then stops his wild dancing,
and the people set to work to catch him. They go to the

forest and set a trap. If he is caught in it he is then accepted as a spirit king (he is supposed to be possessed with the spirit of a dead chief). They cook chickens for him, feast and honour him, and he continues in this profession. (Some of these are very clever dancers and have a very large repertory of songs and ballads.)

A Necromancer. It happens that if a man falls asleep and dreams that there is a demon at his head and he starts up suddenly from sleep he has given proof of his being a necromancer. All gather round him in the night. He tells them his experiences saying, "I have come from afar, please call my medium for me and I'll tell you all things that have brought me here. This year you must sprinkle offerings of meal round the rocks at the river crossings, also offerings of little white beads. Then you shall have good rains, and food shall be plentiful throughout the country. The rivers shall be in flood and fish shall be plentiful. Medium mine, please interpret all these things that have brought me here. When I have told them I must go back. My name is 'the thunderer.'"

Calling a curse on a Supposed Witch. If a mother dies, immediately the children say : " It was a witch that killed her." They say also many other ugly things. During the night the children gather together and address the spirit of their dead mother, saying: " Oh, mother, mother, if you have died a natural death lie peaceably in your grave. If some one has killed you by witchcraft, don't rest quietly but go to the house of that person and kill them also." Now when they find some one has died somewhere, they say, " Behold, to-day the witch has gone away for ever. The tail of the reedbuck has shrivelled up." (Proverb : The first tail from the hunt, i.e. more shall be killed.) They say, " Don't go and join in the mourning. Our dead mother in the ground is venting her anger, saying, ' Be reconciled over my poor body. A pauper's body is a place of reconciliation. No! Hush! keep quiet and don't go to the funeral, children.'"

AUGURY OF LIFE AND DEATH AND THREE FETISHES. Suppose a man compounds three little fetishes when a terrible plague sweeps over the land. He then takes his three fetishes and throws them into his mouth. He lets a certain time elapse while the three small fetishes remain in his mouth. Should one of these come out against his will that is a sign he will die. Should all come out at once then he knows he shall live.

AUGURIES OF THE SNAKE AND WHITE AND RED CHALK. If a man uses a big live snake for fetish purposes, and after that a sickness seizes him, he takes red and white chalk and holds it out to the snake. If the snake accepts the white chalk then he knows he shall live. If it takes the red chalk then he knows assuredly that he shall die.

EXPERIENCE WITH A WITCH OR WIZARD. Now when a witch goes off to bewitch any one it waits till dark and until people are asleep in bed, usually the first watch of the night. On arriving at the house of the person it has gone to bewitch it climbs on to the roof naked, and then jumps down and bursts into the house. The occupant, who is asleep, awakes in a fright. He takes a fetish medicine and holds it inside his mouth. He grasps and pulls out his fetish horn lying at his head and goes outside. On finding that the witch has its fetish horn grasped tightly in its hand he seizes it at once and puts his own fetish in its hand. Then the witch tells him: " You have wronged me by putting the fetish medicine into my fingers. I'm not a witch." The man says to the witch, " Lead the way to your home," but the fetish leads him astray. Then it begs the man not to deliver it up to the people. " Don't tell that you caught me at witchcraft though you found me at your hut trying to bewitch you. Now, you are a wise man, please take me home and I shall pay you handsomely." Then the man leads the way in front and points out the witch's house, saying : " It's there you live." The witch goes in and brings out goods and cloth and pays him to keep quiet. In parting he warns the witch, saying : " Don't repeat this business again, I warn you ! "

FETISH TEST FOR SITE OF NEW VILLAGE. A chief before removing to a new village site first looks out a likely place, and makes the usual fetish test with a handful of white meal. He lays it on the ground of the proposed site, and returns next morning to see if the meal is scattered. If the meal is entire this signifies that the spirits are displeased and they must not remove there at that time. Calling a doctor they say, " Please come and divine for us the reason the spirit chiefs are angry." He comes and drops into his incantations and tells them the result. Says he : " The dead chiefs refuse you permission to remove this dry season, but in the coming wet season we shall agree." Then the doctor says, " I have divined, sirs ; when you confess to a doctor always put your heart into it."

INITIATION OF A HUNTER. Now a man desirous of being a hunter and anxious to receive the initiation drink goes to an experienced hunter of the guild, and says : " Sir, I want you to initiate me as a hunter." They take him, and turning a pot upside down they seat him there with his eyes covered. Then they take medicine and burn it in a potsherd. They stretch out his arm and lance it in a few places and then rub in the burnt medicine. He then takes up a bow, and puts an arrow into it, and goes off to the forest. He hunts, and seeing a buck shoots it and kills it. He returns and calls his " fetish father." The head hunter, called " father of the fetish," cuts two pieces of herbs and plucks leaves. When he reaches the dead antelope he chews some of the medicine and spits it into the animal's ear and on its head. He also blows medicine into its nostrils. Then they place the hunter on the carcase and raise him up with the little finger. They cut open the animal, take out the heart, and give him it to eat. He also eats the fetish medicine. Then they give him four taboos :

(1) Don't eat wild spinach.
(2) Don't eat potato leaves boiled.
(3) Don't eat rabbit.
(4) Avoid your wife each month.

Then they feed him with other meat and he becomes a full-fledged hunter.

FOLK-LORE

Brer Rabbit and the Guinea-Fowl Dinner

The animals went out to hunt one day with the elephant at their head. They had no success, and as it was afternoon and the chief was hungry they sent one animal after another, buffalo, rhino, hippo, etc., but they all came back empty-handed. The rabbit came up to the chief and stood on his hind legs, saying : " Oh, great chief, send me, and I shall bring you eighty guinea-fowl for dinner." The elephant laughed and said, " Go, but I know you won't do any better than the others." Brer Rabbit hustled off and reached the riverside at a spot where guinea-fowl always came to drink. He pulled out his penknife and, setting to work, cut a bundle of osiers with which he commenced to make a big basket trap. He finished by putting a door on the side, which he fastened, and went to sleep. The guinea-fowl came along, cackle, cackle, and woke him up with their cackling. He rubbed his eyes and, looking sleepy, said : " Hullo, you guinea-fowl, how do you do, all of you ? " " What is that big basket for ? " they asked, " Oh," said the rabbit, " if I

were inside that basket all you guinea-fowl couldn't lift me."
They all laughed and said, " Why, one of us could lift you
easily." " All right, try," said Brer Rabbit, as he opened
the door and went inside. They caught the basket and
tossed him high in the air. " Ah, but," said the rabbit,
" that's nothing." " Why," said he, " if all you guinea-
fowl went inside I could lift you up." They laughed,
saying, " Why, you couldn't lift one of us." " All right, all
of you just get inside and you shall see." They hopped inside one after the other until all were in, and Brer Rabbit
quickly pulled out a little string he had kept hidden and
promptly fastened the door. He then hurried off to the
elephant, saying : " Come along at once and see. I have
kept my promise and got you eighty guinea-fowl for dinner."
The animals all hurried excitedly to the spot, and sure
enough, there were the eighty guinea-fowl inside Brer
Rabbit's trap.

FIVE WEDDING SONGS

ON THE MARRIAGE FEAST

" Let's wake up the mill,
    And grind out the meal :
    With Brer Rabbit be kin,
    Who dropped his old skin,
    While working and sweating
    To prepare for the wedding,
    The arrival of guests,
    For the marriage feast."

MARRIAGE REGRETS

" I strutted and swaggered,
    I ogled and courted him.
    Mother, I married him,
    Married a lion grim.
    Now I am sorry,
    And regret my rash folly."

Marital Happiness

" A monkey-nut root
Bears baskets of fruit.
It spreads like a vine,
Which children entwine.
It's pretty to see
Such a family tree."

On a Bad Husband

" Let's catch the man
Who's hard on his wife.
Let's hammer his head
Till he's tired of life,
With heavy sticks
And stones and bricks,
Till he learn the lesson
All good men learn."

Honour to Mothers-in-Law

" When you marry a wife,
See you don't forget
To honour her mother
Each day of your life.
Wherever you go
True marriage is so."

The foregoing, with much that appears elsewhere throughout the book, will give an average idea of native literature, which, if the Bantu peoples knew the art of writing and printing, would all be found in book form.

CHAPTER XXII

Fetishism & Medicine

ONE might preface this chapter by saying that fetish rites and ceremonies with their concomitant customs permeate the whole Bantu fabric, beginning at infancy, and more often prior to birth. The bulk of fetish preparations are preventive and prophylactic, therefore to neglect to provide these, and to consult the oracles in regard to every detail pertaining to Death, Life, and Birth, which is frequently a fresh incarnation, is to expose oneself, or one's child, to the displeasure of the departed spirits. These are more to be feared now in the disembodied state than before. A person may have occupied an infirm, decrepit body while he lived, he may have been despised and ignored as a weakling, but now that, to use an ordinary Africanism, " death has unbound him " and brought him welcome release, he enters a region where his power is unlimited by time and space, and where he will be better able to avenge insults on those whom he knows will have cause to fear him. The Bantu peoples are pronounced spiritists. From first to second childhood they grope in a visionary and illusory world. They see spirits at every turning of the path. They know that to neglect to take the necessary precautions against evils seen and unseen—the unseen being more real and to be feared than the seen—is to court disaster, disease, and perhaps premature death. There is no chance, no unmeaning event. Even the friends of a day that cross the phantasmagoria of his life have been brought athwart his path by invisible beings for unknown reasons. The Bantu must consult his priest and doctor in everything, and make all possible provision against every contingency that may or may not arise. In a word he must cover his family, house, property, and person with potent fetishes and charms and so reduce life's risks to a minimum. In connection with all this there are observances imposed by circumstance and tradition that render the life of the African burdensome and monotonous, nevertheless to ensure safety and success all this rigmarole and these minute details must be gone through for ever and a day.

Fetishism is based on fear of the unknown and unseen. I could tell thrilling stories of three different men who each fought a lion single-handed ; of a man who fought a mother leopard, having stumbled on her two cubs ; of a man who fought a crocodile and killed it, just to show that natives are not void of physical courage. Let any of these same men hear the rustling of a leaf in the forest at night, or see a small snake, or spider of a certain kind in the path, or stub his toe, he will turn and run until he sees and consults the doctor, who will prepare a fetish to counteract the evil influence of the omen met and prevent its recurrence.

PERSONAL FETISHES are of primary and vital importance, as these begin at the birth of the baby and ensure it a good start in life and luck. These are made as a rule by the family doctor, after he by divination and shrewd guesswork finds out the baby's potential idiosyncrasies. They are compounded and compressed inside the shell of a big beetle, or the tiny horn of a very small buck, and tied round the neck, arm, leg, or body of the child. They are sometimes decorated with pretty beads, and a string is passed through for purposes of attaching. Sometimes a few hairs from the head of the father and mother are inserted in a long blue bead, and a string is passed through it with which to tie it round the neck. At various stages of the child's life different fetishes are made and worn, and as it grows up into boyhood, or maidenhood, and passes through one or another of the local clubs, secret societies, or village heathen schools (for instruction putposes), fresh fetish horns are compounded and worn, and so on through life. Every child, boy, girl, man, or woman wears regularly, or on occasions, one or more fetishes which are frequently removed at night and hung up inside the hut to be donned again at sunrise.

FAMILY FETISHES are provided by the parents, who are responsible for the welfare of their families. These are obtained from one or other of the local doctors, who first diagnoses, ascertaining all the details requisite before prescribing, in order to use only the correct ingredients.

CLAN FETISHES also exist, and a very common and much-coveted one is the large *Mantis* called in South Africa the Kaffir God (*Masombwe*). The field-rat clan near the Luapula River have such a fetish which is kept sacred in a small temple. They have some weird theories about its wonderful miracle-working power.

TRIBAL FETISHES are kept at the chief's kraal, or in charge of a doctor or set of priests who are the repositories, and are held responsible. Very often the chief proclaims himself the head doctor, and keeps the tribal fetishes in his own care. These are important and give status to the tribe according to the virtues with which these fetishes are said to be invested. The Ushi tribe in N. Rhodesia have two great Ju-Jus or oracles, called *Makumba* and *Ngosa*, male and female. On May 16th, 1907, I visited these far-famed deities. They are kept in a small temple about ten feet in diameter, where a priestess resides to keep the sacred fire burning. There are several priests in charge, and the chief priest who consults the oracle is a clever ventriloquist and is called *Chilaluka*. On examination I was surprised to find that they were both meteorites of several ounces' weight, hence the legend that, like Diana of Ephesus and the *Kaaba*, or " black stone," at Mecca, " they fell from heaven." Makumba, the male, was wrapped up in python skins with a massive bushy head-dress of white feathers, and surrounded by large Mpande shells, which used to be the native insignia of chieftainship. These were consulted by Msidi, Kanyanta, and other powerful chiefs who sought counsel and aid.

The female, called the sister, lies side by side with the other, and is also wrapped up in python skins. These oracular fetishes, firmly believed to be of miraculous origin, have brought their owners much gain, and still more fame, and many a legend is current as to their origin and history. In the old·days when they were carried before the armies, victory, they aver, was always sure, with the exception of once when the Arab chief Chiwala desecrated the shrine and carried off Makumba, stripping him of much wealth. These are the great tribal deities in N.E. Rhodesia and the heart of the people's religious belief. All natives mention their names and answer questions about them with bated breath as though it were an act of sacrilege. They are the Jupiter Maximus around which constellate the smaller deities of clan, family, and individual worship.

Ubwanga bwilamfya (or " Subjugating Fetish "). This is the great *War Fetish* of the Wemba tribe in N.E. Rhodesia. Its receptacle is a small round shallow basket about six inches wide. About fifty duiker horns are arranged round the outer edge and a large roan antelope horn is inserted through the centre. The basket and horns are filled with the fetish medicine. A small hole is drilled in the middle of the horn of the roan antelope.

The medicine consists of meal, camwood powder, chalk, castor oil, and medicines of various sorts, including a small piece of the skull of the famous Lungu warrior chief called Chikoke. These are compounded in a village mortar with an ordinary native pestle. When Kiti Mukulu and Mwamba, the principal Wemba chiefs, wished to send out their armies to raid they called into the capital the chiefs and the warriors who were to form the raiding parties, and these came in, each with his *Ilamfya* fetish slung across his shoulder. In order to ascertain where to go and whether they would have success or otherwise, all the doctors were set to work to divine. Rods with a spike at each end were stuck in the ground a few feet apart in a row. On the top spike of each was inserted an *Ilamfya* fetish, according to the number of chiefs going to battle. A kilt of *ndibu* (" seed ") rattles was hung round the fetish, and it was set a-spinning.

A man was brought and laid lengthwise on the ground and a hole dug in front of his neck. His throat was then cut and the blood gushed out and ran into the hole. The priest's assistants then came up one by one, each bringing an *Ilamfya* in his hand which he had taken off the spinning rods. Each stooped down and took a handful of warm blood, which he sprinkled over the horns in his *Ilamfya*, pouring some into the roan horn. He then blew into the horn, making incantations while the blood bespattered his face and body. He then waved the horn backwards and forwards, and returning replaced it on the rod stand. All the *Ilamfyas* were then set a-spinning and the doctors and chiefs gathered near eagerly watching the spinnings. Wherever the *Ilamfyas* pointed when they stopped spinning was taken as an indication that they must make war in that direction. After taking all the flowing blood, they pierced the eye of the man with the point of the roan's horn.

Origin of the *Ilamfya* fetish : Chikoko, a Lungu chief, came to attack Mwamba, and Kiti-Mukulu, in the days of Kiti-Muluba, nephew of Kana-Besa, the ancestral spirit and forefather of the Wemba chiefs and people. He was a powerful chief of great repute, but was killed and his skull taken, from which the powerful war fetish is compounded, having this for its base and origin. In each *Ilamfya* there is a small piece of the skull of this great warrior chief. The skull was kept at the Wemba capital, where the high priest of the fetish lived.

The *Mwango*, or " war dance song," when warriors dance with enemies' heads :

> " These shall never hoe again,
> They are dead and gone below.
> These shall never dig again,
> They are dead and gone for ever.
> Fight with heart and hand,
> Kill and never fear, boys."

Form of united oration in praise of Wemba paramount chief when his warriors return successfully :

> " O great chief, your enemies approach :
> They are up within sight of your guns.
> Their shade makes us chill and cold,
> But the Wemba warrior never runs."

Farmers' fetishes are tied to the fences of their fields, so that anything getting into touch with any connected part is held fast until the owner of the field appears. A man protects his canoe, house, property, or animals by means of fetishes, and he has unbounded belief in their power and efficacy. This general belief acts as a great deterrent to crime, and it is only when the native loses faith in his religion, and system of fetishes, that theft, assault, arson, murder, rape, etc., become frequent and the jails are filled. *Fetishism and medicine are two distinct systems*, and are used for the following specified purposes and reasons : *Fetish* comes from the Portuguese word *Feitiço*, meaning a superstitious charm or magic medicine. For this the Bantu word *Bwanga* is used, and/these charms are used exclusively in the practice of the black and white art of magic by qualified doctors, or by wizards and impostors. A man who employs fetishes for his own personal ends, or to injure or kill an enemy, is guilty of sorcery, *buloshi*, and is punished by death. A qualified fetish doctor or wise man, who employs the same system of charms and magic medicines for the tribal good, is a public benefactor, and is so recognised and treated among his tribe.

The Butwa temples are notorious dens, where witches and wizards are made and harboured, but the Society's power protects them. They are said to use Vampire Bats to eat up and carry away the grain and food from the fields of others they wish to injure. They have *Bwanga*, by means of which they induce flocks of these loathsome creatures to go at night and destroy certain enemy fields, and carry the stolen food to their own bins. They also are said to use moles for similar destructive or anti-social purposes. The moles are reputed to carry the food from enemies' gardens at night, and take it to the food stores of these witches and wizards. There also are crocodile doctors, who are said to use crocs to destroy personal enemies or enemies of those who employ them. These sorcerers are said to cause leprosy, pneumonia, twisted neck, and other diseases by their magic medicines. Doubtless many of these are poisons pure and simple. My wife had a very clever native housemaid, who worked hard and earned many pretty cloths. Her married sister (who was a Butwa member),

DEVASTATION.

A desolate scene showing the effects of a raid by a flight of locusts.

MUSICIANS.

A Gourd Piano in Lundaland, played on important occasions.

with whom she sometimes lived, envied the younger sister her dresses, and one day Kalumbwa did not turn up. We were called to see her; she was dying with what the natives call " twisted neck "—her neck was stiff and all awry.

All said that her elder sister poisoned her, and she certainly showed every symptom of death by some powerful poison. I remember a similar case on the Luapula when a native sergeant died. He was said to have been poisoned by a Government headman who publicly expressed jealousy of the other's position. I visited the dying man, who showed every symptom of poisoning. The poisonous plant grew near the station, and I had a cowherd who attempted suicide by means of the juice of the same plant. We saved him by emetics.

Smallpox, chicken pox, sleeping sickness, dysentery, malarial fever, tick fever, enlarged spleen, venereal diseases, and many others are well known and have specific names. *Chifufya*, or " sulphate of copper," scraped off the copper stones and mixed with water and a native medicine in a snail shell, and painted on with a feather, is much used for sloughing ulcers, and fever sores. Transfusion of chicken's blood is used for a dying person. I remember sending back a piece of calico to bury a native boy I left dying at my place; instead I returned to find him well. He recovered as the result of an old doctress's treatment of the aforementioned kind. I knew a Butwa doctor, named Kasenga, who was a chief where I lived for years, who used to use a lizard split down the back, and put against the spleen, where several incisions had previously been made to reduce the painful and swollen organ. He had also many other cures, including one for insanity, and was sent for from all over the country. One of the most common forms of treatment for nearly everything is bleeding and cupping. For headaches, fever, pneumonia, pleurisy, and even for painful ulcers, cupping is resorted to. Animal horns are procured, cut off near the point, and perforated at the blind end. Wax is put over the hole and then pierced to allow of suction. If the cupping is to be done over the temples, behind the ear, or on the head, the place is first shaved clean of all hair. A few incisions are then made while the cupping horn is soaked in water, and when the blood is flowing gently the horn is put over the place, and sucked until the blood flows. When the blood is flowing gently the wax is pressed over the hole to close it, leaving the horn drawing blood. When the horn is full it is removed and the wound is wiped clean. In smallpox, chicken pox, and some forms of venereal disease, the patient is segregated, and lives in a hut or camp some distance from the village.

Prior to the advent of Europeans, inoculation was practised for smallpox. A person coming from a clean, healthy stock—sometimes they would go back three generations to make sure—was taken, and the lymph from his pustules used to inoculate healthy people. During an epidemic I had all my personal and house boys thus inoculated. They were then kept in the segregation camps until recovered, when they were shaved and washed, their old clothes burned, and new ones given to them, after which they were allowed to return to the village. I have never seen a case of blackwater fever among natives, though it is common among Europeans, and often fatal.

The recuperative power of natives is wonderful. I remember a man who, the mission doctor said, would die if not operated on. The man refused to have his leg taken off, and the doctor sent him off with a shake of the head, saying: "I give you five days to live." Some months after, on visiting the village the man came from, he was found quite well, and busy at work.

The fetish doctor goes to the bush regularly to replenish his supplies of leaves, barks, roots, etc., from which he makes up his stock-in-trade of medicines for use. Aperients, astringents, aromatics, soporifics, etc., are well known, and many other medicines whose name and action and locality are kept secret from laymen. Much is done along the lines of " faith healing," and a patient usually enquires about the doctor's credentials before putting his case into his hands for treatment. Much of the treatment and many of the remedies savour of the ridiculous, but one has only to read Mark Twain's " literary fossil " on medicine to see how we ourselves are not so very far removed in point of time from the practices of Africa. How long is it since people in Europe spoke of the doctor as the " Leech," and accepted without question any nostrums he cared to prescribe?

One of the favourite and fashionable Love Charms worn by native women to enable them to gain the affection of a man is made from the hair of an albino. The hair is obtained from albinos when they have their hair cut, and is inserted in the inside of a hollow blue bead which is tied round the top of the head with a cord at a rakish angle. If the albino is old the hair is valueless. I know an albino woman who does a roaring trade with her hair, which she sells at so much per strand. Another love charm is a herbal medicine (*muti*) sold by women doctors to women who want to make certain men fall in love with them. This is mixed in the water they bathe in, and is also supposed to be an unfailing remedy to cure a husband who is running after other women, and makes him fall in love again with his own wife.

CHAPTER XXIII
Theology & Religion

THAT the Bantu races are above all things supremely religious is seen in the thousands of priests, spirit huts and temples, idols and fetish horns, religious objects and new moon services, folk-songs and bush ballads, exogamic, totemistic, and taboo rites, associated with almost every detail that concerns the individual, family, clan, and tribal life of the people. Though fetishism and demonology are two great and important factors in Bantu religion there is also a definite and defined theology. The never-ending cry of the Moslem that " God is great " finds its echo from end to end of Bantuland. He is called " the Great Great One," meaning *great* in point of person, work, and age ; for the three meanings are implied in the same adjective. We find that He may be praised, prayed to, sinned against, appeased, and His help sought in time of trouble and difficulty, though of course for lack of a literature as we know it their ideas of God are more nebulous than ours.

As there is no meaningless event to the negro, so there is no word or name in any of the five hundred and more Bantu languages void of authentic meaning. Each word and name has a specific etymology as well as a current local significance, and nowhere is this feature more in evidence than in the many names, general and particular, used to designate the deity. I shall point out a few of the various names in use for God, and known to me, after which I think the reader will readily admit that the Bantu races, if not theologically inclined to-day, had certainly a theological past.

Among the Ovimbundu tribe of Bihé in Angola the name for God is *Suku*. In that language *usuke* means " poverty," *osuke*, " a poor person." *Uku sukila, suka* means " to be poor or in need," and *Suku*, " God, He who supplies the needs of His creatures." *Njambi-Kalunga*, " God," among the Cokwe, Luena, and Lunda tribes ; *Kalunga*, " the other world," sometimes *the unknown ;* and the full title signifies " the God of the unknown," which was the ancient Greek name for the deity. They also call Him *Sakatanga*, "the father creator who created all countries"; *sa*, " father," *ka* is an honorific prefix, and *tanga* is the verb " to create." The Balomotwa and Katanga tribes called Him, among other names, *Shakapanga upanga no kupangulula*, which means " the father creator who creates and uncreates " ; referring to creation and death, i.e. uncreation or bodily dissolution ; the constructive and destructive theory of the deity. The Lubans call Him *Kafula mova ilunga wa visera*, meaning, " He of many suns, the Eternal God (ancient of days), the bearer of burdens." Another Luban name is *Wamaneme*, " the sorrowful or suffering one." (This is no missionary importation.) Another Luban name still for God is *Vidie Mukulu*, " the great king," and they frequently address the deity, or even a powerful chief, as *Lesa Mukulu*, meaning, " Oh, great God ! "

Before getting to the widely used word current between Congoland and Nyasaland for God, *Lesa*, I should like to suggest a definition of *Mulungu*, used in East Africa, from which the Swahili form *Muungu* is abbreviated and Arabised owing to coast influence. *Mulungu*, I suggest, means " The Righteous One," as the root verb *Lunga*, with its modifications in many Bantu languages, means " to be

right, straight, righteous." The change of the final vowel
—*a* to *u*—is the personal vowel, and the prefix *mu* is the
form of derivative personal nouns. This relates to the
Jehovah Tssaddek of Hebrew. *Lunga, Lungika,* etc., also
means " to arrange, straighten, beautify," so that the idea
of the *God of order and beauty* is contained in this East
Coast word for God.

Now to come to *Lesa* or *Leza,* the most widely used word
for God, and one in use between the Kasai River in the
Congo and Lake Nyasa, I think we shall trace in it a word
of distinctly Semitic origin, which, with other Semitic
words and usages, proves that the Bantus were at one time
in touch with and influenced by the Semitic civilisation of
North Africa. *Lesa* is the causative form of the verb *Lela,*
" to nurse or cherish." The root syllable is *le* and unchangeable, whereas the causative suffix, *sa,* undergoes
quite a lot of changes, according as the idea is causative,
relative, frequentative, intensive, etc. *Le* or *li,* with its
variations *di* and *ri,* is the invariable form of the defective
verb " to be " in Bantu, which would suggest the Jehovah
idea of God, the great I AM of the Jews. *Le* contains the
root idea of a mother nurse, and one hears a lullaby used
to hush the babies wherein " Mother nurses baby for God."
Lesa means also the nurse, and this is a play on the *Lesa*
name for God and the root verb " to nurse." Now what
is the Hebrew name for God Almighty—El Shaddai—if
not the Bantu *Lesa?* and as a vowel may precede or follow
its consonant the *le* therefore gives us *el,* which is both
Arabic and Hebrew for God. *Shadd* is the Hebrew word
for " the breast," so that, in short, the *El Shaddai* of
Hebrew, " the God of the breast," i.e. the great mother
nurse, is nothing more or less than the *Lesa* or *Leza* of the
Bantus of Central Africa ; not mere " Mother of God "
idea, but " God Mother."

Anything great and terrible conveys the real Bantu idea of God, and one need have no hesitation (spite of certain authorities) about accepting the Zulu word for God, *Nkulukulu*, as meaning " the Great Great One and Old Old One," referring to both His Eternal existence and His greatness. *Pe* is another very important root word and contains :

(1) The idea of Eternal, never ending. *Pe*, " eternal, ever, always."

(2) The idea of spirit and spirit world. *Pepo*, " wind, spirit, etc."

(3) The idea of breath, breathe. *Pema*, " to breathe."

(4) The idea of wind. *Pepo*, " wind."

(5) The idea of spiriting or talking to the unseen, from which comes its use in " praying to and worshipping God," *pepa*.

These correspond in many ways to the Hebrew *ruach* and the Greek *pneuma*, with their verbs and derivatives.

" God thunders and God lightens," is a regular wet season expression, and they speak of God descending on the wings of the wind and in fire. When a person dies they say : " *Lesa amulya*," meaning God has eaten him up or taken him to Himself, and *Imfwa lesa* means " a natural or God-death " (as against bewitching).

They have a little song they sing about God, the lizard, and the frog. The lizard plays on the dulcimer and sings :

" I shall sing a song of praise to God.
  Strike the chords of the piano.
  God who gives us all good things.
  Strike the chords of the piano.
  Wives, and wealth, and wisdom.
  Strike the chords of the piano."

The frog speaks. " Quiet," says the frog, " God doesn't hear the singing of an animal with a tail like you. Go and dock your tail." God thereupon descends with a rush on the wings of the wind and enquires : " Who was that I heard singing that pretty song ? " " Croak ! Croak ! Croak ! It was I," says the frog. " No," says God, " that was not the voice I heard singing." Then the lizard replies : " It was I." " Play and sing the words over again," says God. The lizard plays and sings as before :

" I shall sing a song of praise to God.
Strike the chords of the piano," etc.

" Ah, yes," said God, " that was the music and the song I heard," and God gave the lizard all the beautiful colours of life, and left the frog with nothing but his ugly bloated face and his hoarse, rasping, croaky voice.

Natives not only pray to and praise God for success in the business of life, such as hunting, farming, trading, etc., but I have heard them say, " God has given me a good wife and many children." When they narrowly escape an accident or death they invariably say, " God rescued me."

They also pray to God when they worship at their primitive altars and spirit huts. A typical prayer : " Oh my God, if you are on friendly terms with the good spirits of the departed, help me, save me, and grant me a peaceful, quiet life in this world." They are very much given to sending messages to the other world by people who are dying, and many of these I have recorded, with dates, names, and places. When a good man dies they say, " He has gone and will plead my cause with God " ; " he shall speak for me to the good spirits of my departed friends " ; and often add, " and tell them I, too, am coming over soon," etc. Offerings of meal, beer, produce, and live stock, and even human beings used to be sacrificed to the good spirits, and God, as thanksgiving for a successful war, harvest, or success in any department of life, and often to propitiate or appease them.

Africans have holy days when a native will religiously refuse to go to work or to leave his village to do anything on any pretext whatsoever.

At the new moon, or on a heavy fall of hail, or during a period of plague, or mourning, or famine, or war, or any terrible event, all ordinary natural laws are suspended and in abeyance, and no person dare leave his home or village without incurring the severe displeasure of the Spirits and of his fellows.

The Bantu people are very strong in their views about blood sanctification, and I have seen this carried out on many occasions. In the old days slaves were frequently used for this purpose. I remember being present at the inheriting and coronation of Msidi's elder brother. The throats of several goats were cut, and the blood as it spurted warm was caught on a switch of animal tails, and everything, animate and inanimate, was sprinkled. Not only guns, furniture, stock, etc., but all slaves and wives were duly sanctified by the sprinkling of blood. As I stood watching the blood-sprinkling ceremony the old warrior chief Mukembe who was Master of Ceremonies—and who has shed more human blood than any African I know—quaintly remarked in cryptic speech that, if it were not for the white man present, his big, broad-bladed spear would pierce many human hearts. As he said it, he gave me a cunning look and measured about nine inches of sharp steel spear with his fingers for the benefit of those present, who quite understood its significance.

The last war-drum made on the Luapula was made to my order to be used as a school bell, and cost many pounds. Chipampaula said when he finished it and handed it over to me, " Ah, sir, this is the only drum I have made when a slave's throat was not cut and the blood used to paint the drum."

A chief's grave used to be plastered with sacrificial human blood, and blood was employed for sacrificial and sanctification purposes in connection with worship and religious services.

Blood is used at least in four distinct ways :

(1) In blood friendship.
(2) In blood sanctification.
(3) In blood redemption.
(4) In blood feuds.

Blood friendship was a thing without which, fifty years ago, no chief would permit a European to pass through his country. It consisted in making an incision in the arms of the two prospective friends, mixing the blood from the arm of each in native beer, which each had to drink to seal the friendship. Blood feuds were common until recently. I remember a man asking for Government permission to blot out a whole family because one member of it had killed a blood-relation of his own. Redemption by the shedding of blood was also common. The threat " I shall take his blood " was equivalent to " I shall take his life."

There is abundant evidence obtainable about the Bantu belief in the doctrine of immortality and that the soul after death goes to God. When a man dies they say, *Waya kuli Lesa*, " He has gone to God." After a brief interval they say, *Wafika kale*, " He has arrived," death being a journey. Some say, *Lesa wamupoka*, " God has received or taken him." The little grain and other offerings that one sees on the graves of departed Bantus are, they say, " to enable the defunct to buy fire, or light, from God," *Kushita mulilo kuli Lesa*.

One hears natives calling each other " the sons of God." The great leader and founder of the Wemba nation of N.E. Rhodesia was called " the Son of God." One sees from this and previous remarks on the God name that the Bemba people think of God not only as a creator, fierce and implacable, but also as a universal father, and His people *bana ba Lesa*, " the children of God."

Natives are given to using oaths of many kinds, and in early days native commissioners utilised these and their sanctity to swear men in court and get them to be serious and tell the truth. " By my dead father and mother who have gone West." " By the gun that took my brother's life." " By the sharp knife that cut my uncle's ears off." " By the graves of our dead." " By the spirit world." " By Hell." " By God." " As true as God sees me." " Cut my throat and I won't lie " (with finger drawn diagonally across neck). " By the smallpox." " By the sleeping sickness." " As true as God hears us." " May God strike me dead," and many more.

" God is there," says a native, pointing upwards. Always in speaking of the place where God dwells and in their folk-songs they speak of God as " coming down." The Amazulu (or Zulus) means " the people of the skies." They declare that " the stars are the eyes of the dead looking down on the world where they once lived and taking an interest in all." There is a legend that " the sun and the moon had one mother and the mother died, and on the way to the funeral they quarrelled and the sun threw handfuls of mud at the moon, which are represented by the moon's spots. The evening star is the moon's wife because she follows behind the moon. The evening star, by feeding the moon with only a little food, is the cause of its smallness (new moon). The morning star gives the moon, her husband, plenty to eat, hence his increased size (full moon)." The native has a wholesome fear of spirits and fetish medicines. To primitive races nature is an unsolvable problem, it is appalling ! He is in continual dread of the presence of dangers he does not know, cannot measure, and hence is powerless to guard against. He has intelligence to believe more and fear more than brute beasts. Just as the Apostle Paul said to the Athenians, " Sirs, I perceive that in all things ye are *too superstitious*," or as the Greek word puts it, " too reverent to the demons," so it is to-day among Bantus. What applied to the Greeks of St. Paul's time applies with a hundredfold more force to the Bantu races of Bantuland : Too Superstitious.

CHAPTER XXIV

Arabs & Islam

TO speak of Arabs and Islam in Central Africa is to be misunderstood if the reader has in his mind men of the type of Saladin or Abd el Kadir—men who were scholars and soldiers and who possessed the noblest traits of humanity; or mosques with great glittering domes and minarets which shimmer in the bright African sunlight, such as are found in Algiers, Tunis, and Tripoli. The Arab slave traders of Central Africa—with the exception of a few—have been coast men, usually half-breeds born of Arab fathers and slave mothers, while the bulk of Arab personnel were men who attached themselves to them from religious and mercenary motives. We call them Swahilis, men of the *Sawahil* or coast. These, as a rule, were ex-slaves who had obtained their freedom by excelling in cruelty to their one-time slave brothers and sisters during village raids far inland or *en route* to the coast with caravans. The mosques we find in the interior of Africa are similar to the mission village schools, built of mud and poles, and kept in repair by the local natives. In these the faithful gather for daily prayer, and there once a week on Friday— the Moslem Sunday—a few lessons are read from the prayer book and a sermon is given by the *Mallim* with frequent quotations from well-known parts of the Koran.

Arabs have lived and traded along the East Coast of Africa for more than a thousand years, though, until the sixteenth century, they never travelled far inland. From then the lucrative slave trade to provide boys for eunuchs and girls for concubines to fill the harems of Egypt, Arabia, Persia, and even India, attracted increasing numbers of ships to the East Coast, and some of the more daring of these traders went inland with armed caravans, and founded trading colonies in prosperous centres such as Uganda, Tanganyika, Rhodesia, and the Congo. In journeys from the West to the East Coast of Africa I have met Arab traders everywhere, Angola, the Congo State, North Rhodesia, and Nyasaland. Wherever they went they had an ever obvious twofold primary object, viz. to establish Islam and foster the slave trade, and all " in the name of God the Merciful, the Omnipotent," etc. The irony of it reminds one of European nations who not so long ago were engaged in the same slave trade, buying and selling men, women, and children for work on cotton, coffee, and cocoa plantations : " By the grace of God." I have met many Arabs and known not a few personally, and I have ever found them hospitable, courteous, and entertaining, and it was only when the question of the slave trade came up that bitter words resulted and hard things would be said. It certainly was a relief to meet and mingle for a few days occasionally with well-dressed, clean, polite Arabs, after living, month in, month out, with dirty, degraded, undressed, devil-worshipping Bantus.

In 1903 I met Jumbe of Kotakota. He was one of the greatest Arabs of Nyasaland, and he kindly evacuated his own house for me, provided bed and food, and entertained me with proverbial Arab hospitality during the week I spent there. I visited the mosques and schools, of which there were several, and there on his *baraza* of an evening, with his great men and himself, we discussed the " palmy old days " before missionaries and Government officials appeared on the scene, tolling the death knell of departing,

never-to-return slavery and Arab dominion. It was there
I met the local magistrate, my old friend, Mr. Alfred J.
Swann, whose thrilling book, *Fighting the Slave-hunters of
Central Africa*, is well worth reading. On his verandah
we compared notes and had long reminiscent chats of the
early days and life on Tanganyika, and about his experiences
with Tipu Tib and the great gentleman Arab, Rumaliza.
I stayed a few days on my way East that same year (1903)
with Abdullah Ibn Suleiman at his town in N.E. Rhodesia,
near Lake Mweru. He was one of Tipu Tib's clique who
had the good sense to recognise the *force majeure* and to
avoid raising a gun against the British officers of N.E.
Rhodesia. Luckily, he was in the administrative district
of a man who knew Arabs and spoke Swahili fluently.
He is the only Arab chief that remains to-day in N.E.
Rhodesia. Selim Ibn Raschid and a number of lesser
Arabs I have met again and again on my frequent peregrin-
ations up and down the Luapula River. These came into
Rhodesia from German East Africa and settled as traders
near my home at Johnston Falls. Their repeated gunpowder and gun-running into the Congo, and their general
disregard for British laws, led to their eventual expulsion.
Teleka and Muruturula I met at the south end of Tanganyika twenty-six years ago, and I can still remember the
heads stuck on poles around Teleka's walled town. As
we had to cross Tanganyika in a steel Government boat
Teleka supplied us with a crew of Arab sailors, who took
us over to Abercorn. We were three days in getting across,
and as the boat was full of ivory, which rolled about,
and had no keel, caught as we were in one of Tanganyika's
typical storms, we lost control and it nearly cost us our lives.
The " us " refers to the Government official Mr. Knight,
Fred S. Arnot, and myself.

Between Mweru and Tanganyika lakes there used to be

half a dozen *tembe*, or walled towns, occupied and utilised by Arabs and Arabised Bantus engaged in the slave trade. These were loopholed and bastioned, with look-out loopholed towers at intervals round the town. In my journeyings I used to sleep in these. The houses of the principal Arabs were usually fitted with massive, beautifully carved arabesque doors, the envy of all Europeans. Many a plucky, hard fight has been put up by Arabs inside these walled towns. One of the greatest Arab wars in these parts was that fought round Karonga on Lake Nyasa against three Arab chiefs in three strategically built walled towns. Sir H. H. Johnston, Capt. Lugard, and other now notable men, besides traders and missionaries, helped in the struggle, which was one for the supremacy of Europeans, or Arabs, in Nyasaland and Northern Rhodesia. They were defeated, and the head Arab, Mlozi, was hanged. Karonga was the door to Rhodesia and through it poured the Arab hordes, who fed the interior Arabs and native chiefs with guns and gunpowder, while they in return sent out great and regular gangs of slaves which, with ivory, formed the currency.

At the north end of Mweru there lived several Arabs, including Kafindo and Palangwa. On Kilwa Island at the south end of the lake lived Simba (the lion) in a stone-walled town, the only stone wall I ever saw in Central Africa. On the mainland lived his lieutenant, Sename, a Rugaruga, and the terror of the district of North Katanga. Frequently polite messages used to reach us at Luanza to say that "Simba and his men were coming along on a visit to cut our throats," Arab fashion, *ku Chinja*, as poor Emin Pasha was treated by an Arab called Kibonge about the same time. This same Arab, Simba, fought the Belgians twice and repulsed them with heavy losses. Later, as remarked on in *Early Days of North-East Rhodesia*, the British magistrate at Kalunguisi, at Simba's invitation, went across and hoisted the British flag, so that Kilwa Island is not Belgian to-day, but British territory. Simba's end was tragic. He who had prepared and meted out death to so many was destined to end his own life by his own hand. While directing work in his rice field one day, turning, his revolver went off accidentally and he fell dead, the bullet going through a vital spot. Natives declared the white men killed him by their magic.

Another old Arab I knew well was Chiwala away up the Luapula. He had a very large walled town, and with his rascally lieutenant, Chipembere, devastated the countries far and near for slaves and ivory. His town was in the Congo and he was visited twice by Belgian officers and pressed to take the flag. He refused, and instead attacked the State forces, chased them, and plundered their tents and goods. These Arabs were well armed, being supplied with arms and ammunition by the Portuguese at Tette, on the Zambesi. They also had two cannon, which they used, and which were taken later by the Belgians. Captains Brasseur and Verdickt, with an artillery officer, and a big force, attacked Chiwala, who fought hard, and at the beginning of the fight Capt. Brasseur was killed by a bullet from Chipembere. He was shot from a bastion at 300 yards, on seeing which Verdickt, one of the bravest of men, sounded the charge and took the town by storm. The fight was fierce and bloody, and many of the leading Arabs escaped, including Chiwala and Chipembere. The latter, who is alive to-day, is chief of a big village in N. Rhodesia, near Ndola, but old Chiwala is dead. I saw him several times at Ndola before he died, and the last time found him lying on his *angarib*, or bed. He was quite blind. " *Kwaheri Chiwala, tutaonana tena. Mwenyiezi Muungu akurehemia* " ("Good-bye, Chiwala ; please God we shall meet again. May God have mercy on you "), were almost my last words to him, to which he replied : " *Kwaheri Bwana wangu, rafiki yangu* " (" Good-bye, my master, my friend "). Twenty slave boys and girls were handed over to my care on Capt. Verdickt's return from the fight at Chiwala. Some of these are grown up and married and have families and come along to visit me from time to time with little presents in memory of kindness in the old slave days. The State army that fought Chiwala was composed of cannibals, and as they passed my house at Mwena they were laden with bags slung over their shoulders and on their backs, from which projected arms, pieces of legs, and other parts of bodies on which they were feasting. They had been feasting on human flesh of the killed all the way back, the report of which struck terror into the hearts of the natives along the N.E. Rhodesian border.

Unlike the Bihéans of Angola, the Arabs usually settled down beside some powerful or small chief, and made a trading centre. There they traded, and when ivory and slaves were sufficient they sent off caravans to the coast, which brought back guns and powder and other trade goods. After a time of peaceful penetration, having ingratiated themselves with the people, and having built a walled village, the armed Arabs one peaceful morning would attack their erstwhile hosts and friends, killing their men and carrying off women and children. Other villages around, seeing the futility of fighting such strong foes, would, " to save their heads," as they put it, carry ivory and slaves to them and obtain whatever peace terms the Arabs cared to impose. It had to be peace at any price. From then on raids in the more distant villages were the order of the day, while the locals, turned into Arab servants, shared in the plunder. Thus mushroom Arab kingdoms were brought into being and built up throughout Central Africa. I said to Chipembere one day : " Look here,

Chipembere, how many human beings have you killed with your own hands? Hundreds?"—thinking I had hit the mark. He laughed a deep, sepulchral laugh as he said from his throat : " No, Bwana. Thousands, not hundreds." If rumour be true, his estimate is a by no means exaggerated one. Tipu Tib and Rumaliza were the two most powerful Arabs in Central Africa. The father of Tipu Tib was Hamad Ibn Mohamad, a half-breed Arab of Zanzibar, while his mother was a full-blooded interior slave from Tanganyika. His name, Tipu Tib, meant " whistling bullets," from the large amount of shooting that took place wherever he went. Rumaliza means the " finisher off." He usually finished off everything, leaving only empty villages. He was a pure Arab, reputed a gentleman in manner, quiet, courteous, and even cultured. He saved the lives of Europeans again and again because he would not condescend to bandit laws. He and Tipu Tib helped missionaries and travellers times without number, and but for their help Stanley and his party would have perished on the upper reaches of the Congo. Tipu Tib first entered the Manyema country and the West in 1877, the same year as Stanley crossed Africa from Zanzibar to the° Congo mouth. The Upper Congo was at one time an Arab state under Tipu Tib and his armies ; or perhaps I should say his armed trading forces. When Stanley reached the Congo he found Tipu Tib and his Arabs in power, so that he required their help, which they gave at a big price. Nevertheless, they gave it. It is true that out of 600 porters sent by the Arabs to help Stanley, 200 deserted. The Arab chiefs, however, could not (as Swann points out) be fairly blamed for either Major Bartelott's death or any failure of the expedition, as Stanley later blames Tipu Tib and them. At any rate, willy-nilly, Stanley virtually made Tipu Tib temporary governor of the Congo State, with a salary of £3000 a year. When later on he sent forces to occupy the country, the Arabs naturally resented their coming and this resulted in what was called "the Arab war." This was brought to a successful termination by Capt. Dhanis (afterwards Baron Dhanis) and the hordes of Arab soldiers were taken without delay and incorporated into the new State army to be composed of Moslem Swahilis and cannibal Batetelas, a force of some 17,000 men.

What kind of chicken came out of this egg we shall see later. Sometimes, as natives say, snakes and crocodiles as well as birds are hatched from eggs, and this time the egg produced *a brood of snakes*. Meanwhile, the old lingo of Chimoyo we all spoke died, and Swahili as a lingua franca took its place. White men learned it, natives in far-away districts picked it up, and it became the Esperanto of the Congo State. At a *poste* on the Kasai River, in 1894, owing to some grievance of, I believe, an Arab woman, plus corporal punishment meted out to soldiers for serious offences which under Arab dominion had been ignored, the Moslem Swahili soldiers revolted and were later joined by the cannibal Batetela. This resulted in a serious mutiny in which over thirty Belgian officers lost their lives, one of whom, Capt. Bellen, was a personal friend of my own. These revolters went from *poste* to *poste* burning buildings, killing whites, and taking all arms and ammunition found. They razed town after town to the ground and destroyed the inhabitants, settling for a long time on the Lualaba River. Cannibalism became rampant and the terrible stories that reached our ears at Luanza where I lived have been depicted for English readers in sufficiently lurid colours by Crawford, and may be read in his book. Batta, an old Batetela soldier, was one of the worst type of cannibals. He would catch a woman on the road, kill her, cut her up, and bring her home for consumption in his hut. He it was who carried his own baby up to the Commandant one day, saying: "Sir, I haven't tasted baby beef since I left my own country. I want permission to eat my baby." After years and years of big districts being devastated by Moslem and cannibal revolted soldiers, during which our own lives were more than once threatened, Major Malfeyt, with strong State forces, drove them back in battle after battle, further and further towards Angola, until finally they made their last stand and eventually capitulated on the Luburi River. Thus ended the military mutiny chapter of the Congo, which was essentially due to Arabs and Islam, and which cost the lives of so many brave Belgian officers.

Arab power in Central Africa has been broken. Congoland, Rhodesia, and Nyasaland are now for ever free from the menace and possible domination of Moslem Arabs. The Arabs we have known who swaggered, turbanned, in their white *kanzus*, dangling silver swords and jewelled revolvers and daggers, the rulers of the land, their only boast that " the gun is king," have now become absorbed and are now almost quite unrecognisable. One hears that they make good engine-drivers and stokers. I met one such on a Katanga train not long ago. We talked of the old days before the iron horse began to spin his iron web from east to west and north to south. He could only say like many another of his ilk, with a sigh for the old golden days, " *Ah! Bwana wangu, tumeshindwa*" (" Alas, master, we are beaten ").

CHAPTER XXV

The Story of the Katanga

PAST

BY an apt philological coincidence, the Katanga signifies in local parlance *the leading country*, and the aborigines who, from time almost immemorial, have lived among and worked the copper hills are called the *Ba-Sanga*, which means "the discoverers." Where they came from originally, and when they first discovered this rich copper country, would doubtless, if traceable, take us back to a date coeval with the Bantu migration. The earliest local history locates them where they are to-day. All that is known of the Katanga prior to about fifty years ago is found in the language, legends, and camp fire literature of the tribal inhabitants, and the stories of a few travellers and traders. For over a century Katanga was known to the Arabs and Portuguese and current legend avers that many of the early kings of Uganda were buried in copper coffins made from Katanga copper.

In 1886 Arnot wrote that "The Arabs have been long in communication with the 'Garenganze' country, known as Katanga, famous all over Eastern Africa for its copper and salt. Caravans come from Lake Tanganyika and the north for copper to supply the markets of Uganda."*

* See A. J. Swann's *Fighting the Slave Hunters in Central Africa*. Mr. Grohun explains the name "Tanganyika" as embodying a legend of a copper trader from Tanga (Katunga), who found a spring which native tradition held sacred, and by interfering with it caused it to burst its bounds and become a lake.

Copper hoes were in continuous and universal use until about thirty-five years ago, when they commenced to be replaced by iron hoes which were manufactured by the Lubans, and the Ushi tribe on the east side of the Luapula River. It is believed that certain families possessed the lost art of copper-hardening but that the secret of this art died with them; Arnot in his book, *Garenganze*, 1886, says: "The copper mines are wrought and the copper smelted out of the ore by certain families. This business is handed down from father to son and the instructions of the forefathers are followed with the greatest accuracy. At one place the copper is cast in the form of a capital H, and the angles of this figure are perfect. At other times it is cast in the form of a Maltese Cross, the mould being made in the sand by the workers with their fingers; and out of twenty casts from such moulds scarcely one-eighth of an inch difference is discernible. The malachite from which the copper is extracted is found in large quantities on the tops of bare rugged hills. In their search for it the natives dig little round shafts seldom deeper than fiftee to twenty feet." (A friend of mine who was manager at the Star of the Congo mine tells me there are native shafts eighty feet deep to water level). "They have no lateral workings, but when one shaft becomes too deep for them they leave it and open another." These words were written over thirty-five years ago when the Katanga native copper trade was in progress. Traders from Uganda, Stanley Falls, Angola, the Zambesi, and Zanzibar, as well as Nyasaland, met and mixed in this great Central African copper market. Again Arnot says: "At Msidi's capital I have met with native traders from Uganda, the Unyamwezi country, the Ungala to the east of Tanganyika, the Luba country as far down as Stanley Falls, the basin of the Zambesi, Zumbu, Bihé, and Angola, as well as Arabs from Lake Nyasa and Zanzibar. Copper, salt, ivory, and slaves, are the chief articles of commerce. In exchange for these Msidi purchases flint-lock guns, powder, cloth, and beads, besides many other curious things that these natives and Arab traders bring. It is, indeed, quite an entertainment when Msidi opens out his stores and exhibits his treasures, in doing which he seems to take a peculiar pleasure. His collection contains tins of meat unopened, musical boxes, concertinas, guns, and pistols, all kinds of opera glasses, scientific instruments (generally out of order), trinkets of every imaginable description, watches, and jewellery; also cast-off clothing, varying in quality and colour from the sombre blue of the London policeman's uniform to the gorgeous dress of some Portuguese governor." Copper axes, spears, knives, beads, with copper wire of many gauges besides ornaments, rings, and decorations for powder horns, belts, etc., show but a few of the many uses to which Katanga copper was put.

Everywhere all through these countries just referred to, any and all of the above forms of manufactured copper were used as a currency in travelling. I have used them on several journeys from Katanga to Angola, and vice versa, otherwise travelling would have been both difficult and expensive. Although the Katanga of to-day comprises a congeries of tribes whose origin, languages, and customs are allied and similar, the people who claim undisputed aboriginal rights are the Ba-Sanga. Their principal chief is Mpande, whose capital, thirty years ago, lay alongside the site of the present Kambove mine. They were famous elephant hunters, and Mutwila, the brother of Mpande, again and again brought down his three bull elephants per diem. Elephants were once so plentiful in the vicinity that at one hunt on the Lufira near Sampwe two hundred elephants were killed in a few days.

LAKE MWENE CHIEF, KATANGA.
HEAD-DRESS STYLE, BANTU WOMAN.

MATIEMVO, THE GREAT CHIEF OF
LUNDALAND.
CONGOMAN WITH TWO HORN FETISHES
HANGING DOWN IN FRONT.

Buffalo in thousands and nearly every kind of game used to roam the Katanga plains until 1892, when, after Msidi's death, the rinderpest swept over the land and exterminated the larger fauna save elephant. When I lived at the Lufoi River the game was so tame around there that they used to come up to the front of the house where I lived. I have sat on the verandah of the house and watched herds of game feeding all round. The plains there used also to be black with buffalo and most kinds of game.

Next to Mpande in importance were two other large chiefs. Mutwila, Mpande's brother, who stockaded himself on an island on the Lufira and defied the State forces under Captain Brasseur, though he was eventually driven out and was pacified. Mulowanyama (whose name means the game wizard) was a veritable modern Nimrod who lived in the caves towards the Lualaba West, into which he was driven and killed by a strong State force under Lieut. Froment. Froment was also killed in the attack at the cave's mouth. For previous offences against Msidi Mulowanyama had his ears cropped off by order of the chief for insolence, and this insult he never forgave. For this he hated Msidi and his tribe, the Ba-Yeke, with a fierce, implacable hatred. The last time I saw him was twenty-five or more years ago, when I remember he wore a turban to cover the disfigurement.

The Ba-Sanga are surrounded by a number of other tribes whose language and customs are akin. I refer here to the administrative area of the Katanga. Southwards as far as the British boundary at Ndola live the Balamba, whose three principal chiefs are Katete, Ntenke, and Dilanda. This tribe was under tribute to Msidi, who periodically raided the villages to keep up his supply of slaves for the East and West Coast markets. Part of the Balala and Baushi tribes live round the south bend of the

Luapula River. Eastwards towards the Luapula River live the Batembwe and Bashila tribes ; the latter, a fishing folk, are the originators of the great secret society called Butwa, already described. North-east, along the western slope of the Kundelungu range, live the Balomotwa, a mountaineer tribe, who are great game and honey hunters. They cultivate the rich fertile valleys at the mountain foot which are enriched by the annual wash of the rainy season from the hills.

Northward lives one of the greatest tribes of Central Africa, the Baluba, who are of undoubted Semitic origin. The name Baluba means "the lost tribe," and their language and customs have many Hebrew affinities. Their name for, and idea of, God, with their word for water, and people, and many other words and ideas, show their Semitic strain. West of, and along the Western Lualaba River live the Basamba and the Balunda tribes, whereas further south, along the Lualaba on both banks, live the Bena-Kaonde, whose full-dress name is Benakaondebamulundampanda. This Teuton-like tribal name describes the origin of the people and has reference to the Tower of Babel story. The legend runs : " Away back in the world's history our ancestors were occupied in building a great tower (*chamba*) to reach heaven. While they built the white ants were at work on their wooden pillars, and down they came one after the other. They struggled on, adding pillar to pillar, but the white ants were more successful than they, and after years of labour, down came their tower, leaving them nothing but the long name by which they now describe themselves."

Last and not least in the congeries of tribes that compose the heterogeneous population of the Katanga, and one that has all to do with the past five decades of development, is the Ba-Yeke, an exotic people from the north end of Tanganyika, and who, under their chief Msidi, founded an empire that has held sway for nearly half a century. The personal, family, and clan history of this mushroom autocrat, where he came from, and how he obtained and retained possession of this great tract of rich country reads like a chapter from the Spanish conquests of Peru and Mexico.

Msidi was a son of Mwene Kalasa (Lord Kalasa), who was a minor chief under Mirambo, the king of the Nyamwezi country on the east side of Tanganyika. His tribe, which lived at the north end of the lake, was called the Basumbwa. Msidi's father, Kalasa, was a copper trader who did business in Uganda and often travelled to the East Coast in pursuit of trade. He also made frequent journeys to the Katanga, and a close friendship sprang up between him and the old chief Mpande. On one occasion Msidi, who was Kalasa's second son, made a trip to Katanga instead of his father. Mpande had just been attacked by bands of marauding Balubas under a powerful chief from the north who invaded his country. Msidi came to the rescue with four guns, a new weapon of war, unheard of before, and attacked the Lubans, killing many of them, the remainder fleeing home northwards. The old Sanga king was so pleased that he decided to reward Msidi handsomely. He did so, handing him over large presents of ivory and requesting him to return to Katanga as soon as possible. Msidi, seeing and seizing every advantage to be derived from Mpande's friendship, returned to his home in the Nyamwezi country, and after a stay there he started again for the Katanga with his wife and children and such friends as were willing to follow him. On reaching the Katanga again he found that his friend Mpande had grown old and feeble, and Msidi promised to remain in the country to receive the chieftainship that had been promised him for his help in driving off the Balubas. Shortly after this the chief, perceiving that his end was near, gave up to Msidi the Omande shell—which answers to a European crown—and installed him as chief of the Ba-Sanga. In the exercise of his newly acquired power, Msidi put to death every one who opposed him, and all who were likely to do so, and carried aggressive warfare into all the countries adjacent. He defied even the powerful chief Kasembe on the eastern bank of the Luapula River, who had formerly received tribute from the Sanga chief. Kasembe then determined to punish Msidi for his rebellion, and to this end he invaded his country. Msidi, however, was successful with the help of Angola traders from Bihé in resisting Kazembe and asserting his independence. He next added to his kingdom the Luba country to the north, and encouraged the immigration of refugees from the Lunda country who were ready to flee from the oppression of the great Mwate Yamve power, now nearly extinct. Thus by fair means or otherwise Msidi gathered round him a large number of followers, inviting also many of his own tribe from the Nyamwezi country to come and join him and occupy prominent positions in the new kingdom he had thus so recently founded.

Several Portuguese travellers passed through the Katanga, pre-eminent among whom were two naval officers named Capello and Ivens, who took the only existing photo of the old chief Msidi, which appears in their book, *D'Angola ao contra costa*. They also give a description of the country with a few good pictures of game and native life.

Later, Herr Reichard, a German traveller, reached the source of the Lufoi River, overlooking Msidi's capital, but he, hearing of Msidi's doings, returned north with his caravan. About 1885 Fred Arnot came to the Katanga in search of a healthy and suitable mission centre for work,

He lived for three years alone with Msidi at the most interesting period of the Katanga history—which story may be read in his modest narrative called *Garenganze* (publ. Pickering and Inglis), and in his Biography (publ. Seeley, Service and Co.). He was relieved by Messrs. C. A. Swan and Faulkner ; then came Thomson, Lane, and Crawford, after which came three Congo Free State expeditions to annex the Katanga on behalf of King Leopold and the newly founded State. Previous to this Mr. Alfred Sharpe reached the Katanga on a diplomatic mission, that failed owing to an Englishman, Captain Stairs, in the employ of King Leopold, intercepting the letter sent by Msidi to recall Sharpe with the British flag.

As Katanga had been included in the newly founded Congo Free State three expeditions were sent there to hoist the State flag, to establish stations, and take over the country officially. One expedition was in charge of Captain Bia, who died at Ntenke near the present town of Elisabethville ; the second was in charge of Capt. Delcommune, and the third, from the East Coast, was in charge of Capt. Stairs, who accompanied Stanley on his trans-African trip. All sorts of pacific measures were tried on Msidi, liberal presents and promises, etc., but the old chief repelled all attempts at conciliation, and shifted and shuffled until all patience was exhausted. At last two officers were despatched by Stairs to bring the king to terms, the Marquis de Bonchamps and Capt. Bodson, with a body of soldiers. Bodson approached Msidi to insist on his accompanying them to the head camp ; Msidi made a thrust at the captain with a sword, and the captain, seeing treachery, shot Msidi dead with his revolver, and was himself shot by Masuka, one of the chief's soldiers. Msidi's head was cut off, the blue flag with the golden star (*le drapeau bleu avec l'étoile d'or*) was hoisted on the hill overlooking Msidi's capital.

Capt. Bodson was buried with military honours, and a mountain peak near there (Bunkeya) commemorates his name (*le pic* Bodson). Thus ended the *coup d'état* of 1892 by virtue of which the Katanga is to-day a Belgian colony.

Capt. Legat established the first *poste* on the Lufoi River where I lived. He retired and was succeeded by Capts. Brasseur and Verdickt, who later removed the *poste* to Lukafu. Lieuts. Serckel and Delvienne were their under-lieutenants and helpers, and did a lot of rough pioneering work. As stated earlier, Capt. Brasseur was killed in a fight at the Arab town of Chiwala, near to the present Chinama on the Luapula River. He was buried by Verdickt and Delveux, though the grave would be difficult to find. Lieut. Froment was killed at the caves in the fight referred to previously. Perhaps one day we shall find in the well-laid-out centre of the town of Elisabeth-ville *une pierre commemoratif* to remind the present-day dwellers of the Katanga of the three captains B.—Bodson, Bia, Brasseur, with Froment and other brave Belgian officials who laid down their lives in the early pioneering days to open up the country.

Capt. Van den Broeck and others followed, taking up the hoe laid down by Bodson, Bia, and Brasseur, and furrow after furrow is being dug up, seeds are being sown of mining, commerce, and other industries. Let us hope that—whatever the past has been—the Katanga will, in the near future, be one of the garden colonies of Central Africa—a model of industry, enterprise, and commerce; and, may I add, that along with our civilising efforts the missionary enterprise will not be forgotten, and that the true foundation of society—the Church of Christ—may raise its head high where the old regimes of the past, which we have sought to describe throughout the book, have held sway from time immemorial.

Nearly thirty years have passed since some of us came to the Katanga, a Katanga given over to war, bloodshed, and the horrors of the slave trade. The fairy wand of civilisation has touched and transformed the land and people almost beyond our recognition. If those we have watched dancing the weird, wild *Tomboka* war-dance, with heads in their hands, or dangling from their mouths or at their waists, fresh back from the slaughter of Lubans, Lambas, or Sangas, who burned their wizards and witches under our eyes and threw their children to the crocs and hyenas, could appear among us to-day and see the changes that have come over the land of their birth—what would they say?

PRESENT

Katanga is still *the leading country* of Central Africa and the Belgian people its modern *discoverers* and inhabitants. The railway known as the C.F.K. (Chemin de fer du Katanga) runs through it from the Rhodesian boundary to Bukama on the Lualaba River, where steamers ply carrying the commerce of the interior : palm oil, nuts, ivory, and produce of many kinds, not least being the boat-loads of *Africa's great asset*—workmen for the mines and farms under the care of a well-organised, though still young, Labour Bureau called locally the B.T.K. In Elisabeth-ville, the rising metropolitan town of the Katanga, are to be found natives from far-off tribes, including Bangala, Azande, Budja, Basoko, and many other cannibal repre-sentatives of the Equator, each with their peculiar tribal tattooings, styles of hairdressing, and teeth chipping, filing, and extraction. Many copper mines are being worked, also tin mines, gold and diamond mines, with the great coal-fields of Sankishia on the Lualaba River, now producing large quantities of coal, for which previously the Katanga was dependent on South Africa. A number of towns have sprung up along the railway, and there is a fair-sized white population of a very miscellaneous and cosmopolitan character.

There are not only Belgians, who naturally preponderate, but there is also a proportion of Britishers, Italians, Greeks, French, Russians, Spaniards, Portuguese, and Jews from many lands. There are Indians, Arabs, Turks, and a sprinkling of many different tribes from Capetown to the Senegal. Elisabethville is the official centre of the Katanga, with Government and mining offices and buildings that would do credit to South Africa. It is well laid out in streets and avenues with a boulevard, all named after notable men, rivers, lakes, and tribes. In the centre of the town and not far from each other are the law-courts, Government offices, post office, club, theatre, and a Belgian and British bank, plus a British Vice-Consulate.

There are great trading companies such as the S.C.M., Société Commercial et Minière, the Belgo-Katanga, the Mercantile Anversoise, the Intertropical, and a dozen others. There are three churches, an American Methodist Episcopal Mission, and a cathedral is being built by M. de Hemptinne of the Benedictine Fathers, who is Préfet Apostolique of the Katanga. There are three European and two native hospitals with an adequate medical staff and service. There are seven hotels and an unfortunately large number of " Bars." There are two weekly papers, *L'Étoile du Congo* and the *Efforts de Katanga*, and there is a daily paper called the *Journal du Katanga*. All three are printed in French with part in English to meet the need of the large English-speaking population. The public works and mines department have made a network of hundreds of miles of good motor roads. The native interests are well looked after by a number of intelligent, sympathetic judges and Government officials, and if there is any leaning shown towards natives in the law-courts it is certainly in the direction of leniency.

The native problem in the Katanga is now in large measure recognised by men at the heads of departments, and let us express the hope that the Government's recent policy of trying to understand and enter into the perplexing and ever-emerging native questions will be rewarded with success, so that *Africa's chief and permanent asset,* its population, may live contented and peaceful throughout the Katanga under the ægis of the Belgian flag.

CHAPTER XXVI

Sport & Travel

IN 1892 I set out from Benguella on the West Coast for my first trip into the interior of Africa with a native caravan, and spent my first Christmas alongside a slave camp by the Catumbella River. At that camp I contracted my earliest malarial fever with a temperature of 105°, and before I reached the Bihé I was taking quinine in 35-grain doses that made me stagger along the path like a drunken man. The use of the daily prophylactic 5-grain doses of quinine we all take to-day was then unknown.

Turning my back on the sea, thirty-five miles from the first camping place we crossed the Esupwa Pass through the "door of Noah's Ark," as the Bihéans call it, and thence, climbing all the time for 150 miles, we reached Bihé—a white man's land—where I passed my first eighteen months in Africa.

While there, the call from Katanga reached me in the form of a pressing letter from the Interior, and as I was the only member of the mission eligible and free to go, I responded, and turned my face east with a big slave caravan which was then on the point of starting. The thirty carriers who formed my personal equipment, and who, with the wages I gave them, would return laden with slaves and ivory, shouldered my travelling household in the form of kitchen utensils, clothing, tools, and trade goods, and in a few days we had left Bihé behind and reached the Quanza River, on the other side of which was the terrible "Hungry Country."

A crowd of natives gathered at the ferry to watch us cross and listen to the haggling over canoes and payment. I left my headman to settle, and being a good swimmer, I decided to swim across. I stripped, dived off the high bank, and struck out for the opposite shore. Foolishly, however, I forgot that African rivers are dangerously cold and that crocodiles abound, until I got fully half-way over, when in a flash it dawned on me, and with the thought of crocs and the numbness of my body, it was all I could do to reach the other bank. Once, in after years, I was hunting on the Luapula, when over went my canoe and I was plunged into the water with crocs all round me, and I had to swim ashore holding my rifle above my head.

A thousand miles on foot through hostile tribes of whose language and customs one was ignorant was a by no means enviable experience. This took me three months, and we were often held up for days with a gun at our heads by some local petty chief, who demanded tribute. We had to pay up or fight, for of course this blustering, loud-mannered " nobody " was the representative of a " powerful somebody " within call of the war drums. Besides, my carriers were never tired of quoting the Bantu proverb that " A tortoise never climbed on to a tree stump." However, with one stop at a hospitable mission station we eventually reached Katanga, where I settled *pro tem.* at the Lufoi River, and later joined D. Crawford at Lake Mweru.

Arnot, the pioneer of the Katanga, came back on a visit about this time, but his health failed, and I accompanied him to Abercorn on Tanganyika. Returning to Lake Mweru from Tanganyika, I got together a caravan of a hundred Lubans and made a seven months' journey of three thousand miles on foot to Bihé and back to bring in provisions and goods which we were in need of. On the way out west and back I was attacked and, with my caravan, fired on three times, and one night I remember a war party dancing a war dance round our camp, singing : " White man, white man, we'll dance to-morrow with your head on the end of a spear." I returned from Mweru and built a station at Msidi's capital, and after some five years in the Katanga I travelled out to the East Coast via Nyasaland and had stirring experiences by the way. We trekked through countries where the Angoni were at war with the Government, and through others in the adjoining Portuguese territory, where intertribal warfare was in progress, and I had some narrow escapes. But for the fact that my men were all armed and accustomed to fighting, events might have ended differently, and this story remained untold.

Unexpectedly and without warning we were attacked one day by an Impi of Angoni in Portuguese territory. My men loaded their guns, charged, and chased the Angoni, and as some of them did not return to camp till sundown I fear my orders were exceeded. My orders were, *unless the men were shot at, not to shoot.* The following day we were threatened several times by armed raiding parties, but got through unscathed until 5 p.m. During the morning of that day we rescued sixty-nine fugitive women and children, who were pursued by Angoni warriors, and whose villages had been burned and most of their men-folk speared. But for our timely appearance they would have been killed or captured. About 5 p.m. we ran into a regiment of Angoni who were returning from the slaughter. We could not avoid them. My men were so maddened at the sights they had witnessed that they rushed at the brutes, gun in hand, and disarmed them. I caught their Induna by the throat and held a revolver at his head. " You rascal, you have been murdering defenceless women and children," I said, and as I did so, a bundle containing two severed heads fell at our feet. I told them to hurry home and be thankful their lives were spared. I returned to my men, who were examining a pile of shields, head-dresses, spears, and battle-axes, many being stained with blood. I took several loads of these trophies to Blantyre in Nyasaland, and several to England as curios.

The two days following I shall never forget, for the whole country seemed to be ablaze. As we passed we saw, lying outside the doors of huts in deserted and burned villages, large numbers of corpses of men who had been speared while trying to escape. The blood was still oozing out of the wounds, which were mostly around the heart and neck.

We hurried on for two days more through scenes of carnage, and once during the night my own life was attempted by two warriors with stabbing spears. One of these escaped in the dark, the other was caught at my tent door and, but for my intervention, my men would have killed him. The following day I was glad to leave the rescued women and children at a mission station of the Z.I.M. in the Shire Valley and hurry on to Blantyre ; thence to the East Coast.

I went home, married, and returned again to the Katanga in 1900, and for years travelled through Angola, the Katanga, and Northern Rhodesia, gaining experiences, some of which are related in this book.

On my first trans-African trip I had no tent, but my men built a rough hut for me of branches of trees. Sometimes if the day's trek was long and the men tired, I occupied an old hut in a village, but these were usually full of vermin, and one suffered in consequence. I am not likely ever to forget an attack of tick fever I got travelling from Nyasa-land to the Luapula seventeen years ago, as a result of sleeping in native huts. One's style of camp is usually determined by tribal notions, and carriers from different countries have each their own mode of transport and standard weight of load. A West Coast porter travels in comfort and builds a daily camp composed of round huts. He will carry, plus his food and pots, a box or bale of 60 lbs. weight, but will travel no more than 10 to 15 miles a day. An Interior native usually argues, " I won't live in this hut to-morrow, so why should I trouble ? " Hence he puts up a shack that, according to a facetious native saying, " lets the nose get wet," i.e. covers every part when standing but the nose. He carries as light a load as possible—45 lbs.

An Arab's camp is usually comfortable and roomy enough to hold his goods. Swahili boys, like Congo porters, will carry from 70 to 80 lbs. weight. I have seen a man carry two loads tied together, weighing in all 120 lbs., plus food and pots, in order to get the double pay offered by the trader.

A West Coast caravan used to number anything from 300 to 1000 men, with women and boys, so that the camp was more like an organised travelling village. There was the master of the caravan with his big flag, and small traders each with their private flags. There were camp rules and regulations that had to be obeyed, and the Camp Crier announced each evening the orders for the following day's trek. Caravans travelled as big as possible for protection.

Native paths are mere ruts trodden by men from generation to generation. In the Congo, Rhodesia, and Nyasaland to-day, wide, well-kept roads have replaced some of these, and the usual form of native taxation in the initial stage of civilisation is, year by year, a month of road-making.

In early days the people who lived by river and lake were the most inaccessible and troublesome, but to-day river and lake travelling has become popular and these water peoples have become important. On Lake Bangweulu in N. Rhodesia, a flotilla of over a thousand canoes, with paddlers, was commandeered during the late war, and these carried war loads along the river from near the railhead at Ndola and over the lake through the swamps to Kasama, for the use of troops in German East Africa. The best shooting and fishing is found along these waterways, and almost any day on the West Lualaba you can see from the deck of the river steamers herds of hundreds of elephants and buffalo. On Lake Bangweulu among the marshes I have actually seen herds of thousands of Lechwe antelopes, and have brought down three with one shot of my 303°.

" Mushroom and elephant " is ringing in my ears as I remember my first experience with Jumbo Africanus. I left the lakeside with a caravan of meat-hungry boys who were smacking their lips in anticipation. We got two-thirds of the way across the Mweru-Congo range when a boy ran up to me with a large white mushroom in his hand, shouting, " Master, you're going to shoot elephant to-day." (This particular white mushroom signifies hunter's luck with elephants). An hour or so afterwards we ran into a small herd of five. I got my old Martini-Henry and a handful of cartridges and gingerly stalked His Majesty to leeward. I got to within about 25 yards of him when he scented me and turned to see what was the matter. I fired and wounded him. He charged, and I fired again. Remembering the native theory that Jumbo won't climb an anthill, I took the hint and did so myself, but in scrambling up it I rolled down to the bottom and sprained my ankle (which kept me, later, indoors for six months). I got up again, fired a few more shots, to which a native added more, and then, staggering from side to side, the magnificent brute fell over dead. A few days after there was an elephant dance at Luanza, when " mushroom and elephant " were the subjects of the song. Native hunters danced the " elephant dance " to drum and song with a tusk under the arm, going through the antics of a hunted, wounded, and dying elephant. One of the songs ran :

> " Elephant spoor is fresh
> Through the new-burnt grass,
> Breaking twigs and leaves
> For the herd to pass."

I shot my first buffalo at the north end of Lake Bangweulu, Rhodesia, in what is called the " buffalo bush." I was travelling from Nyasaland to the Luapula and cut through this spot to cross the lake. We came on a herd feeding, and as they moved off I shot this one with my new 303°. I was so surprised to see him drop stone dead with one shot that I concluded that buffalo-hunting and its dangers had been greatly overrated. I have changed my views since, and now know that buffalo is the most dangerous four-footed animal in Africa.

As I required meat to feed over 200 people I determined to make my mark on a herd of buffalo whose haunts were near the Belgian *poste* of Kasenga. I spoored them and came on the herd. I got to within some 200 yards and fired at the biggest, which was standing shoulder on. It ran and dropped, while the herd cleared off. I saw it fall and knew it must be near. The grass was three feet long and I cautiously picked up the blood spoor. I followed, looking well in front, but could see nothing at first. Going on I saw a long black body lying in the track, its head turned towards me and a wicked look in its eye. I grabbed my rifle, stuck a spear in the ground to steady my hand,

A STOCKADED VILLAGE.

The poles forming the stockade used to be decorated with human heads.

and as I did so the brute got up on to its feet, and, swerving round at me, charged, roaring, with its head down and tail in air. I fired, and it fell with a crash only a few yards from where I stood. I followed up the herd, and at about half-past five in the evening came on the buffalo in the open, with not a tree near. We wanted the meat badly, so I crawled up and taking steady aim shot one after another of the remaining five. I went over to look at them. The animal farthest off was moving, and my native threw two spears at it. It was a cow. She jumped to her feet, my man bolted, and I was left alone face to face with the wounded buffalo and not a single cartridge in my belt or gun. She charged, I dodged, she hunted me with head down, I ran, zigzagging, she after me until I got absolutely winded. I was done. I wheeled round and faced her at ten yards with empty rifle clubbed. Luckily for me she stood. She shook her head and tail and bellowed. I shook my head, waved my arm behind, and roared in an attempt to imitate the buffalo. How long we faced each other I don't know, but I kept moving backwards until I had got a little distance away, then I ran. She still stood, and later my boys came along with more cartridges from the camp, and I gave her the *coup de grâce*. A narrow shave, indeed.

Three years ago, during a famine on Lake Bangweulu, where I lived for many years, people were dying on every hand from starvation as the crops had failed. We brought many children to the station and fed them there, but in the villages the old people and the weak were going to the wall. To try and relieve the situation I went out to hunt as I had done on two previous occasions during famine. I shot some hartebeeste and water-buck and then ran on an enormous herd of buffalo (I had hunted the same herd before, when, though I followed them for four days, I did not even see them). This time I was destined to pay them back. I determined to stalk them carefully. I got up behind an anthill only a dozen yards from the herd, picked out the biggest and nearest, and raised and lowered my rifle slowly three times before I fired. The first rolled on his back with legs in air and never moved. Then the herd stampeded. I shot one, then another, then two with one shot (I was using a 400° express rifle, D.B.). I followed on and got, in all, eleven. The last was an old bull, who, when he fell, was merely stunned. My boys ran up and began sticking spears into him. He suddenly woke up, wriggled to his feet, and promptly charged us. The boys made for the nearest trees. I stood and fired, and it took five shots more to finish him. The horns are lying outside my house as I write this, a trophy and a reminder of the danger of buffalo-hunting. One white man was killed by a charging buffalo near that same place, and another I knew was charged and tossed on the horns of a buffalo, and lay on the plain where the brute left him for a day and a half. He was eventually picked up unconscious, and never quite recovered from the effects.

Hippo afford good sport when hunted in the water from canoes. On the Chifunabuli, an arm of Lake Bangweulu on the west side, I got some natives to join me with canoes and went out hippo-hunting in mid-lake. The hippo were well out, and we paddled right up to them. We got a few shots in as we chased them, the hippo diving under our canoes or coming up close to us; but though we had an exciting hunt I did not succeed in killing one, since it is difficult to aim straight from a coggly canoe. On the Luapula River the natives harpoon them, and I have seen a hippo with thirty or more harpoons sticking in his body like a giant pin-cushion.

Hippo are pugnacious, and I have been charged by them on Lake Mweru times without number, also on Lakes

Bangweulu and Tanganyika. Once while travelling on a little trading steamer that used to ply between Lake Mweru and Johnston Falls on the Luapula, on turning a bend of the river we came on a big school of hippo. We decided to steam up close to the herd and try our luck. We got safely in among them and turned off steam to wait for a good shot. They were bobbing up all round us and grunting, seemingly amused at our coming so near, when we felt something we couldn't see bumping the bottom of our boat, and lifting the little s.s. *Scotia* out of the water. The captain rushed to the engine to back out when suddenly we were lifted again and this time we saw the cause, for a big black bull hippo head with jaws open came up alongside, scraping the boat's bottom and grabbing the gunwale in its mouth. We snatched a rifle, crammed in a cartridge, just in time to fire a bullet down his throat, which made him let go and quickly submerge. We were glad to get a safe distance between us and Behemoth, and thankfully left them in undisputed possession of their favourite pool.

I once shot a cow-hippo, and as the calf refused to go away, I shot it—when cooked it was the most delicious meat I ever tasted. I got £5 locally for the hippo head, which was a fine specimen. Looking for marrow fat (for cooking) in the hippo leg bones, I found none, but after going through the other bones I found it in the lower part of the mandible.

Sable, roan, eland, and all the other bigger game I have shot, save rhino. A wounded sable is dangerous with his long scimitar-shaped horns, and I have known a lion and a sable found dead side by side.

CHAPTER XXVII

Sport & Travel (*continued*)

"HERE are lions " used to be writ large over one of the earliest maps of Africa, and the author of *Gulliver's Travels*, writing later, put it rather quaintly, though not without truth :

> " Geographers in Afric's maps,
>   With savage deserts filled the gaps,
>   And o'er inhospitable downs
>   Placed elephants instead of towns."

Many men tell of having seen lions after a few days' residence in the Interior, and our facetious Dutch friend, Pete K—— of Catumbella, returned late one night, quite scared, to say that he had seen a white lion which attacked him. We all laughed, as it had happened after a protracted dinner. I have myself seen only four live lions during twenty-nine years, and that on three different occasions when we hunted them. I wounded one and killed one with strychnine after he had eaten my cook— having previously bumped against my bed in my tent whilst I was asleep and wakened me.

At Broken Hill a Mr. Thornton got his hand and arm chewed by a lion while he was asleep in his tent, but in answer to his cries his boys rushed in and shot it. W. R. Johnstone, a Government official at Mpolokoso in North Rhodesia, twenty-five years ago, after a fight with Arabs who were smashed up and expelled, went out for a shoot the latter, seeing a big tree in front, jumped, and climbed up until it reached the top, where it clung. The lion jumped almost simultaneously, but in the spring it missed the baboon and landed in the big fork of the tree, where it got wedged. Some days after, the local natives were passing the tree and saw the dead lion in the tree-fork, and looking up they saw the baboon, dead, still clinging and looking down. It had died of fright. It is strange that Africans should call an old person *chikolwe*, "big monkey," owing to their stooping as they walk. The negro has also his views on the simian origin of humanity, and considers the baboon as a mere case of atavism.

A native hunter saw what he thought was an antelope and crawled up to shoot it. It turned out to be a leopard, which sprang at him. He dropped his gun and, catching the leopard in its spring, fell with it, breaking its back in two. I met an Arab once who was attacked by a lion, which he fought with nothing but a spear, and killed. He showed me the marks of the brute's claws on his body.

When hunting in Uganda, George Grey, one of the brothers of Viscount Grey and one of the best of Englishmen, the man who opened up the Katanga, had his promising career cut short by *Felis Leo Africanus*.

Lake Bangweulu and its surroundings might well be called a *hunter's paradise*, for there is an enormous variety of game and great herds of most kinds, besides birds of eighty different names, and I have also the names of forty different kinds of fishes. There are herds of elephant, buffalo, rhino, a small herd of giraffe, eland, sable, roan, hartebeeste (three kinds), puku, water-buck, Sititunga, and Lechwe in herds of thousands in the marshes of Lungaland and Butwaland, round the islands and at the south end of the lake.

While out shooting Lechwe and duck among the swamps

and saw what looked like a herd of eland. This turned ou
to be a troop of five lions. He crawled up and shot ther
one after the other. As he went to examine his luck,
lioness which had been only wounded came for him. He
made for an anthill and climbed up a low tree, dropping
his rifle as he did so. The lioness climbed after him and
caught him by the leg and clawed him, trying to drag him
down. He fought it while his strength lasted, but the
brute eventually pulled him down and he got into grips
with it. To save his head, he stuck his arm into the brute's
mouth. It chewed his fingers and hand, then his arm,
and mauled him badly all over the body. He eventually
threw it off and it fell, being badly wounded. He crawled
over to his rifle, crammed in a cartridge with the other
hand which was also badly torn, and raising the rifle with
his torn arm, he levelled it and fired. Both man and
lioness fell over. His native soldiers were up trees watching the struggle, but were afraid to come down. When
they saw the lioness was dead they descended from their
perches and went to their master. They bandaged him
up and carried him in a hammock to Kambole, the L.M.S.
Station, three days off, but he was so weak from loss of
blood that he died after the amputation of the arm.

At Johnston Falls, where I lived many years, a native
called Kinyanta went into a thicket near by for firewood,
and did not notice an old lion asleep at the opening. As he
came out, the lion woke up and sprang on him, clawing his
head, but being a man of powerful build he got a grip on
the lion and threw it down, crying aloud for help. The
villagers came to his aid, and found him on top of the lion.
They rushed in with their spears and finished it.

I passed a spot in Bihé years ago where a chase took
place between a lion and a baboon which cost them both
their lives. The lion ran the baboon almost to earth, when

on the Luapula, I witnessed a battle once between two bull Lechwe antelopes. A herd of these water-antelopes was quietly feeding on the green grass in an open spot among the papyrus, and while stalking other Lechwe I came upon this lot evidently holding a council of war. All at once they scattered and opened up, when two bulls sprang out, swerving, bellowing a challenge, dropped their heads and charged each other. They backed to a respectable distance, and with lowered horns they charged again and again, coming on sideways. The loud thud as their heads met and the noise of their horns in trying to lock, the scraping and tearing of ground as they fought, with the roaring and the excitement of the cows was a sight to remember. I sat in hiding and watched the battle for what seemed to me two hours, then I shot the one Lechwe, and as the other would not go away I shot him also.

The most disgusting and ungentlemanly creatures in all Africa are the crocodiles, which are half-fish and half-animal. I have again and again known them to crawl into canoes and drag natives out, and I have known them to catch fishermen who were paddling or fishing and drag them into the water. These animals frequent ferry crossings, where they hide and catch women and children as they come to draw water. I have seen one of our caravan-men caught and dragged down as he tried to reach our boat, and I know many natives who have fought crocs and bear the marks of their teeth on their bodies. A white man was once caught while swimming, and in sight of his friends, who were helpless to save him, was dragged over a sandbank in the brute's mouth, and carried off to be eaten.

Kasambanika, a lad who travelled with me, was caught by a crocodile near Chinama's village on the Luapula and dragged to the bottom of the river. The brute stowed him away under the roots of a submerged tree and left him.

He turned round to look at the boy again and again as he swam away. As the boy saw him go off for good, he crawled out, got to the surface of the water, and drew himself ashore, where he lay torn and bleeding. He has recovered, though his chest and back are badly scarred, and he boasts a new name as the result, namely, " The man who swam the river." Marolela, another boy of mine, was dragged out of his canoe by a crocodile and pulled under water. He had his hands free, and fought it, making it let go its hold by sticking his fingers into its eyes, after which he succeeded in reaching his canoe, and crawled back into it. He has great ugly teeth-marks on his chest.

I have shot crocodiles often and never considered a cartridge at them wasted. An enormous man-eater which I shot had moss on its back and one paw chewed off. This is the only crocodile photo I possess. A monster!

I was putting up a cottage of several rooms on Lake Mweru some twenty-five years ago, and to be near my work I occupied one of the unfinished rooms. The temporary doors and windows were made of reeds, and though the roof was up the ceiling space was open, and so with all the other rooms. Leopards frequently came into the other rooms, and on one occasion a leopard jumped over my head in chasing a chicken. I fired up at it in the dark and the bullet went through the roof.

At another house I occupied a leopard sprang through the calico window-frame and, falling over some empty tins in the dark, got a fright and jumped out again. My cook was chased several evenings while bringing my dinner, and was nearly caught by a lion.

One night I had gone off to sleep and my cook and houseboy were sleeping by the fire in the middle of my room, when at 2 a.m. I was roused by an unearthly noise at the other end of the house, and my boys shouting: " A

lion, Bwana, a lion in the house." I awoke and jumped
out of bed, lit a candle, and the boys blew up the fire
at which we sat crouching. The noises in the other room
made us nervy. There were intervals of quiet, then the
tramp and noise was resumed. It was pitch dark, the
village was some distance away, and the brute could have
climbed over the partition wall. I felt jumpy, and decided
that the time for action had come, so grabbing my rifle
I said to the cook, " I'll open the door and cover you with
my rifle while you run to the village and call the men."
I did so successfully, but the noise was renewed, so I decided
to have a shot at the brute myself. " Goi," I said to my
houseboy, " hold the lantern over my head and I will go
out and shoot the lion myself." " Right, sir," he replied,
so I opened the door and moved cautiously in the direction
of the lion. I got there with nerves highly strung, and was
ready to shoot the first thing that showed. To my surprise
and amusement the lion turned out to be a puppy-dog
that had got its head inside an empty 4 lb. sugar tin, and
couldn't get it out !

" Monkeys are not qualified to judge forest law suits,"
runs the proverb in Bantuland. They have certainly a
weird, semi-human appearance, so that we forgive the negro
when he says " monkeys were once human beings, like us,
but to escape work they fled into the forest and grew tails."
Hard pressed, I have shot and cooked monkey for food, but I
confess I never quite finished that meal. My Belgian
neighbours used to have a dish of monkey-stew once a
week, but it was prepared according to the magician's art,
so that you could not detect the difference between it and
venison.

I remember setting out to visit some friends and pay
my respects to the new baby, and decided to take a present
of two black monkey-skins. On the way my boy was

preparing lunch by the thicket where the black monkeys lived, and in the meantime I set out monkey-hunting. I shot a fine, big fellow, and the boy proceeded to skin him. I started lunch, but hearing a queer noise, turned round, and to my horror the monkey, who had only been stunned by the bullet, was sitting up and turning over with his fingers some inches of the skin the boy had removed to examine it. He turned to me with anything but a simian expression, with great wide-open human eyes, as much as to say, " What are you doing with me ? " Since that most gruesome experience I have never shot a monkey.

Travelling in Angola many years ago, a friend of mine went off the path to where a peculiar clicking and laughing noise was in progress. Looking over the steep bank of the Zambesi River, he saw a great crocodile with its body half out of the water looking eagerly up, with his mouth wide open, while at the end of the overhanging branch of a tree was a monkey who was playfully swinging down to the crocodile. Each time he reached the croc, snap went the great jaws, and back swung the monkey with screeches of laughter and chuckles of delight.

Famine used to follow quadrennial floods along the Luapula River and Lake Bangweulu, so to save the situation and to carry the natives through the next hoeing season I would take my rifle and shotgun and go out, not for sport, but to kill as much as possible. I fed the natives who, as a *quid pro quo*, came and cultivated a hundred acres of food that later, during another famine, saved many of their lives. My biggest bag was seventeen head of game in one day, inclusive of six buffalo. I got seventeen duck with a " right and left " the following day on a sandbank, as it was evening and they were close together preening their feathers for homeward flight. Another day I got eleven buffalo, plus hartebeeste and water-buck. Another day again

I got six eland, two hartebeeste, and a reed-buck, and another time a bull elephant that had been destroying gardens, and two hippos.

Marabout, stork, flamingoes, with cranes, cormorants, and many other kinds of big birds, including the crested crane, whose calls and antics when in love have led to the popular songs and dances adopted by the " African Butwa Musical Association "—a powerful secret society referred to elsewhere—widgeon, duck, and teal of many kinds abound, besides a variety of geese. I have seen the plains black with spur-winged and Egyptian geese during the season, and we used to dry, smoke, and salt them. Pigeons and partridges of several varieties help the larder in these shopless lands. Egrets, kingfishers, ospreys, and bewildering flocks of gaudy waterfowl live among the marshes or take up their abode in the season on uninhabited and uninhabitable islets at the north end of the lake. I have seen these islets white or blue with waterfowl eggs.

Many native songs are bird songs, or contain allusions to bird life or bird characteristics, and all bird names are, without exception, onomatopœic. Owls are looked on as birds of ill omen and are called " witches " and " death birds." Their cry is " Fwi, Fwi," which is their name, and means " Die, Die." Natives are past masters at imitating bird-calls, and need no artificial help. I have had them call guinea-fowl for me again and again, when they would flock to within a few yards of us. I can do so now myself.

The following are some Bantu bird songs :

SONG OF THE HAWK

" Hawk, Hawk, why do you cry ?
Say, have you lost your mother ?
Up in the sky, flying, flying,
There you'll find another."

Song of the little Deserted Village Bird

" The little bells are ringing,
And the little babies singing,
But a tiny bird is calling
In the village ruins near."

Song of the Sparrow

" Oh, you little sparrow
That sits on the leafy bough,
Just wait until to-morrow,
I'm after elephant now."

Song of the Night-jar

" Oh, night-jar, Oh, night-jar,
Come, stretch out your wings.
Lie low, lie low, just so, just so,
The night-jar sings."

Tiger fish is about the best angling one can get in Africa. We used to get seven to nine pounders at Johnston Falls. He is most destructive and consumes immense quantities of young fish in the season. Carp is good eating, and on a small inland lake of an evening I have caught as many as sixty-eight with my net. Caviare, made from the roes of a cod-like fish, and smoked, I have found good eating. I used to go out at nights in Africa (as I have done in Scotland for mackerel) wrapped up in a mosquito-proof coat and with lights in the bows of our canoes, when we got really large hauls of fish. The crocodile is the fisherman's enemy, and he tears their nets to get at the fish within them. The osprey, kingfisher, diver, and otter also account for a few fish.

One of the best and bravest hunters I ever knew bore the name of Richter, a well-chosen one, for he was a judge of beasts and men, and wore his black robe with dignity.

He was a gift to me by a Dutch missionary, with the sole recommendation that he had held up a hyena until his master arrived and shot it, and that he permitted no familiarity. From the first day we " hit it off " and struck up a friendship that stood the test of years. He was a little fellow, stout, with black body, short legs, long ears, and curly hair. He was a peculiar mixture of ferocity and faithfulness—a bull spaniel, a real hunter's favourite. Though he has been dead now nearly fifteen years, the natives on the Luapula River still speak of him with respect, and not a few white men remember him. Again and again I have, even after the lapse of years, to recount anew by request to his many native friends and admirers oft-told stories of his prowess on the hunting field ; of the buck he ran to earth ; of the leopards he worried, of the hyenas whose legs he bit as he chased them, and of the lion he attacked that killed him.

I have seen him on more than one occasion jump into the Luapula River, which is several hundred yards wide, full of crocodiles. Once he swam the river three times after a wounded buck, drove it on to a sandspit and fought it for over an hour until we came to the rescue with a canoe. An attack on a troop of baboons once on the Koni Hills nearly cost him his life. He returned to me torn and bleeding, but with head up and tail wagging.

Only twice did I ever see him turn away from animals, once on reaching a buffalo, and the second time after hunting a porcupine. The latter experience I don't think he ever forgot, for the quills were stuck all over him, and he looked like a pin-cushion.

One evening at about 8 o'clock a leopard sprang at his mate, Katie, a yellow wolf-dog, and bit her badly. It would possibly have killed her, but for Richter, who came for it and caught it by the under-jaw. True to the bull,

he held on while the leopard howled, helpless. It was
pitch dark, but my hunter boy came up with a grass torch,
by means of which I saw Richter and the leopard in grips.
I fired, and bowled the leopard over, when Richter let
go the brute, who was then *hors de combat*. The skin and
skull with the dog's teeth-marks adorn a corner of my
father's sanctum.

The lion that killed the plucky dog at last was prowling
around our house for something human, and my chum
used to declare that Richter saved one of our lives.

TO AN OLD RIFLE.

" You're worn in the barrel, you're gone in the stock,
 Your sights are deceptive and battered askew,
 You're foul in the breech and you're crank in the lock,
 Yet I love you far more than I loved you when new!
 I've done a fair quotum of stalking and shooting, old
  rifle, with you."

C. G.

CHAPTER XXVIII

Early Days of North-East Rhodesia

THIRTY-FIVE odd years ago when A. J. Swann wandered round Tanganyika getting chiefs' signatures to treaties and helping to establish a British hold round the Lake, the country was a no-man's land. Arabs, east and west, north and south, dominated the situation and these supplied the Wemba, Ngoni, and other warlike tribes with guns and gunpowder, by means of which for many years they preyed on each other and resisted foreign interference.

The earliest reliable local history tells that about the year 1730 the first Kazembe (Kanyimbe) came from Lundaland in the West and established himself, and people, among the Bisa and Senga tribes. In 1796 Peréira, a Portuguese traveller, visited Kazembe and about the same time the original Wemba leaders crossed from Ngwenas in the Kola country on the Eastern Lualaba River in Lubaland and settled in what was then known as Lunguland. In 1798 Dr. Laçerda, another Portuguese traveller, visited Kazembe-Lukwesa, and in 1802 Pombeiros visited Kazembe-Chireka. Again, in 1831–32 Monteiro and Gamitto, two other Portuguese, also visited Kazembe, whose name was Kapumba, son of Chireka. In 1853 another Portuguese visited Kazembe, and about 1856 the Arab, Ibn Saleh, came to Kazembe's country, who was called Chinyanta, son of Chireka, who later was succeeded by Lukwesa, also a son of Chireka. In 1862, Muonga, another son of

Chireka by a slave woman, expelled Lukwesa, and in 1867 Dr. Livingstone visited Kazembe while en route from Tanganyika to Lake Bangweulu and Katanga, and there more reliable history begins.   (Ina-Kafwaya, Kazembe's queen, referred to in the chapter on "Polyandry," was then alive and a lady of importance whose picture appears in Livingstone's *Last Journals*.)   Kazembe's capital was then not far from the spot where it is to-day, at the extreme S.E. corner of Lake Mweru.   About 1868 the Arab, Tipu Tib, appeared, fighting and travelling round the north end of Lake Mweru ; he was heading for Manyema in Congoland, where he settled.

Considering that all the European travellers who visited Kazembe (save Dr. Livingstone) were Portuguese, Portugal naturally considered that they had a first claim to the country, but like many another claim, their pretensions rested on very flimsy foundations.   On similar grounds and for like reasons one had heard them volubly claim not only Angola, but N.W. Rhodesia and the Congo. The only extant and detailed description of the now Wemba country, as it existed then, was given first by Lieut. Gerard, a French naval officer, and afterwards by Dr. Livingstone, both of whom visited the capital of the paramount chief, Kiti-Mukulu, then named Chita-pangwa, " the Uncreated One," which visits they describe in their journals with photos of the chief and country. They both circumnavigated Lake Bangweulu, from which the former returned to the East Coast and at the south end of which the latter died.

The first British station in N.E. Rhodesia, which was chosen by Sir A. Sharpe and established by Capt. Crawshay, was at Chienji, at the extreme north end of Lake Mweru, where the first British flag was hoisted.   Kidd and Bain-bridge followed him, but both died at their post, one a week after the other, and are buried at Kalunguisi. Later, the Chienji station was removed to the Kalunguisi River and administered by Dr. Blair Watson and Hubert T. Harrington, with a sub-station at Choma under Cecil Warringham. The following year, 1893, Fort Abercorn was established by Mr. Marshall with a sub-station at Sumbu, at the south-west corner of Tanganyika. H. C. Marshall was vested with powers as Consular Judicial Officer at Abercorn, and a Mr. Knight was put in charge at Sumbu. Marshall's force consisted of half a dozen Sikhs and a few trained Atonga from Lake Nyasa, for N.E. Rhodesia was, until 1895, governed from the British Central African headquarters at Zemba in Nyasaland. The country was full of Arabs, so that gunpowder and gun-running, with war and the slave trade, were in full swing in every quarter. I travelled to Abercorn from the Katanga in 1893 with Fred S. Arnot, pioneer missionary of the Brethren's Mission in Central Africa, and the three frontier posts of Choma, Sumbu, and Abercorn had their hands full, chasing, fighting, and capturing Arabs. These posts formed an outer cordon along the northern border, including the Belgian Congo and German East Africa, and many a stiff little fight was put up against Arabs, Rugarugas, and native slavers that never appeared and never will appear in print.

Many a time round the camp fires of an evening or at the fire in front of the pioneer huts of officials or missionaries, or of Andrew Laws, a Scotch ex-R.H.A. man who had seen service in India, the only existing representative of trade, have we listened to stories of fights with Arabs and natives in which the missionary and trader took an honourable part. One missionary I knew was called " the bullet maker," because he served out and made ammunition for the natives with which to defend themselves from hordes of raiding A-Wemba. The story of Laws' running fight with Sename in the Congo near Kilwa Island and of his smashing up of the walled town of the Arab Teleka, are two of a score of interesting items from the early days. Round the African Lake Corporation's store at Kituta I remember seeing several disabled natives who were employed as watchmen and did light work, having been shot and got broken limbs in these unofficial fights with slave traders and cut-throat Arabs and natives. I remember at Abercorn in 1893 seeing several gangs of Arab and other slavers in chains, some gaudily dressed in silk turbans and wearing silver swords. The original Fort Abercorn was represented by a few mud and thatch huts, offices, and a prison. These were built and the country was administered by H. C. Marshall, formerly a big-game hunter, and one of the best men I have ever met. He is to-day Acting-Administrator of the whole of Northern Rhodesia. These were the palmy days of transition, when there were no game laws, reserves, or licences necessary, and when men could and did shoot scores of elephants, the ivory of which brought good prices. In those days also there were no questions asked if a man in self-defence armed his camp carriers and burned a village, a number of men being shot on both sides. One has seen diaries of plucky prospectors which read like this : " 20th. Found a quartz outcrop and noticed indications of . . . Went on and was attacked in the afternoon by a horde of armed natives who fired on our men, wounding two and killing one. We replied shooting seven, and following them up, burned their village. 25th. Travelling along low hills crossed three streams—formation . . . Were surrounded by a band of slavers who attacked us in our camp and who shot two of our men. We made a sortie and chased them, killing five and wounding three, who fell into our hands," etc.

In 1895 Major Forbes with three other troopers trekked up across the Zambesi from the south and that year took over the administration of baby N.E. Rhodesia. He established a number of stations, forming a strong outer cordon of posts, and then others were run into the Wemba country, where the Arabs had fostered resistance among the natives. Four great chiefs, Mwamba, Kitimkulu, Mpolokoso, and Kazembe, after a number of small scraps tendered their submission, and welcomed the administration and posts at or near their various centres and capitals. Major Forbes was invalided home in 1897, and in October, 1898, Mr. Codrington came north, extending and consolidating the young colony. In 1899 the headquarters of the British South African administration was removed from Zomba to Fort Jameson in Mpeseni's country. During the transition period for three months the country was administered from Fife and Abercorn, and in 1900 Mr. Robert Codrington was made Administrator of N.E. Rhodesia, with headquarters at Fort Jameson. During these early years, as I said, British Central Africa and N.E. Rhodesia represented identical interests and were under one administration, which helped to simplify operations against the Arabs, who were the backbone of resistance and everywhere endeavoured to retard progress and the advance of the British flag. Sir H. H. Johnston, A. J. Swann, and other early pioneers, made every effort to settle matters amicably, but the Arabs, at the back of whom were many powerful turbulent native chiefs, refused to listen to reason or accept any terms save gun-terms as they called them. " Let the gun speak," or, " We only hear a gun " (*tusikia bunduki tu*), were their oft-repeated answers to all attempts at conciliation. " Guerre à outrance " was the only possible alternative, and Mlozi Kopakopa and other Arabs were smashed up at Karonga in their three

walled towns. Mlozi was hanged after trial by the Konde
chiefs and people, who had been his victims for long years,
a large part of whom had been driven into the lake to be
eaten by crocodiles while the Arabs stood by to shoot any
who might attempt to escape. Saidi Mwazungu was
hanged further south by Swann for the murder of two
Europeans. Jumbe of Kotakota, Mwasi, Makanjira, Zirafi,
and many other Arabs and underlings had their power for
evil permanently broken, and all felt the keen edge of
British justice. Thus civilisation went forward in Nyasaland, and trading companies, missionary societies, coffee
and cotton planters, joined hand in hand to help to heal
Africa's " open sore," and to keep the flag flying.

As in British Central Africa so in N.E. Rhodesia the question of Arab domination and evil influence had to be
settled once for all. A fight at Mpolokosos in the Wemba
country settled the Arabs there. Palangwa, Kafindo,
Abdullah Ibn Suleiman, with Chiwala, Simba, and many
others, were sitting on the fence watching their chance.
Simba, on Kilwa Island, Lake Mweru, fought and expelled
the Congo State forces by which he had been twice attacked, and eventually asked for the protection of the
British flag. Kilwa was thus annexed by Dr. Blair Watson
and the British flag was hoisted. Abdullah at Kabuta,
though he played fast and loose and kept a horde of Swahili
and Rugaruga robbers under leash, eventually rendered his
submission to Dr. B. Watson and accepted the flag.
Chiwala let N.E. Rhodesia severely alone, and confined his
filibustering and slave-trading expeditions to the Congo
State. On one occasion when he came to a British camp
with a conciliatory present of ivory I was present and was
asked to interpret, and tell him that if he wanted to live in
N.E. Rhodesia (he had been driven out of the Congo) he
would get short shrift if he repeated his Congo slave

practices. The Arabs Palangwa and Kafindo cleared out, and a number of others who came later, ostensibly to trade on the Luapula River near to my home, were also expelled by the Magistrate, G. Lyons, and were sent back to German East Africa, whence they came, a good riddance. Thus after a few years' hard work in N.E. Rhodesia by a small and inadequate handful of officials the only Arab remaining was old Abdullah, whose power for active harm became nil, so that, instead of trading or stealing ivory and slaves as formerly, he latterly grew rice and bred milk goats and fat-tailed sheep, for which good prices were obtained. Abdullah was one of Tipu Tib's lieutenants and representatives, and told me he knew Dr. Livingstone, of whom he spoke respectfully as Bwana Daud (or Lord David), for so he was called by the Arabs.

For many years one of the least known and most difficult and inaccessible corners of N.E. Rhodesia was Lake Bangweulu, with its many islands. The Bisa, Batwa, Baunga, and other peoples who occupied various parts of the lake were among the last—if not the very last—to submit to the Government and pay hut tax. Among their swamps and floating islands they considered themselves impregnable and immune from attack, and insulted and shot at Government officials and messengers again and again with impunity until they got a few sharp lessons. It is one of the largest of the four lakes found encircling N.E. Rhodesia. I reckon it approximately 120 miles long by about 80 miles wide, its length and width altering with the wet and dry seasons. There are large plains along the east side and at the south end, where live the three water tribes, Bisa, Batwa, and Baunga. These plains are alive with Lechwe and Sititunga antelopes, duck, and geese, and with waterfowl of many kinds. The upper surface of the boggy plains is covered with stretches of peat which, during

the grass fire season, burn steadily until the heavy rains
come and put out the fires. Enormous quantities and
many varieties of good fish are caught everywhere, besides
fresh-water shrimps and otters, with which these lake
peoples used to pay tax. The east side and south end is
entirely swamp, whereas the west side has a few hills.
Lycanthropy is practised round the lake, and a few notorious
doctors whom I know have earned a great reputation
(Kasoma and Chama), and do a profitable business with
their reputed lion packs. The natives have an implicit and
unshakable faith in this form of black magic. (See
Gouldsbury's poem on the *Chisanguka.*)

The three chief islands are Chirui, Kisi, and Mbawala,
which had about thirty villages each, and were well popu-
lated and cultivated. Formerly there were herds of cattle,
but such is not the case to-day. I have been all round the
lake, and on its many islands again and again during the
past twenty odd years, and I should say that Bangweulu
has a great future as a fishing and boating centre. Otter
skins, Lechwe skins, and shawls, with fat-tailed sheep and
goats, as well as fish and antelope flesh, are in great demand
in Northern Rhodesia and the Congo, whence many
traders come to buy. The hut tax, which has been raised
from 3s. to 5s. and now to 10s., is more easily paid by them
than by their land neighbours. All round the big lake there
are dozens of little lakes from several hundred yards to
several miles long. There are also a number of arms of
the lake that remind one of Loch Long and other Scottish
lochs. The people belong chiefly to the anthill clan, and
cultivate little patches of grain round the foot of these
termitic structures. They also live on the roots and seeds
of the water lily, besides edible roots and leaves of many
kinds, on which I have lived myself when on a journey and
when food was scarce.

As previously referred to the Arabs stirred up the Wemba chief Mpolokoso, who decided to put up a fight against the Government with Arab help. It cost the chief and people dear and the Arabs dearer still, for few of them escaped. W. R. Johnston was left as official in charge of the first administration station there. Hunting one day he shot five lions ; the fifth, a lioness, charged him and chased him up a tree, from which he was dragged down, and the experience cost him his life. This story is told elsewhere in the chapter on " Sport and Travel."

Kalunguisi station, one of the first to be built, was in charge of Blair Watson for many years. As he kept an Arab teacher and spoke and wrote Swahili fluently, besides having a good knowledge of natives and native law, he did much to pacify the natives along the Congo border, and inaugurated the first hut tax, and cut the first road by purely native labour.

About this time the Lunda chief Kazembe gave trouble, fired a few guns, and refused to take the flag. Dr. Watson, with a small force of Europeans and native levies, attacked Kazembe, who fled to Johnston Falls, and was eventually, on a promise of pardon, handed over to the Government by the missionary lady there. He was reinstated, and shortly after this Fort Rosebery was built by G. Lyons at Johnston Falls, which falls were named after Sir Harry Johnston by Sir A. Sharpe while on a political mission to Msidi in the Katanga. I lived here for a dozen years or more. Mr. Harrington succeeded Lyons, and the latter trekked to the south bend of the Luapula River and built another station at Sekontwe where good work was done, though it was afterwards suppressed. Thus, step by step, the administration of the country went forward, while taxation was peacefully instituted everywhere and roads were made, rivers bridged, while in course of time posts were established in every important centre of the new territory. There was little noise and no newspaper reports, but the work of civilisation progressed without a single revolt or costly war. Of course in the early days men had to endure hardships and privation, with sugar and flour at 1s. 6d. per lb. and tea at 7s. 6d., while they lived in mud huts surrounded by strong stockades to prevent surprise attacks from quarrelsome natives or slave-trading Arabs who hated our anti-slavery administration. Every official had to hammer out his little band of soldier police and native servants from the raw material to hand, and one can still hear the tootling of the old brass bugle that did duty, played by a sturdy local ex-fisher lad who had been taught the various calls by his Bwana. When the official was doing a round of the district sometimes the local missionary or trader would be left in charge to receive mails and despatch them, and as there was always the possibility of a surprise attack the guns had to be kept clean.

The hoisting and lowering of the flag was always a solemn occasion in those early days. Next to this was the arrival of the monthly or bimonthly mail. Sometimes the letters were intact and dry, but sometimes they had been dropped in a river by the way. On one occasion the mail failed to turn up, and searching along the road a red fez cap was found, a bit of the postman's skull, and a lot of scattered letters, and alongside, the spoor of a big lion. Newspapers were common property and passed round from one to another. " The simple life " describes pioneering in the early days of N.E. Rhodesia. In 1900 Fort Jameson was established as Government headquarters after the Angoni were smashed and Mpeseni pacified. The era of burnt brick, collars and ties, and ladies set in, so that from 1900 onward the real civilised development of N.E. Rhodesia began. Stockades were pulled down and one by one Government stations were built to a paper plan, built of brick and tile under the supervision of a white builder. European doors and windows were put even in the prisons and stores. " Fort Jim," as we called it, assumed importance with a Residence, its orderly built and kept offices, its public works and prison, with printing presses and materials turning out official documents and papers *the pride of old Crowther's life*. I have seen old Crowther (the printer) at work in his office in pyjamas and dressing-gown, shaking all over with fever when he should have been in bed with a hot-water bottle. Mr. Codrington, the administrator, had kindly asked Crowther to print a little " In Memoriam " card for me as I had just lost my younger son at Karonga. This I prize and keep, for now both the administrator and the head printer have also passed on : two pioneers of the early days of N.E. Rhodesia.

The water tribes of Lake Bangweulu were the last to submit and pay hut tax. Now annually the natives roll up with their previous tax-papers stamped with duck, axe, or hoe (by which names the natives call the year's tax-paper) to pay their current taxes, and defaulters are comparatively few. A network of good roads intersects almost the whole country, even through many of the swamps. Rivers are bridged, and in road-making and bridge-building the natives turn out with their chiefs and work with a will. The Government laws are becoming better understood, and the natives now know as they did not in earlier days what they may and what they may not do. Years ago some natives were sent to catch a murderer and bring him back " dead or alive." They caught him and killed him, and tying the dead body to a pole they brought him in to the official. As the law was not well known then, and there was no malice, the men were let off with a severe public warning. Sometimes there are attempts made to evade the law, but many of these are found out and punished. Cases of infanticide and witch-killing occur, but most of these eventually come to the light. One mission boy I know was caught by means of a letter he wrote to a friend in which he told of the killing of an " unlucky child." Still I should say that in proportion to the population crime is greater almost anywhere in Europe than it is in Northern Rhodesia.

There have been lots of petty troubles along the Belgian boundary from Bangweulu to Tanganyika, though, on the whole, friendly relations exist among both British and Belgian officials. Some natives to escape hut tax play fast and loose, and often criminals escape from one side to the other.

The Kabwalala robber gang is the most glaring instance of frontier difficulty. A frontier native is facetiously called " Mr. Facing-both-ways " (*Mpumi Kubili*).

Sleeping sickness and the removal of the population from the river-banks led to a wholesale exodus of natives into the Congo, for the Belgians did not enforce their law as strictly as they were supposed to do, and left the villages on the bank of the river. Fish was the attraction. Johnston Falls is a stretch of rapids extending for seventeen miles, and at the north end enormous quantities of fish are caught, split, smoked, and sold. Large herds of game, including buffaloes and elephants, used to roam here, and leopards and lions are still a perfect nuisance. On the Belgian side the tsetse fly are bad, whereas on the British side we keep herds of healthy cattle. The sleeping sickness fly, *glossina palpalis*, is found along the banks of the Luapula here, and the *morsitans* in the forests around. The natives are now made to clear the grass and vegetation along the river-banks and round their villages, as the fly feeds on the mosquito larvæ found on the vegetation on the river-banks. There is good fishing and shooting here, as also along the valley of the Luapula River.

Farming and mining in N.E. Rhodesia are in the initial stage and no great fortunes are likely to be made in these lines for many years to come. Cattle are few in N.E. Rhodesia save round Fort Jameson and on the Saisi River, Abercorn, where good bulls have been introduced and the stock improved.

Recruiting is the great asset of N.E. Rhodesia, and two great recruiting companies are at work throughout the territory; the Rhodesian Native Labour Bureau and the Robert Williams Co., or " Tanganyika Concessions." The former recruits boys for the farms and mines of Southern Rhodesia, whereas the latter recruits for the Union Minière du haut Katanga (Katanga copper mines). Last year over twelve thousand were recruited by the Robert Williams Co., and each boy is well cared for, fed, and tended medically, receives half his pay in the Congo and the other half on returning to Rhodesia. The native is, I believe, the one and only permanent asset of Africa, and the future progress and peace of the country depends largely on the intelligent understanding and just treatment of the native races. As Inspector of Recruiting for Robert Williams and Co. in connection with Angola and Rhodesian natives, I have on visiting the boys at work, or in their well-kept compounds, been often amused. " For whom are you working ? " I have asked again and again. " Tuli bantu ba Robert "— " We are the people of Robert," they have replied. The recruits of R. Williams and Co., like little Topsy, prefer to think they belong to somebody. The British South African Co. are jealous of the treatment of their natives, and will only confide recruiting licences to those who are in a position to accord the best possible treatment and pay to the natives.

At present N.E. Rhodesia is marking time while waiting for the advent of the iron horse to replace " Adam's bus," and the antiquated system of native porters. Even the Congo is ahead in this respect, and it is to be hoped that —mines or no mines discovered—a line of railway will soon run through N.E. Rhodesia, joining up the Cape with Tanganyika. I have heard it said that the money spent on the carrying of war loads between Ndola and Kasama across Bangweulu, and the making and maintaining of a motor road from Kashitu to Abercorn would more than have paid for the construction of a permanent railway and a supply of rolling stock for use from Broken Hill to Tanganyika.

" Mieux tard que jamais ! "

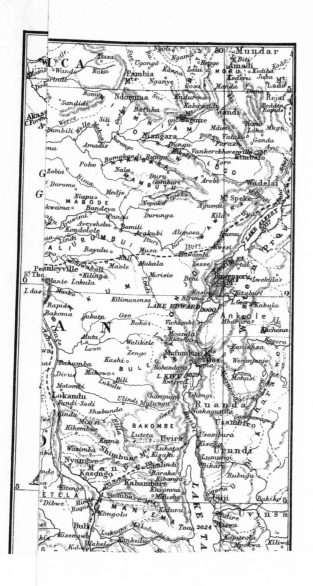

INDEX

A

Aborigines Protection Society, 30
Abortion, 92, 226
African Lakes Corporation, 298
African Nimrods, 192
Amusing mistakes, 203
Ancestry, pride of, 144
Angola, 18
Anti-Slavery Society, 30
Arab chief, blind, 257
Arabs, 26 ; and Islam, 253 ; Nyasa-
  land, 300 ; Rhodesia, 301
Army, native, 38, 39
Arnot, F. S., 225, 262, 297
Augury of life and death, 229

B

Babel, the Tower of, 260
Baby, birth and names, 167 ; a
  lucky, 169
Bag, biggest, 290
Bailundu, 23, 24
Baker, Sir S., 188
Balala, 265
Balomotwa tribe, 266
Bandits, 63
Bangweulu, 190, 302
Bantus, the, 17 ; language, 17 ;
  tyranny, 43, 167, 204, 213, 223
Bartelott, Major, 259
Basanga, 264
Bashila tribe, 195
Batetela, 260
Battle between two bull antelopes,
  287
Batwa tribe, 195
Baunga tribe, 195
Baushi tribe, 265

Bay, Lobito, 18, 21
Beads, 141
Beer, 136, 137
Beeswax, 19
Bellen, Capt., 260
Belmonte, 19
Benguella, 18, 20
Bia, Capt., 270
Big devils, 32
Bihé, 19, 22
Birds and birds' songs, 291
Black, eating, 133
Black ivory hunters, 20, 29
Blood sanctification, 249
Bodson, Capt., 269
Bonchamps, Marquis de, 269
Boys and girls, 170
Brasseur, Capt., 257, 265
British, first station in N.E. Rho-
  desia, 296
British, first officials in N.E. Rho-
  desia, 296
Broeck, van den, Capt., 270
Buffalo, 189, 280, 281
Bulindu, 109
Bumbuli, 107
Burning a robber, 50
Bushman folklore story, 181
Butwa secret society, 96, 106 ;
  temple, 240 ; doctor, 241
Buyembe, cannibal society, 108

C

Calling curses on witch, 228
Camps and carriers, 278
Cannibal soldiers, 258
Canoe digging, 124
Cape to Cairo Railway, 308
Cape Verde Islands, 19

309